The
EVERYING.
Whole-Grain, High-Fiber Cookbook

Dear Reader,

If you're looking for a delicious way to add whole grains and fiber to your diet, this book is for you! I've put together 300 recipes using fruits, vegetables, whole grains, and alternative grains, augmented with tips and tidbits. Julie Negrin has supplied nutritional information for each recipe.

Over the years I have cooked many recipes based on my culinary school education and professional restaurant experience. My work in the pastry department at Chez Panisse included providing wholesome desserts containing fresh fruits, nuts, and interesting grains. Polenta Pear Tart, Buckwheat Crepes, and Fig Raspberry Compote are a few examples. I also spent a year in Eugene, Oregon, soaking up the organic produce at the Saturday open-air market; making baby food from scratch with no preservatives; and creating candy recipes using ingredients such as brown rice syrup, sunflower seeds, and soy milk. I enjoyed making this book, and I hope you will find it a valuable tool for making delicious high-fiber snacks and meals.

Bon appetit!

Lynette Rohrer Shirk

Welcome to the EVERYTHING® Series!

These handy, accessible books give you all you need to tackle a difficult project, gain a new hobby, comprehend a fascinating topic, prepare for an exam, or even brush up on something you learned back in school but have since forgotten.

You can choose to read an *Everything®* book from cover to cover or just pick out the information you want from our four useful boxes: e-questions, e-facts, e-alerts, e-ssentials. We give you everything you need to know on the subject, but throw in a lot of fun stuff along the way, too.

We now have more than 400 *Everything®* books in print, spanning such wide-ranging categories as weddings, pregnancy, cooking, music instruction, foreign language, crafts, pets, New Age, and so much more. When you're done reading them all, you can finally say you know *Everything®*!

QUESTIONS?
Answers to common questions

FACTS
Important snippets of information

ALERTS!
Urgent warnings

ESSENTIALS
Quick handy tips

DIRECTOR OF INNOVATION Paula Munier

EDITORIAL DIRECTOR Laura M. Daly

EXECUTIVE EDITOR, SERIES BOOKS Brielle K. Matson

ASSOCIATE COPY CHIEF Sheila Zwiebel

ACQUISITIONS EDITOR Kerry Smith

DEVELOPMENT EDITOR Elizabeth Kassab

PRODUCTION EDITOR Casey Ebert

Visit the entire Everything® series at *www.everything.com*

THE
EVERYTHING®
WHOLE-GRAIN, HIGH-FIBER COOKBOOK

Delicious, heart-healthy snacks and
meals the whole family will love

Lynette Rohrer Shirk
Technical Review by Julie Negrin, M.S.

Avon, Massachusetts

The nutritional information provided with all of the recipes
in this book was calculated using NutriBase Clinical Version 7.0.

An Everything® Series Book.
Everything® and everything.com® are registered trademarks of F+W Publications, Inc.

Published by Adams Media, an F+W Publications Company
57 Littlefield Street, Avon, MA 02322. U.S.A.
www.adamsmedia.com

ISBN 10: 1-59869-507-X
ISBN 13: 978-1-59869-507-6

Printed in the United States of America.

J I H G F E D C B A

Library of Congress Cataloging-in-Publication Data
available from the publisher.

This publication is designed to provide accurate and authoritative information with regard to the subject matter covered. It is sold with the understanding that the publisher is not engaged in rendering legal, accounting, or other professional advice. If legal advice or other expert assistance is required, the services of a competent professional person should be sought.

> —From a *Declaration of Principles* jointly adopted by a Committee of the American Bar Association and a Committee of Publishers and Associations

Many of the designations used by manufacturers and sellers to distinguish their products are claimed as trademarks. Where those designations appear in this book and Adams Media was aware of a trademark claim, the designations have been printed with initial capital letters.

The Everything® Whole-Grain, High-Fiber Cookbook is intended as a reference volume only, not as a medical manual. In light of the complex, individual, and specific nature of health problems, this book is not intended to replace professional medical advice. The ideas, procedures, and suggestions in this book are intended to supplement, not replace, the advice of a trained medical professional. Consult your physician before adopting the suggestions in this book, as well as about any condition that may require diagnosis or medical attention. The author and publisher disclaim any liability arising directly or indirectly from the use of this book.

This book is available at quantity discounts for bulk purchases.
For information, please call 1-800-289-0963.

Dedication

To Grandma and Daddy Joe Metzendorf

As always, I would like to thank my husband, Jeff, and daughter, Zelda, for their patience and appetites while I worked on this book. Thanks also to everyone at Stringfellow School in Coppell, Texas, especially the moms who watched over my daughter this school year, and Miss Kennedy McCann for sharing her friendship bread starter. Thanks also to Kerry Smith and June Clark for providing me the opportunity to write about whole grains and high fiber. And special thanks to Nancy Maar!

Contents

Introduction

The importance of whole grains and high fiber in the human diet cannot be overstressed in this modern era of overprocessed foods. It's possible to get all the fiber you need from fruits, vegetables, and grains; there's no need to rely on supplements. The purpose of this book is to inform the reader of the wide variety of available foods containing fiber, then provide recipes for delicious meals using those high-fiber ingredients. While the current American diet averages only about 10 grams of dietary fiber per day, upping your daily intake to 25 to 40 grams of fiber per day could reduce your risk of developing a host of chronic diseases, including cancer, heart disease, and gastrointestinal conditions.

Fiber is found in plant foods and comes in two forms. Soluble fiber is the part that dissolves in water (sources include oatmeal, broccoli, bananas, and citrus fruits). Insoluble fiber is the roughage part that doesn't dissolve in water (sources include the outer husk of whole grains like wheat bran, and nuts, seeds, and most vegetables). Each type of fiber has different benefits, so most people are advised to increase their intake of foods that feature both soluble and insoluble fiber. Research suggests that soluble, not insoluble, fibers are helpful in protecting against heart disease by lowering triglyceride levels. Fiber also improves blood sugar control, which is important for people with type 2 diabetes. Diseases such as colon cancer and diverticulosis can also be prevented with a diet high in insoluble fiber. Insoluble fiber stretches and exercises the walls of the intestines. It relieves constipation and moves any harmful substances through and out of the intestines more quickly, leaving less time for the toxins to be in contact with the intestinal walls.

Whole-grain foods, such as whole-wheat flour and brown rice, are higher in fiber than their processed counterparts (white flour and polished rice) because the outer husk has not been removed from the grain kernel. Fruits and vegetables provide fiber in their cellulose and pectins. Apples and blueberries are sources of high fiber in both their skins and flesh. Their skins provide the insoluble fiber the body needs, and their flesh provides soluble fiber in the form of pectin. Raw fruits, vegetables, and whole grains are an easy way to bump up the fiber intake of the diet, and dried fruits, cooked vegetables, and fruits offer variety and flavor to make a high-fiber diet palatable and pleasurable. Soluble fiber from beans, oats, psyllium seed, and fruit pectin not only lower cholesterol levels but can lower appetite. With the recipes in this book you may improve your health by increasing your fiber intake without having to add fiber supplements, which can be costly and unpleasant. Say good-bye to gritty stir-in drink supplements and sawdust cereal with the 300 creative and flavorful recipes in this book.

Chapter 1
Fiber and Whole Grains

Getting enough fiber and whole grains in the diet is essential to your health and well-being. This book will inform you why your body needs fiber and how to get it. It will show you the foods that contain fiber and how to prepare them. By incorporating the recipes in this book into your cooking repertoire, you will be able to easily calculate your family's fiber intake from home-cooked meals, snacks, and desserts.

What Is Fiber?

Fiber is made up of a variety of plant compounds that the human body uses to maintain good digestive-tract health. Plant products contain phytochemicals, which protect first the plants themselves and then the humans who consume them. Whole grains, nuts, seeds, legumes, vegetables, and fruits are all important for a high-fiber diet. There are two main types of fiber: soluble fiber and insoluble fiber. The body needs both to perform different functions.

The American Heart Association recommends that people eat 25–30 grams of fiber a day, but it estimates the average American only gets about 15 grams per day. Increase your fiber intake slowly to prevent bloating, and drink plenty of water to prevent constipation.

Soluble Fiber: Nature's Sponge

The body cannot digest fiber as it digests fats or carbohydrates. Fiber makes its way through the digestive system, helping the body maintain overall health. Soluble fiber dissolves in water to form a gel-like substance. It helps the body by absorbing cholesterol and keeping blood sugar levels healthy. Soluble fiber is important in keeping the body's energy level balanced. Oatmeal, legumes, barley, and fruits are high in soluble fiber. These foods also provide more nutritional value than do insoluble fibers.

Insoluble Fiber: Nature's Broom

Also known as roughage, insoluble fiber does not dissolve in water. Its benefit is that it is not digested but moves through the digestive tract, helping to flush waste out of the digestive system quickly. Whole grains and most vegetables are high in insoluble fiber. Breads, pastas, and pastries made with whole grains rather than refined white flour are higher in insoluble fiber. Popcorn is another good source of insoluble fiber—but use unbuttered popcorn, not the stuff that's laden with lard and/or butter.

Health Benefits of Fiber

Fiber is instrumental in keeping your digestive system running smoothly. It helps keep bowel movements regular and decreases your risk for irritable bowel syndrome. Low-fiber diets leave you at risk for developing diverticulosis—pouches in the colon—and diverticulitis—inflamed pouches in the colon.

Besides keeping your digestive system in good working order, fiber can reduce your risk for colon cancer and heart disease. It makes you feel full longer and may actually prevent the body from absorbing fat, which is helpful in losing weight. Fiber also helps the body maintain a lower blood glucose level so that less insulin is necessary to ferry energy to the body's cells. Eating a diet rich in fiber is one way to help prevent type 2 diabetes, and fiber can help people with diabetes control it. Dietary fiber helps the body eliminate cholesterol and is crucial in lowering cholesterol levels.

Whole Grains

Botanically speaking, grains are members of the grass family. Among the many varieties of grasses that humans eat are wheat, oats, rice, barley, corn, and rye. The seeds of the grasses are eaten whole or processed into smaller pieces or ground into meals and flours. But remember—when wheat kernels are stripped of their outer hull, they are not considered whole wheat or wheat berries anymore. This stripping process produces white flour, which is not as nutritious as whole grains. Look for whole-grain breads and pastas and opt for brown rice over white rice.

Whole grains are a source of dietary fiber, mostly insoluble. They also have large amounts of vitamins, which are soluble. Wheat is the most common whole grain. The edible parts of wheat are the seeds or kernels.

The unprocessed wheat kernel, commonly known as a wheat berry, is made up of three major parts: bran, germ, and endosperm. Wheat berry contains vitamins, minerals, and nutrients, including vitamin E, twelve B vitamins, essential fatty acids, protein, iron, copper, zinc, manganese, phosphorus, and magnesium. It also contains folic acid, which is vital to developing fetuses.

Fifteen percent of the wheat berry is wheat bran, which comes from six fibrous protective layers. Around 3 percent of the wheat berry is wheat germ, which is located in the center of the kernel. It is nutritionally the richest part of the wheat berry and contains insoluble fiber. Cracked wheat consists of wheat berries that are coarsely chopped and can be eaten as porridge or incorporated into breads and cereals. Kamut and spelt are heirloom varieties of wheat and can be consumed by people with sensitivity or allergies to the gluten in common wheat and oats.

Oats are a high-protein grain with amino acids similar to wheat. Oats also help stabilize blood sugar, which helps the body to maintain stamina. They contain the highest percentage of unsaturated fat among the grains. Brown rice is high in insoluble fiber because the outer bran layer is left on the grain. Wild rice, also a water-growing grain, is loaded with insoluble fiber and soluble vitamins.

Buckwheat, quinoa, and amaranth are seeds that are treated as whole grains and are high in fiber but are not actually from the grass family. Quinoa is grown in the Andes and contains the highest amount of protein of all the grain-like foods.

Nuts and Seeds

Both nuts and seeds provide dietary fiber. Sprouts have plant fiber; bean and alfalfa sprouts are easily grown on the kitchen counter and are full of crunch and goodness. Nuts are a source of energy. They provide essential fatty acids, vitamin E, calcium, phosphorus, potassium, and magnesium. They rival meat in protein content and are the most concentrated vegetable source of oils. Substitute walnut oil for olive or canola oil for extra flavor in your salad dressing.

Nuts include almonds, cashews, peanuts, pistachios, walnuts, pecans, hazelnuts, macadamias, Brazil nuts, chestnuts, pine nuts, and coconuts. Seeds, such as sesame, sunflower, flax, poppy, pumpkin, caraway, celery, and fennel, are an excellent source of protein and minerals. They also have higher iron content than nuts and are high in unsaturated fats. Add them to salads and cooked vegetables as a healthy garnish.

Natural food stores usually have a variety of quick energy bars, which usually include nuts and seeds. These bars are convenient to have handy when you're on the run and need a pick-me-up. You can also carry the nuts themselves to snack on.

Nuts

Nuts are basically seeds with a hard shell. They are high in good fat and fiber. They are good to snack on because the fiber found in nuts helps you feel full quickly. However, if you are trying to lose weight, nuts should be eaten in moderation because of their fat calories. Eating fresh fruit, such as an apple or grapes, with a small handful of nuts will help fill you up faster and you will feel full longer.

Many specialty stores now sell toasted nuts with herbs or spices. Delectable rosemary-toasted or pepper-toasted nuts make wonderful garnishes for salads. Chestnuts, peeled and boiled or home roasted, are excellent in stuffing for game birds or turkey. French glazed chestnuts are wonderful as part of a dessert, such as a pudding, tart, or stewed fruit.

Seeds

Like nuts, the fiber found in seeds helps to make you feel full quickly. They are a delicious and satisfying snack to stave off hunger and increase your fiber intake. Seeds are loaded with fiber; in fact, the seeds from the psyllium plant are used to make commercial fiber supplements.

There are many exciting ways to add seeds to your diet to enrich it. Toss some toasted sesame seeds into your vegetables. Add caraway seeds to coleslaw, cooked carrots, and cooked cabbage. Sprinkle celery seeds over hot pasta and mix them into pasta salads.

QUESTION?

How can I promote the health benefit of beans to my family when I don't like kidney beans or wax beans?
If the ubiquitous "three-bean salad" of salad bar fame grosses you out, make your own. You don't have to use the traditional kidney beans, wax beans, and chickpeas if you don't like them. Substitute one or all for other legumes, such as black-eyed peas, green beans, or black beans. Toss equal amounts of the cooked, drained beans together and toss them with a little Italian dressing for seasoning.

Legumes

The numerous varieties of dried legumes are an inexpensive way to get soluble fiber into your diet. They are also high in protein and make excellent meat substitutes. Lentils, split peas, pintos, black beans, white beans, navy beans, garbanzo beans, black-eyed peas, and kidney beans are all common legumes that can be easily found in any grocery store. More exotic varieties, such as adzuki beans, calypso beans, and cranberry beans, are available in most health food stores. Fresh legumes, such as lima beans, fava beans, peas, and soy beans (edamame), are also good sources of fiber. A high-fiber diet is easy to accomplish when legumes are included as a mealtime staple.

Getting kids to eat their legumes can be a challenge, but there is hope. Exposing them to cuisines in which beans are prominent, such as Mexican refried beans or Middle Eastern hummus, is a start. Make bean dip using a recipe for hummus and substituting cooked white beans for the garbanzo beans and serve it with carrot sticks and pita bread for the next football game snack spread. Adding cooked beans to soups and salads is an easy way to sneak them into kids' diets, too. Try using red or yellow lentils in soups. The gray-green color of regular lentils may turn kids off. Add just a few red beans to your chili, slowly increasing the ratio of beans to meat and sauce.

Vegetables and Fruits

High-fiber vegetables include sweet potatoes, corn, broccoli, cabbage, greens, carrots, celery, lettuces, snow peas, string beans, tomatoes, and avocados. There are a lot of vegetables out there, but they are not equal in fiber content. For example, choose more fiber-rich field greens over iceberg lettuce. Follow the rule "the greener the better" when shopping for lettuce and other green vegetables.

Dehydrated vegetables, such as corn, carrots, and sun-dried tomatoes, are a nice snack alternative to have around the house. They can be simmered in chicken or vegetable broth for a quick vegetable soup.

Vegetables and fruits eaten raw with their skins on are a better source of fiber than cooked and peeled vegetables. For example, a fresh apple has more fiber than cooked applesauce in a comparable serving. However, some vegetables cannot be eaten raw (think artichokes) or are simply not appealing unless cooked (think Brussels sprouts).

Not all preparations of vegetables are a good source of fiber: French fried potatoes are not, but a baked potato with the skin is. A healthy alternative to fried potato chips with a sour cream–based dip could be corn tortilla chips with fresh tomato salsa and avocado dip. Raw carrots, radishes, or celery sticks in place of potato chips as a side for a sandwich are a good way to start adding fiber to the diet.

King Cabbage

Cruciferous vegetables—the cabbage family—are high in dietary fiber and offer a variety of shapes and colors to choose from. Cabbage is found in different cuisines around the world and is the foundation for dishes such as American coleslaw, German sauerkraut, and Korean kim chee. It is a filling in Hungarian strudel and Polish pierogies and a must-have ingredient for Russian borscht.

Cabbage comes in different varieties such as white head cabbage, purple head cabbage, bok choy, wrinkly Savoy head cabbage, and Napa cabbage. Other members of the cruciferous family to look for include broccoli, cauliflower, broccoli rabe, broccolini, Brussels sprouts, kale, collard greens, arugula, mustard greens, and watercress. Eat raw broccoli, cauliflower, and carrots as crudités. Chomp on celery and radishes between meals. Make your own coleslaw and add lots of celery seeds or caraway seeds to boost the fiber.

Corn, the All-American Vegetable

The Pilgrims would never have survived that first winter in New England if Native Americans had not supplied them with corn. Dried corn was boiled, popped, added to meat stews, and ground for bread. Corn's insoluble fiber content retains much of its original form as it goes through the digestive system. The increased bulk in the stool after eating a vegetable like corn is what makes the high-fiber diet effective, by toning the colon.

Pickled vegetables are good to have in the pantry for the times when you need a side salad to go with a sandwich and there are no greens in the fridge. Italian beef sandwiches in Chicago are served with giardiniera (pickled carrots, onions, celery, zucchini, and cauliflower) right on the sandwich, and Vietnamese pork sandwiches come with pickled carrots inside. Pickled veggies are also great added to salad greens, shredded cabbage, and sautéed onions.

There is nothing exactly like corn for cleansing the colon. However, there are many vegetables when eaten with their skins on that will do pretty much the same thing. Red, green, and yellow peppers and hot peppers all have edible skins. Snow peas and sugar snaps are very high in fiber and deliciously sweet as a snack, stir-fried, or tossed in salads. Asparagus and artichokes are extremely high in fiber. Asparagus can simply be blanched, but artichokes must be well cooked with the spiny, indigestible "choke" cut out. Parsnips are usually cooked or added to stews, but they're worth a try raw.

Fruits

Fruits of all kinds are another excellent source of dietary fiber. Eat raw fruits to get the most fiber out of them. Cooked fruits have less fiber but are a better source than fruit juices. The general rule is: the less processed the more fiber. However, dried fruits like apricots, raisins, and prunes are a very good source of fiber and are easy to take along for on-the-go snacking.

Berries, such as strawberries, raspberries, and blackberries, are an extra-good source of fiber due to the seeds in them. Blueberries are another because of their skins and pectin content. Citrus fruits are loaded with fiber, as are figs (both fresh and dried), bananas, mangoes, melons, pineapples, and cranberries. Dried apricots can be added to tapioca pudding, rice, cookies, or stuffing to add fiber and flavor, making them a flexible choice for a high-fiber diet. Try adding dried cherries or cranberries to rice, stuffing, and pudding or sprinkle them into apple, peach, or other fruit pies for added flavor. There are so many possibilities, both sweet and savory, for adding more fruit to the diet.

Feeding the Family

Making the shift to a fiber-rich diet may not be the easiest change for you and your family. The key is to do it slowly and gently. Start by making slight changes to your normal recipes. Substitute almond meal for some of the all-purpose flour in your favorite chocolate chip cookie recipe. Sprinkle nuts and seeds over your salads. Stir granola and fresh fruit into plain or vanilla yogurt. It's likely no one will notice the changes in the early stages.

Make Changes

Slowly phase out the unhealthy elements of your diet. Replace the chocolate chip cookies with oatmeal cookies. Snack on trail mix with M&Ms instead of a bag of just M&Ms. Stock your cupboards with dried fruits and nuts, and replenish your supply of fresh fruits and vegetables every time you go grocery shopping. Get different fruits and vegetables each time to increase variety and stave off boredom.

FACT

If you are a doughnut lover, you can substitute the fried, refined-flour rings with a healthier breakfast. Try making a batch of whole-grain or bran-enriched biscuits filled with stewed prunes, nuts, and no sugar. If you were scarred at an early age by being forced to eat canned prunes, you may want to try dried apricots instead.

Find the type of bread your family likes the best. If you've been buying plain white bread for years, change to a multigrain bread and work your way up to a whole-grain bread. Using cookie cutters to make the bread into fun shapes makes the healthier bread more fun for kids. Make sure the texture of the bread is smooth; fiber-rich breads often have nuts and seeds in them, but picky kids and adults might object. Take a similar approach with pasta and rice. Mix whole-grain pasta and regular pasta together and slowly increase the ratio of whole-grain pasta until you can eliminate the regular pasta altogether. Do the same for brown rice and white rice.

To slow the release of sugar into the system, add celery, lettuce, cabbage, and fruit to various dishes. Every meal should include a salad laced with red onions, radishes, cucumbers, extra nuts, sprouts, and jicama. Try making salads with an extra kick—black beans, fresh corn, and cherry tomatoes for a large serving of fiber, protein, and happiness.

Plan Ahead

When it comes to feeding a busy family, there is a lot of temptation to grab fast-food meals at a drive-through to save time and effort on the way to and from school and extracurricular activities. A little planning can help you stay on track and resist temptation. Pack easy sandwiches made with whole-grain bread the night before. Include fresh fruits such as apples, oranges, and bananas. Keep a bag of granola and boxes of raisins in the car for quick snacking with bottles of water for hydration.

Plan out your meals a week in advance and vary the sources of fiber. This allows you to stay ahead of the game so you don't have to scramble to throw something together at the last minute. It also lets you calculate your fiber intake each day so you can be sure you're getting enough.

Feeding your family a fiber-rich diet can help them be healthy and happy for years to come. If you encounter resistance, don't give up. Instead, try to pinpoint why your family is rebelling. You might have to slow down or even temporarily reverse course to satisfy them, but keep your eye on the end result—a family with general good health.

Chapter 2
Breakfast

Peach Yogurt Smoothie

Serves 2

Calories: 308.71
Protein: 7.64 grams
Carbohydrates: 68.62 grams
Fiber: 3.84 grams
Fat: 1.89 grams

½ banana
1½ cups peaches, cubed
1 cup vanilla yogurt
¼ cup orange juice
1 teaspoon honey

You may use frozen peaches in this for a sherbet-like texture. The combination of yogurt and fruit will give your day a delicious boost. You can substitute yogurt for cream in many dishes and add it to fruit for a delicious dessert.

1. Place all ingredients in a blender and blend until smooth.
2. Pour into two glasses and serve as a quick breakfast.

Fiber Fact

If you use orange juice with pulp in it you increase your fiber content without even thinking about it, so don't pick up the pulp-free variety anymore. The same goes for grapefruit juice. For added color and fiber, eat a handful of fresh raspberries along with your juice.

Blackberry Mango Smoothie

Serves 2

Calories: 194.09
Protein: 3.62 grams
Carbohydrates: 45.82 grams
Fiber: 6.36 grams
Fat: 1.22 grams

½ banana
1 cup frozen mango cubes
1 cup blackberries
½ cup vanilla frozen yogurt
¼ cup orange juice
1 teaspoon honey

The fiber in bananas, mangoes, and blackberries will help you stay full for longer than if you drink plain juice for breakfast. The yogurt will add just enough protein to burn the sugar in the juice.

1. Place all ingredients in a blender and blend until smooth.
2. Pour into two glasses and serve as a quick breakfast.

Blueberry Lemon Smoothie

The classic combination of lemon and blueberries makes for a tasty breakfast shake. Bananas are the most filling of fruits, and they are also easily digestible.

1. Place all ingredients in a blender and blend until smooth.
2. Pour into two glasses and serve as a quick breakfast.

Blueberry Heaven
The United States produces 95 percent of the world's supply of blueberries. Maine produces the bulk of U.S. blueberries, followed by other northeastern states and Oregon. Many farms in these regions allow you to pick your own berries when they're in season.

Serves 2

Calories: 218.80
Protein: 6.51 grams
Carbohydrates: 40.43 grams
Fiber: 3.09 grams
Fat: 4.39 grams

½ banana
1 cup frozen blueberries
1 cup lemon yogurt
¼ cup grape juice
1 teaspoon honey

Strawberry Banana Smoothie

A classic combination, strawberries and bananas, forms the fiber-rich base of this breakfast beverage. Smoothies save the day when you are in a rush; if you are worried about getting enough protein into the family, toss in a tablespoon of wheat germ.

1. Place all ingredients in a blender and blend until smooth.
2. Pour into two glasses and serve as a quick breakfast.

Bananas and Strawberries
Bananas are a very tasty source of soluble fiber. Strawberries have the added benefit of being high in both soluble and insoluble fiber in the form of pectin and seeds. Both are also higher in minerals than any other soft fruits.

Serves 2

Calories: 207.44
Protein: 5.46 grams
Carbohydrates: 45.88 grams
Fiber: 3.63 grams
Fat: 1.45 grams

1 banana
1 cup frozen strawberries, cut up
1 cup vanilla frozen yogurt
¼ cup orange juice
1 teaspoon honey

Raspberry–Almond Milk Frappe

Serves 2

Calories: 134.24
Protein: 4.15 grams
Carbohydrates: 25.91 grams
Fiber: 4.43 grams
Fat: 2.06 grams

1 cup frozen raspberries
¾ cup vanilla frozen yogurt
½ cup almond milk
⅛ teaspoon almond extract
1 teaspoon honey

*The seeds in whole raspberries are a fabulous source of fiber.
You can also substitute maple syrup for honey in this recipe for a different
flavor. You can substitute other flavors of frozen yogurt to add variety!*

1. Place all ingredients in a blender and blend until smooth.

2. Pour into two glasses and serve as a quick breakfast.

Cornmeal Grits

Serves 4

Calories: 161.27
Protein: 2.54 grams
Carbohydrates: 23.46 grams
Fiber: 2.23 grams
Fat: 6.85 grams

4 cups water
1 teaspoon salt
1 cup polenta meal
2 tablespoons butter

*This warm cereal is similar to oatmeal. It can be eaten in a variety
of ways: as a breakfast cereal, as a side with ham and eggs, with
cheese stirred in it and shrimp on top, or with gravy.*

1. Put water and salt in a saucepan and bring to a boil.

2. Gradually add polenta and stir constantly over medium-low heat until it has thickened, about 15 minutes. Stir in butter.

3. Serve immediately for soft grits or pour into a greased loaf pan and let cool. When cool, grits can be sliced and fried or grilled.

Blackberry Buckwheat Flapjacks

Blackberries are a good source of fiber because of their seeds. For a quick fix, try a Blackberry Mango Smoothie (page 14) for breakfast. The good part is that blackberries are available fresh and frozen all year round.

Serves 4

Calories: 366.40
Protein: 11.41 grams
Carbohydrates: 53.91 grams
Fiber: 4.24 grams
Fat: 12.31 grams

*1 cup all-purpose flour
½ cup buckwheat flour
3 tablespoons sugar
1½ teaspoons baking powder
½ teaspoon baking soda
½ teaspoon salt
2 eggs
3 tablespoons melted butter
1½ cups buttermilk
1 cup blackberries*

1. Whisk together flour, buckwheat flour, sugar, baking powder, baking soda, and salt in a large bowl.

2. Whisk together eggs, melted butter, and buttermilk in another bowl.

3. Stir egg mixture into the flour mixture until combined. There will be lumps; be careful not to overmix.

4. Pour about ⅓ cup batter for each pancake onto a hot oiled griddle or pan. Scatter several blackberries on top of batter. Flip pancake when bubbles have formed and started to pop through the batter. Cook on other side for a minute.

5. Serve hot with maple syrup.

Kernel Knowledge
Whole grains that have been ground into flour can have varying degrees of fiber. Buckwheat flour can be light, medium, or dark depending on the amount of hull left in it. The black hull or outer shell of the grain is a good source of the amino acid lysine, so try to find the darker version.

Blueberry Cornmeal Pancakes

Serves 4

Calories: 373.18
Protein: 10.63 grams
Carbohydrates: 55.67 grams
Fiber: 2.94 grams
Fat: 12.35 grams

1 cup flour
½ cup yellow cornmeal
3 tablespoons sugar
1½ teaspoons baking powder
½ teaspoon baking soda
½ teaspoon salt
2 eggs
3 tablespoons melted butter
1½ cups buttermilk
1 cup blueberries

You get a double dose of fiber in the blueberries and the cornmeal in these pancakes. These are dense and filling, great for a frosty morning when you are sending the kids out in the cold, or on your way to shovel some snow.

1. Whisk together flour, cornmeal, sugar, baking powder, baking soda, and salt in a large bowl.

2. Whisk together eggs, melted butter, and buttermilk in another bowl.

3. Stir egg mixture into the flour mixture until combined. There will be lumps; be careful not to overmix.

4. Pour about ⅓ cup batter for each pancake onto hot oiled griddle or pan. Scatter several blueberries over batter. Flip pancakes when bubbles have formed and started to pop through the batter on top.

5. Cook on other side for about a minute. Serve hot with maple syrup.

Purple Power

It's an interesting experiment to substitute purple cornmeal for standard cornmeal. The flavor is the same, but they look really fabulous. By dripping the batter in the shapes of snowmen, dragons, or animals, fussy eaters will become fast fans. Covering the cakes with fresh fruit adds to the fun and the nutrition.

Banana-Nut Stuffed French Toast

This delicious recipe imparts fiber through whole grain, fruits, and nuts. You can vary the French toast with different kinds of nuts and fruits.

1. Peel and slice the bananas. Whisk together eggs, milk, vanilla, brown sugar, and cinnamon in a bowl.

2. Dip four slices of bread in the batter and immediately fry in a little canola oil over medium heat.

3. Divide the banana slices and nuts evenly among the four slices of cooking bread. Dip the remaining four slices of bread into the batter and put them on top of the bananas to create four sandwiches.

4. Add remaining canola oil to the pan, flip the sandwiches over and fry over medium heat until golden.

5. Halve the French toast diagonally and arrange slices on a platter. Scatter the raspberries over the French toast triangles and sprinkle them with powdered sugar.

Serves 4

Calories: 587.63
Protein: 21.91 grams
Carbohydrates: 54.85 grams
Fiber: 9.06 grams
Fat: 33.94 grams

2 bananas
6 eggs
1½ cups milk
1 teaspoon vanilla
1 tablespoon brown sugar
½ teaspoon cinnamon
8 slices day-old whole-wheat bread
2 teaspoons canola oil
1 cup chopped walnuts or pecans
handful of fresh raspberries
powdered sugar

Double Corn Waffles

Serves 6

Calories: 434
Protein: 11.16 grams
Carbohydrates: 34.55 grams
Fiber: 5.05 grams
Fat: 29.16 grams

3 eggs
4 ounces canola oil
1½ cups plain yogurt
1¾ cups yellow cornbread mix
½ cup corn kernels
oil for waffle iron

*Cornmeal plus corn kernels equal whole-grain fiber heaven.
You can use canned or frozen corn, but this is a real treat if you
can get corn in season at the end of summer.*

1. Whisk together eggs, canola oil, and yogurt.

2. Stir egg mixture into the cornbread mix to combine. There will be lumps; be careful not to overmix.

3. Fold the corn kernels into the batter.

4. Pour or ladle about ½ cup waffle batter onto preheated and oiled waffle iron and cook according to manufacturer's instructions.

5. Serve hot with honey butter spread.

Good Company
Honey Butter Spread is a good partner for cornbread and cornmeal muffins. Whip 2 tablespoons of honey with ½ stick softened unsalted butter with an electric mixer for a delicious butter spread to accompany double corn waffles.

Oatmeal Raisin Scones

These luscious scones pack a whopping punch of fiber from oats, wheat germ, and raisins. Try using Irish oatmeal for these scones, but soak them first. Steel cut oats have the most fiber and instant oats have the least.

1. Preheat oven to 400°F. Line a baking pan with parchment paper or spray lightly with oil. Grind half of the oatmeal into flour in a food processor.

2. Combine remaining oats, oat flour, all-purpose flour, wheat germ, sugar, salt, baking powder, and butter in a food processor with a metal blade. Process until mixture resembles cornmeal.

3. In a large bowl whisk together eggs, buttermilk, and vanilla. Stir in raisins with a spatula or wooden spoon.

4. Add dry ingredients and fold in with spatula. Drop scones into rounds onto prepared baking sheet.

5. Brush scones with egg white and sprinkle with raw sugar. Bake for 15 minutes.

Edible Oats

Oats are one of the best sources for soluble fiber, which is important in regulating cholesterol in the bloodstream. Oats also lose only the outer husk during the milling process so they are more nutritious than refined wheat.

Serves 6

Calories: 372.76
Protein: 8.88 grams
Carbohydrates: 54.01
Fiber: 3.62 grams
Fat: 14.67 grams

1½ cups rolled oats
½ cup all-purpose flour
2 tablespoons wheat germ
3 tablespoons sugar
½ teaspoon salt
1⅛ teaspoons baking powder
6 tablespoons cold, unsalted butter, cut in pieces
2 eggs
⅔ cup buttermilk
½ teaspoon vanilla
1 cup raisins
1 egg white
2 tablespoons raw sugar

Olallieberry Polenta Scones

Olallieberries are ⅔ blackberry and ⅓ raspberry. If you don't have any olallieberries, substitute blackberries. Add about five minutes, baking time for frozen berries. You will find that frozen berries stand up a bit better when baked—as long as they are not thawed prior to mixing.

Serves 6

Calories: 343.48
Protein: 7.65 grams
Carbohydrates: 45.69 grams
Fiber: 2.38 grams
Fat: 14.45 grams

1½ cups flour
¼ cup polenta meal
3 tablespoons sugar
½ teaspoon salt
1¼ teaspoons baking powder
6 tablespoons cold, unsalted
    butter, cut in pieces
2 eggs
⅔ cup plain yogurt
½ teaspoon vanilla
1 cup olallieberries
1 egg white
2 tablespoons raw sugar

1. Preheat oven to 400°F. Line a baking pan with parchment paper or spray lightly with oil.

2. Combine flour, polenta meal, sugar, salt, baking powder, and butter in a food processor with a metal blade. Process until mixture resembles cornmeal.

3. In a large bowl whisk together eggs, yogurt, and vanilla. Stir in olallieberries with a spatula or wooden spoon.

4. Add dry ingredients and fold in with spatula. Drop scones into rounds onto prepared baking sheet.

5. Brush scones with egg white and sprinkle with raw sugar. Bake for 15 minutes.

Sneaking Fiber into Scones

Using cornmeal and berries turns the dull, old, white buttery scone into something special. The healthful corn of polenta will give the scones "shoulders," making them not only more delicious but higher in fiber.

Raspberry Almond Turnovers

*Delicious for breakfast but also a good dessert or snack,
these turnovers are a versatile part of the high-fiber diet repertoire.
If you are a weekend warrior, make a double recipe and freeze them
in individual plastic bags for use later in the week.*

Serves 4

Calories: 562.24
Protein: 11.28 grams
Carbohydrates: 47.67 grams
Fiber: 5.8 grams
Fat: 37.1 grams

1 cup sliced almonds
1 sheet puff pastry, thawed in the refrigerator
1 egg white
4 teaspoons almond paste
1 cup frozen raspberries
4 teaspoons sugar
2 teaspoons cornstarch
1 tablespoon wheat germ
2 tablespoons powdered sugar

1. Preheat the oven to 400°F. Grind half of the almonds in a food processor. Set aside.

2. Roll the puff pastry into an 11" × 11" square on a floured surface. Cut the square into four smaller squares. Paint the egg white on the pastry squares.

3. Put a teaspoon of almond paste in the middle of each square, layer ¼ cup raspberries on top, then sprinkle the ground almonds, sugar, cornstarch, and wheat germ over the berries.

4. Fold each square over to make a triangle to encase the filling. Press down on the outer edges with your fingers or a fork to seal.

5. Brush the egg white on the turnovers and sprinkle them with the remaining sliced almonds and powdered sugar. Bake for 10 minutes, turn the oven down to 350°F, and continue baking for about 10–15 minutes longer. Let cool before eating.

Puff Pastry

Unfortunately, you can't buy whole-grain puff pastry, but you can fill it with fruit and nuts for wonderful turnovers. Wheat germ is also an excellent source of vitamins and fiber, which can be added to everything from meatloaf to pancake batter.

Granola

Serves 6

Calories: 565.50
Protein: 16.55 grams
Carbohydrates: 69.07 grams
Fiber: 11.56 grams
Fat: 26.59 grams

4 cups rolled oats
1 cup sliced almonds
½ teaspoon cinnamon
1 teaspoon vanilla
4 ounces orange blossom
  honey
2 ounces canola oil
½ cup wheat germ
¼ cup sesame seeds
¼ cup millet
¼ cup flaxseeds

Serve this granola with fruit and yogurt or just eat it out of hand for an on-the-go breakfast. You can also turn this into trail mix by adding dried apples and/or raisins.

1. Preheat oven to 350°F.

2. Toss oats, almonds, cinnamon, vanilla, honey, and canola oil together in a big bowl. Spread the mixture on a baking pan and bake for 10 minutes.

3. Stir and add wheat germ, sesame seeds, and millet. Bake for 15 minutes.

4. Stir and add flaxseeds. Bake for 10 minutes.

5. Remove from oven. Cool and break up large chunks.

Oatmeal

Serves 4

Calories: 193.22
Protein: 4.44 grams
Carbohydrates: 35.37 grams
Fiber: 3.91 grams
Fat: 4.83 grams

2 cups water
1 cup rolled oats
¼ teaspoon salt
½ cup dried currants
1 teaspoon ground cinnamon
4 teaspoons honey
1 cup almond milk, chilled
2 tablespoons cream

This is the comfort food of the high-fiber diet—warm, cozy, and delicious. This will keep a family going happily until lunch. You can also eat it for supper when you aren't feeling quite right.

1. Bring water to a boil. Add the oats and salt and stir. Turn the heat to low and simmer 5 minutes.

2. Stir in the currants and simmer for 10 minutes, stirring occasionally.

3. Remove from heat and spoon cooked oatmeal into four bowls.

4. Sprinkle ¼ teaspoon cinnamon and drizzle 1 teaspoon honey on each bowl.

5. Mix the cream with the cold almond milk and serve it on the side in a small pitcher.

Chapter 3
Salads to Live For

Avocado Grapefruit Salad

Serves 4

Calories: 340.63
Protein: 2.94 grams
Carbohydrates: 22.81 grams
Fiber: 8.28 grams
Fat: 29.02 grams

2 avocados
1 ruby red grapefruit
¼ cup pomegranate seeds
1 tablespoon minced shallot
¼ cup olive oil
1 tablespoon pomegranate juice
salt and pepper, to taste

This pretty pink and green salad is studded with jewels of ruby pomegranate seeds. Pomegranates are loaded with protective phytochemicals, which include antioxidants. Try to incorporate them into different salads and desserts.

1. Cut the avocados in half and remove the pits. Cut the avocado halves, still in the skin, into long thin strips. Scoop the meat out of the skin with a large spoon. Fan the strips out on a serving plate.

2. Peel the grapefruit skin. Cut sections off the grapefruit with a sharp knife.

3. Squeeze the juice from some of the grapefruit sections onto the avocados. Scatter the remaining grapefruit sections over the avocados. Sprinkle pomegranate seeds over the salad.

4. Whisk the shallot, olive oil, pomegranate juice, salt, and pepper together in a bowl.

5. Drizzle the mixture over the salad and serve at room temperature.

Grenadine

The pomegranate used in this salad recipe is a source of ruby red juice. Grenadine is a tart-sweet syrup that is made from pomegranate juice and sugar. It is used to make mixed drinks, including the nonalcoholic Shirley Temple and Roy Rogers. Try mixing a little grenadine in your lemonade.

Coleslaw

*This is a mayonnaise-free version of the shredded cabbage salad
classic. You'll find that the sesame oil adds a wonderful nutty flavor.
You can also garnish the slaw with toasted sesame seeds.*

1. Mix all ingredients together.
2. Refrigerate at least 60 minutes before serving.

Serves 4

Calories: 162.28
Protein: 1.23 grams
Carbohydrates: 4.65 grams
Fiber: 1.95 grams
Fat: 16.03 grams

*3 cups shredded cabbage
¼ cup shredded carrot
¼ cup green onion, sliced on
the bias
¼ cup canola oil
1 teaspoon sesame oil
2 tablespoons rice vinegar
1 tablespoon sesame seeds
salt and pepper, to taste*

Broccoli Slaw

*Broccoli, carrots, raisins, and almonds provide lots of fiber and
flavor in this salad. It's especially good for kids who won't eat cooked broccoli.
You can give them this in place of a hot vegetable.*

1. Mix all ingredients together.
2. Refrigerate at least 60 minutes before serving.

Serves 4

Calories: 169.20
Protein: 4.22 grams
Carbohydrates: 13.09 grams
Fiber: 2.95 grams
Fat: 11.76 grams

*3 cups blanched broccoli
florets
¼ cup shredded carrot
2 tablespoons mayonnaise
1 teaspoon Dijon mustard
1 tablespoon red wine
vinegar
1 tablespoon minced shallots
¼ cup golden raisins
½ cup toasted sliced almonds
salt and pepper, to taste*

Tabouli Salad

This whole-grain salad is made from bulgur wheat, which is simply whole wheat berries that have been steamed, dried, cracked, and rehydrated. Much of the Middle East relies on various versions of tabouli to stretch its meat supply. It absorbs the flavors of spices, aromatic vegetables, and meats.

Serves 6

Calories: 141.52
Protein: 2.34 grams
Carbohydrates: 12.95 grams
Fiber: 2.99 grams
Fat: 9.69 grams

½ cup medium bulgur wheat
1½ cups water
⅓ cup lemon juice
2 tablespoons chopped fresh mint
1 teaspoon salt
1 teaspoon pepper
¼ cup extra-virgin olive oil
1 cup chopped fresh parsley
½ cup chopped green onions
2 large tomatoes, diced
1 tablespoon minced garlic

1. Soak the bulgur in the water for at least 2 hours.

2. Drain the excess water and put the bulgur in a large bowl.

3. Add the remaining ingredients to the bulgur and mix well.

4. Let sit at room temperature for 60 minutes or refrigerate overnight.

5. Serve chilled or at room temperature.

Prepare Your Own Bulgur

If you soak 2 cups of wheat berries in 4 cups of water overnight, you can make your own bulgur the next day. Drain the wheat berries, simmer them in 4 cups of water for 60 minutes, and drain. Dry the wheat berries on a baking sheet pan in a 250°F oven for 45 minutes or until dry. Chop up the dried, cooked wheat berries in a food processor and store in a large jar.

Carrot Salad

The raw carrots and green onions in this recipe provide a great source of fiber. You can use plain mustard if you want to avoid the honey or substitute maple syrup.

Serves 4

Calories: 305.67
Protein: 1.20 grams
Carbohydrates: 12.01 grams
Fiber: 2.21 grams
Fat: 28.90 grams

½ cup salad oil
2 tablespoons honey mustard
1 tablespoon white wine vinegar
salt to taste
pepper to taste
4 medium carrots
2 green onions

1. In a blender combine salad oil, honey mustard, and vinegar and blend until smooth. Add salt and pepper to your taste. Set aside.

2. Peel and shred the carrots and put them in a mixing bowl.

3. Slice the green onions and toss them with the shredded carrots.

4. Pour the dressing over the carrot mixture and toss well to combine.

5. Refrigerate overnight to let the flavors develop.

Carrots

Carrots are native to Afghanistan, cultivated from Queen Anne's Lace, which is a wild white carrot. The orange version we know and love is loaded with vitamin A, sugar, and beta-carotene. A red version contains lycopene, which is the same nutrient that gives tomatoes their red color. Other members of the carrot family include caraway, celery, chervil, cilantro, cumin, dill, fennel, parsley, and parsnips.

Curried Shrimp Salad in a Papaya

*Chilled shrimp and toasted almonds complement the fruits
and vegetables in this knockout luncheon salad. You can add some
toasted sesame seeds to increase the nutrition and fiber value.*

Serves 2

Calories: 314.21
Protein: 8.58 grams
Carbohydrates: 24.33 grams
Fiber: 4.80 grams
Fat: 21.71 grams

2 tablespoons olive oil
¼ cup plain yogurt
1 tablespoon lemon juice
1 teaspoon grated lemon zest
½ teaspoon curry powder
salt and pepper to taste
1 cup cooked peeled shrimp,
    chilled
¼ cup diced celery
¼ cup diced cucumber
¼ cup seedless green grapes,
    halved
1 medium papaya
¼ cup toasted sliced almonds

1. Whisk together olive oil, yogurt, lemon juice, lemon zest, curry powder, salt, and pepper in a mixing bowl.

2. Add the shrimp, celery, cucumber, and grapes and toss to coat with the dressing. Chill salad until ready to serve.

3. Cut the papaya in half lengthwise through the stem area and scoop out the seeds.

4. Fill the papaya with the shrimp salad, mounding it up on top.

5. Sprinkle the almonds on top of the shrimp salad. Serve with a fork and spoon so the papaya flesh can be scooped and eaten after the salad is gone.

Exotic Fruit Salad

This fruit salad is a kaleidoscope of magenta, ruby, jade, sapphire, yellow, orange, and gold with a whole spectrum of flavors to match. The more fruit you put in any salad, the better it is for you in terms of fiber and nutrition.

1. Gently toss everything but the ginger in a large bowl.

2. Chill salad before serving.

3. Sprinkle the ginger and coconut on the salad and serve on individual plates or in one large bowl.

Serves 6

Calories: 103.87
Protein: 0.88 grams
Carbohydrates: 23.29 grams
Fiber: 2.11 grams
Fat: 1.71 grams

*1 blood orange, rind removed
    and cut into segments
½ cup pomegranate seeds
1 kiwifruit, peeled and cut
    into rounds
½ cup blueberries
½ cup quartered strawberries
½ cup fresh pineapple chunks
½ cup peeled mango chunks
¼ cup chopped candied ginger
¼ cup shredded coconut*

Waldorf Salad

This salad is high in fiber because of the apples with skin, celery, grapes, and walnuts. It's delicious for the same reasons.

1. Combine apples, celery, grapes, walnuts, mayonnaise, and yogurt in a bowl.

2. Spoon salad onto lettuce, either on a platter or individual plates.

3. Serve chilled.

Sesame Twist

To add a distinctly Asian flavor and even more fiber to this recipe, stir about 1 teaspoon of toasted sesame oil into the mayonnaise first and then sprinkle the finished salad with a generous amount of sesame seeds.

Serves 4

Calories: 273.93
Protein: 3.67 grams
Carbohydrates: 20.05 grams
Fiber: 3.88 grams
Fat: 21.84 grams

*1 cup diced red apple, skin on
1 cup diced Granny Smith
    apple, skin on
1 cup diced celery
½ cup halved seedless grapes
½ cup chopped walnuts
¼ cup mayonnaise
¼ cup plain yogurt
4 butter lettuce leaves*

Orange and Onion Salad

Serves 4

Calories: 116.89
Protein: 1.35 grams
Carbohydrates: 13.93 grams
Fiber: 2.89 grams
Fat: 7.02 grams

2 navel oranges
1 blood orange
1 small red onion, peeled
2 tablespoons olive oil
2 teaspoons lime juice
salt and pepper to taste
1 tablespoon chopped fresh
parsley

This salad is best served with a Moroccan tagine or stew, and it also goes well with a roast chicken. The lime juice and the onion neutralize each other's sharpness, and a sweeter, finer flavor comes through.

1. Cut the top and bottom off the oranges and stand them up on their cut ends. With a small serrated knife, cut away the rind in strips. Remove as much white pith as you can.

2. Turn the oranges on their sides and cut crosswise into the slices. Arrange the orange slices on a plate.

3. Cut slices from the onion crosswise and scatter them across the orange slices.

4. Put the olive oil, lime juice, salt, pepper, and parsley in a jar with a lid and shake the ingredients to combine.

5. Pour the vinaigrette over the oranges and onions and serve at room temperature or chilled.

Shaved Fennel, Kumquat, and Frisée Salad

Chicory, frisée, curly endive—whatever you call it, the bitter green tastes good with the tart-sweet kumquats and sweet anise-y fennel.

1. Combine olive oil, orange juice, orange zest, shallot, whole-grain mustard, and fennel seeds in a blender and blend until smooth. Add salt and pepper to taste.

2. Thinly slice the fennel bulbs and kumquats and toss them together in a bowl. Remove any kumquat seeds.

3. Divide the frisée among four salad plates and top with the fennel/kumquat mélange. Drizzle the dressing over the salad.

Kumquats

Kumquats are great snacks to pack in a lunch. The olive-sized orange citrus fruits are entirely edible, skins, seeds, and all. The skin is sweet and the interior is sour. Try adding them to your next relish tray along with black and green olives. The only problem with kumquats is that they are only available during the fall-winter season.

Serves 4

Calories: 360.02
Protein: 3.31 grams
Carbohydrates: 28.48 grams
Fiber: 7.11 grams
Fat: 28.20 grams

½ cup olive oil
2 tablespoons orange juice
1 teaspoon grated orange
   zest
1 tablespoon minced shallot
1 teaspoon whole-grain
   mustard
1 teaspoon fennel seeds
salt to taste
pepper to taste
2 fennel bulbs
6 kumquats
2 large handfuls frisée

Wild Rice Salad

Wild rice isn't really rice—it's a different type of grass—but it is prepared like rice is. It lends itself to all sorts of additions, hot or cold. Once cooked, it keeps for a week in the refrigerator.

Serves 4

Calories: 239.05
Protein: 7.23 grams
Carbohydrates: 26.71 grams
Fiber: 2.97 grams
Fat: 12.54 grams

2 cups cooked wild rice, warm
¼ cup diced yellow bell pepper
1 tablespoon minced shallots
¼ cup dried cranberries
½ cup chopped walnuts
2 tablespoons balsamic vinegar
1 tablespoon walnut oil
salt and pepper to taste

1. Mix everything together while the wild rice is still warm. This allows the rice to absorb more flavor.

2. Chill mixture.

3. Adjust seasoning and serve cold.

Wild Rice

For years wild rice was harvested by hand by Native Americans in the lake country of northwestern United States and Canada. Watch for the rice to go from spikes to blooms. It's loaded with fiber and flavor. Plus, you can add dried berries, prunes, apricots, and nuts to give it extra fiber and flavor.

Celery Root Salad

Sometimes celery root that is peeled and cut into julienne strips is available in cans, so check your supermarket for this timesaver.

Serves 4

Calories: 153.81
Protein: 1.08 grams
Carbohydrates: 7.88 grams
Fiber: 1.49 grams
Fat: 13.63 grams

½ pound celery root(s)
¼ cup minced shallots
¼ cup olive oil
2 tablespoons lemon juice
1 teaspoon grated lemon zest
1 teaspoon Dijon mustard
salt and pepper to taste
2 tablespoons chopped chives

1. Peel the celery root(s) and cut them into ¼"-thick slices. Stack the slices a few at a time and cut them into matchstick strips (julienne). Place the sticks in a large bowl.

2. Put the shallots, olive oil, lemon juice, lemon zest, mustard, salt, pepper, and chives in a jar with a lid and shake to combine.

3. Pour the dressing over the celery root and toss to combine. Cover and refrigerate for at least 60 minutes.

4. Serve as part of a salad sampler plate or as a side salad.

Raw or Cooked?

The celery root in this recipe is not cooked but served raw. You may blanch the celery root if you prefer a less crunchy salad. Bring a large pot of water to a boil and plunge the peeled and julienned celery root into it for 5 minutes, then shock them in a large bowl of ice water. Drain them in a colander when they have chilled and proceed with the recipe.

Corn and Tomato Salad

*This salad is a great example of how a diet high in fiber is not
a taste sacrifice. It's a perfect late-summer salad. Make it when local corn is
young and the tomatoes are bursting with juice. Try growing your
own arugula for the spiciest of green flavors.*

Serves 4

Calories: 181.78
Protein: 3.62 grams
Carbohydrates: 26.20 grams
Fiber: 3.65 grams
Fat: 9.08 grams

2 cups fresh sweet corn
2 tablespoons olive oil
½ teaspoon grated lemon
   zest
1 tablespoon fresh lemon
   juice
pinch ground cumin
¼ teaspoon salt
¼ teaspoon pepper
2 tablespoons minced green
   onions
¼ cup diced red bell pepper
¼ cup diced green bell pepper
¼ cup pitted black olives
¼ cup chopped arugula
2 medium tomatoes

1. Steam the corn for 2 minutes and then spread it on a sheet pan to cool.

2. Put the olive oil, lemon zest, lemon juice, cumin, salt, and pepper in a jar and shake to combine.

3. Toss the corn, green onions, bell peppers, black olives, and arugula together in a large bowl.

4. Pour the dressing over the corn salad and toss to combine. Chill for 60 minutes.

5. Slice the tomatoes and serve the corn salad on top.

Green Lentil Salad

Green lentils are smaller and plumper than other lentils, which makes them look like the caviar of lentils. The French have been making lentil salad for centuries. When you make it yourself, you can cook the lentils to your preference.

Serves 4

Calories: 292.21
Protein: 11.57 grams
Carbohydrates: 31.94 grams
Fiber: 8.06 grams
Fat: 13.85 grams

1 cup dried French green
    lentils
5 cups water
1 bay leaf
2 tablespoons olive oil
1 carrot, finely chopped
1 stalk celery, finely chopped
2 tablespoons minced
    shallots
1 teaspoon minced garlic
2 tablespoons extra-virgin
    olive oil
¼ cup lemon juice
1 teaspoon grated lemon zest
1 tablespoon chopped fresh
    thyme
1 tablespoon chopped fresh
    parsley
¼ teaspoon ground coriander
salt and pepper to taste

1. Put the lentils, water, and bay leaf in a saucepan. Bring to a boil, reduce heat, and simmer for 20 minutes. Drain in a colander, remove the bay leaf, and let the lentils cool. Put them in a large bowl and set aside.

2. Heat the olive oil in a sauté pan and cook the carrot, celery, and shallots over medium heat until tender, about 5 minutes. Add to the lentils.

3. Add the garlic, extra-virgin olive oil, lemon juice, lemon zest, thyme, parsley, coriander, salt, and pepper to the lentils. Toss to combine and chill.

4. Serve chilled or at room temperature.

Beans Count

You can soak them overnight and then cook them or buy them canned without losing much of their nutritional makeup. Beans are a substitute for animal proteins in vegetarian cooking, and they add to any meal, vegetarian or not.

Cabbage and Chicken Salad with Peanut Dressing

Serves 4

Calories: 552.77
Protein: 36.06 grams
Carbohydrates: 73.00 grams
Fiber: 4.66 grams
Fat: 13.06 grams

2 egg whites
4 teaspoons Chinese rice wine or dry sherry
1 tablespoon cornstarch
1 teaspoon kosher salt
2 boneless skinless chicken breasts, cut into ¼" strips
¼ cup rice vinegar
¼ teaspoon red pepper flakes
¼ cup chopped cabbage
2 tablespoons tahini
2 tablespoons chopped roasted peanuts
1 tablespoon diced jicama or water chestnut
1 clove peeled garlic, sliced thin
4 cups shredded cabbage
2 tomatoes, cut into cubes
½ cup sliced mushrooms
½ cup julienne zucchini
2 cups crisped cellophane noodles (optional)
¼ cup maltose peanuts

Maltose peanuts are a type of sweet and salty peanut available in Asian grocery stores. They can be replaced by honey roasted or chopped roasted peanuts if desired. Asian cooking relies heavily on peanuts for protein. Rice, soy, and many wonderful veggies stretch a bit of protein.

1. Combine the egg whites, rice wine, cornstarch, and kosher salt in a food processor and blend to a smooth consistency. Put the sliced chicken in a bowl, pour the egg white mixture over it, and toss to coat. Cover and marinate in the refrigerator for 60 minutes.

2. For the dressing, purée the rice vinegar, red pepper flakes, chopped cabbage, tahini, peanuts, jicama, and garlic in a blender. Set aside.

3. Heat 6 cups of water to a simmer and poach the marinated chicken in it for about 5 minutes or until cooked through. Strain the chicken pieces and then place them in a large bowl to cool. Pour half of the dressing over the chicken and toss to combine. Let cool completely.

4. When the chicken has cooled, add the shredded cabbage, tomatoes, mushrooms, and zucchini to the bowl. Pour the remaining dressing in and toss the salad well.

5. Spread the cellophane noodles on a platter and place the chicken salad on top of them. Sprinkle the maltose peanuts over the salad.

Cellophane Noodles

Cellophane noodles, also called glass noodles or bean threads, are dental floss–thin translucent noodles made from mung bean starch. To make crisped noodles, heat peanut oil in a wok to about 400°F. Turn off the heat and immediately add ¼ ounce dry noodles to the hot oil and flash-fry them for about 2 seconds. They will puff up and turn white, like little Styrofoam yarns. Remove immediately and drain on paper towels. Store crisped noodles in an airtight container until ready to use.

Chapter 4
Hearty Soups

Black Bean Soup

Serves 6

Calories: 172.40
Protein: 6.77 grams
Carbohydrates: 24.73 grams
Fiber: 6.85 grams
Fat: 5.25 grams

¼ cup minced shallot
2 tablespoons olive oil
1 large potato, peeled and
    diced
4 cups chicken broth
2 cups cooked black beans
1 teaspoon dried thyme
½ teaspoon ground coriander
1 tablespoon dry sherry
2 teaspoons salt
6 lemon slices
2 tablespoons chopped
    chives

You can use canned black beans to make this recipe immediately or soak dried beans and then cook them before starting this recipe. Traditional garnishes for black bean soup include shredded cheddar cheese and sour cream.

1. Sauté shallots in olive oil. Add potato and chicken broth and simmer for 30 minutes.

2. Add black beans, thyme, and coriander and simmer 45 minutes.

3. Purée ⅓ of the soup in a blender and return it to the pot.

4. Stir in the sherry and salt.

5. Serve hot garnished with lemon slices and chives.

Soaking Beans

To help keep the gas factor down, dried beans need a soak. Fill a saucepan with 1½ quarts water and add 1 cup beans. Bring the water and beans to a boil and simmer for 2 minutes. Turn the heat off and let the beans sit in the water overnight, at least 8 hours. Most of the gas-causing elements will dissolve into the water. Discard the soaking water and add fresh water to cook the beans.

Split Pea Soup

Legumes, like peas, are a source of high fiber and a good source of protein in vegetarian diets. To make this meal completely vegetarian, omit the ham bone and use vegetable stock.

1. Simmer water, split peas, and ham bone for 60 minutes.

2. Add carrot, celery, and onion and simmer for another hour.

3. Remove the ham bone, season the soup with salt and pepper, and serve hot.

Serves 6

Calories: 266.45
Protein: 20.38 grams
Carbohydrates: 43.25 grams
Fiber: 17.64 grams
Fat: 2.00 grams

8 cups water
2 cups split peas
1 ham bone
½ cup diced carrot
¼ cup diced celery
1 cup diced onion
salt to taste
pepper to taste

White Bean Soup

Like the black bean soup recipe, you can use canned white beans to make this recipe immediately or soak dried beans and then cook them before starting this recipe. For added fiber, you can increase the quantities of celery and onion.

1. Sauté the carrots, onion, and celery in the olive oil for 10 to 15 minutes.

2. Add tomato paste and stir to combine.

3. Add chicken broth, beans, and thyme, bring to a boil, and simmer for 25 minutes.

4. Remove the thyme sprig and purée half of the soup in a blender.

5. Return the purée to the pot. Stir and season the soup with salt and pepper. Serve hot.

Serves 4

Calories: 253.34
Protein: 11.10 grams
Carbohydrates: 35.29 grams
Fiber: 8.38 grams
Fat: 7.77 grams

½ cup diced carrots
½ cup diced onion
¼ cup diced celery
2 tablespoons olive oil
1 tablespoon tomato paste
4 cups chicken broth
2 cups cooked white beans
1 sprig fresh thyme
salt and pepper to taste

Lentil Soup

Serves 8

Calories: 199.86
Protein: 15.08 grams
Carbohydrates: 33.99 grams
Fiber: 16.35 grams
Fat: 1.00 grams

2 cups dried lentils
4 cups water
8 cups chicken broth
1 cup peeled, diced potato
½ cup diced carrot
¼ cup diced celery
1 cup diced onion
1 tablespoon kosher salt
3 tablespoons sherry vinegar
pinch of ground cloves
1 cinnamon stick
1 bay leaf
1 teaspoon dried thyme
salt and pepper to taste

Only Americans discard the tasty celery leaves; they're perfectly healthy for you, so keep them in. You can garnish this soup with grated, raw celery root for added flavor and fiber.

1. Soak the lentils in water for 2 hours in a soup pot.

2. Add the chicken broth, potato, carrot, celery, onion, salt, vinegar, cloves, cinnamon stick, bay leaf, and thyme to the pot and simmer for 3 hours.

3. Remove the cinnamon stick and bay leaf and season with salt and pepper to taste. Serve hot.

Fast and Easy

Lentils are faster cooking than other legumes and beans. They are smaller than beans and they don't need to be soaked before cooking. Lentils like assertive flavors like garlic and herbs. Children seem to prefer the yellow or red lentils to the gray-green ones.

Harvest Stew

*Add fresh herbs from the garden to this soup to suit your taste,
and throw in any extra vegetables you may have on hand.*

1. Brown the beef cubes in olive oil. Sprinkle the flour over the meat and stir to coat and distribute.

2. Add the onions, carrots, celery, leek, garlic, zucchini, potato, turnips, tomatoes, bay leaf, thyme sprigs, and beef broth. Bring to a boil, then lower the heat and simmer for 60 minutes.

3. Remove the bay leaf and thyme sprigs. Add the Worcestershire sauce, salt, and pepper. Serve hot.

Serves 6

Calories: 358.19
Protein: 16.70 grams
Carbohydrates: 18.89 grams
Fiber: 2.99 grams
Fat: 24.18 grams

1 pound stewing beef cubes
2 tablespoons olive oil
¼ cup flour
¾ cup diced onions
½ cup sliced carrots
½ cup diced celery
1 leek, cleaned and diced
6 garlic cloves, peeled
2 cups diced zucchini
1 potato, peeled and diced
3 turnips, diced
2 tomatoes, chopped
1 bay leaf
3 sprigs fresh thyme
4 cups beef broth
2 tablespoons Worcestershire sauce
salt and pepper to taste

Celery Soup

Fiber and phytochemicals protect the colon, and celery has both in abundance. Buy only the very greenest celery, not the stripped to the heart offerings.

Serves 6

Calories: 171.93
Protein: 1.69 grams
Carbohydrates: 11.34 grams
Fiber: 2.13 grams
Fat: 14.71 grams

2 tablespoons olive oil
2 cups chopped celery
1 medium onion, chopped
3 tablespoons flour
½ teaspoon salt
½ teaspoon pepper
3 cups vegetable broth
½ cup cream
1 cup thinly sliced celery
1 tablespoon butter

1. Put the olive oil in a soup pot. Sauté the chopped celery and onion over medium heat for 5 minutes. Sprinkle the flour, salt, and pepper over the vegetables and continue cooking for 2 minutes.

2. Gradually add the vegetable broth and bring to a boil. Turn the heat down and simmer for 15 minutes. Purée the soup in a blender and return it to the pot.

3. Stir in the cream and keep the soup warm on low heat.

4. Melt the butter in a sauté pan and sauté the sliced celery until tender, about 5 minutes.

5. Stir the sautéed celery slices into the soup and serve hot.

Creamy Soups

Creamy soups are the most elegant of offerings, suitable for a first course at a sit-down dinner party—and it doesn't take much cream to enrich them. The fiber in these soups is especially digestible for people with diverticulosis or diverticulitis who cannot have seeds or the shells on corn or beans. Fiber is added with a garniture of fresh herbs or grated raw vegetables, such as radishes.

Beet and Cabbage Borscht

A pretty alternative to the red beet is the baby golden beet.
These are delicious and certainly have a more subtle flavor than red beets.

1. Put the olive oil in a soup pot and sauté the caraway seeds, onion, carrots, and celery in it over medium heat until tender, about 15 minutes.

2. Add cabbage, potatoes, tomatoes (with liquid), tomato paste, and beef broth, bring to a boil, and simmer 45 minutes.

3. Add the beets (with liquid), dill, and vinegar and simmer 10–15 minutes.

4. Season with salt and pepper to taste.

5. Serve hot garnished with sour cream and chopped fresh dill and sliced pumpernickel bread.

Red or Green?

Either red or green head cabbage may be used for this recipe since the beets color the soup dark red. The cabbage has a goodly amount of fiber if it's not overcooked. You can also add shredded raw cabbage as a garnish.

Serves 8

Calories: 119.41
Protein: 3.45 grams
Carbohydrates: 11.30 grams
Fiber: 2.54 grams
Fat: 7.35 grams

2 tablespoons olive oil
1 teaspoon caraway seeds
½ cup diced onion
½ cup peeled and diced carrots
½ cup diced celery
2 cups shredded cabbage
½ cup peeled, diced potatoes
1 cup peeled, diced tomatoes (canned)
2 tablespoons tomato paste
6 cups beef broth
2 cups diced beets (canned)
2 tablespoons dried dill weed
¼ cup red wine vinegar
salt and pepper to taste
½ cup sour cream
3 tablespoons chopped fresh dill
pumpernickel bread

Gazpacho Mary

This is a chilled soup with the flavors of tomatoes, celery, and horseradish,
like a puréed virgin Bloody Mary. It will enhance your daily intake
of fiber exponentially and delectably.

Serves 4

Calories: 196.05
Protein: 3.18 grams
Carbohydrates: 16.71 grams
Fiber: 3.84 grams
Fat: 14.33 grams

3 large tomatoes
5 celery hearts
½ yellow bell pepper
1 shallot
½ cucumber
¼ cup lemon juice
¼ cup extra-virgin olive oil
¾ cup tomato juice
½ teaspoon cayenne pepper
   sauce
1 teaspoon Worcestershire
   sauce
1 tablespoon grated
   horseradish
1 teaspoon celery salt
½ teaspoon black pepper

1. Chop the tomatoes and place them in a blender. Chop up one celery heart and save the others for garnish. Add the chopped one to the blender.

2. Chop the pepper, shallot, and cucumber and add them to the blender.

3. Add the remaining ingredients to the blender and purée until smooth and there are no large chunks.

4. Pour into glass tumblers and garnish with celery hearts. Serve chilled.

Coconut Curried Ban-Apple Soup

Bananas, apples, celery, potatoes, and onions all have plenty of fiber, and their flavors marry nicely with the coconut milk and a pinch of curry powder. Adding some roasted peanuts as a garnish ups the fiber too.

1. Put the vegetable broth in a soup pot.

2. Peel the banana and potato, chop them, and put them in the soup pot. Core the apple, chop it, and add it to the soup pot. Chop the celery heart and onion and add them to the soup pot.

3. Bring the soup to a boil, then lower the heat and simmer for 10 to 15 minutes. Add the coconut milk, curry powder, and salt.

4. Put the hot soup in a blender and purée.

5. Serve the soup hot. Garnish with toasted coconut and cilantro.

Cut the Fat

To cut the fat in this recipe, substitute some other creamy liquid for the coconut milk. Try unsweetened soymilk, half-and-half, milk, or plain yogurt. Coconut milk does add a rich and exotic flavor to the soup.

Serves 4

Calories: 255.11
Protein: 3.75 grams
Carbohydrates: 31.87 grams
Fiber: 5.11 grams
Fat: 13.99 grams

2 cups vegetable broth
1 ripe banana
1 large potato
1 Granny Smith apple
1 celery heart
1 sweet onion
1 cup coconut milk
1 teaspoon curry powder
1 teaspoon salt
¼ cup toasted coconut
2 tablespoons chopped fresh cilantro

Minestrone Vegetable Soup

This Italian soup is full of high-fiber vegetables and legumes, such as cabbage, celery, zucchini, navy beans, and garbanzos.

Serves 6

Calories: 202.73
Protein: 9.09 grams
Carbohydrates: 14.79 grams
Fiber: 4.45 grams
Fat: 12.44 grams

½ cup chopped onion
½ cup chopped carrots
¼ cup chopped celery
2 tablespoons olive oil
2 cloves garlic, minced
1 cup chopped cabbage
4 cups chicken broth
1 cup chopped, peeled
*   tomatoes*
2 cups chopped zucchini
½ cup cooked navy beans
½ cup cooked garbanzo
*   beans*
½ cup broken whole-wheat
*   spaghetti*
salt and pepper to taste
¼ cup basil pesto
½ cup grated Parmesan
*   cheese*

1. Sauté the onions, carrots, and celery in the olive oil for 15 minutes.

2. Add garlic and cabbage and cook until cabbage is wilted.

3. Add chicken broth, tomatoes, zucchini, navy beans, and garbanzo beans and bring to a boil.

4. Simmer for 15 minutes. Add the broken spaghetti and simmer 15 minutes longer; then season with salt and pepper.

5. Serve hot with pesto and Parmesan cheese in each serving.

Corn Soup

Fresh corn kernels have an abundance of fiber, both soluble and insoluble. You will also get a good amount of vitamin C as well as fiber from the red pepper.

1. Simmer the corn cobs in the water for 15 minutes.

2. Meanwhile, sauté the carrot, celery, and onion in olive oil in a separate pan until tender. Add the corn kernels and sauté 5 minutes.

3. Remove the corn cobs from the water in the soup pot and discard them. Add the sautéed vegetables to the soup pot and simmer 15 minutes. Purée soup in a blender; then return to the pot.

4. Dissolve cornstarch in ¼ cup cold milk. Add remaining milk to soup pot and bring to a simmer. Stir in the cornstarch mixture and cook stirring until thickened, about 3 minutes. Remove from heat and season with salt and pepper.

5. Serve hot. Garnish with roasted red bell peppers, baby corn, and chives.

Summer Soups in Winter

During the chilly season when farmer's markets are closed and your garden is brown, you can still get wonderful fresh produce and an abundance of excellent frozen vegetables. Of course, you can always find cabbage, zucchini, and tomatoes. The nutrition of brightly colored food is undisputed. The fiber is there—use it!

Serves 6

Calories: 160.09
Protein: 4.34 grams
Carbohydrates: 24.88 grams
Fiber: 3.70 grams
Fat: 6.01 grams

*4 ears corn, kernels cut from
    cob and cobs saved
5 cups water
1 carrot, peeled and diced
1 stalk celery, sliced
1 small onion, diced
2 tablespoons olive oil
1 tablespoon cornstarch
1 cup milk
salt and pepper to taste
½ cup roasted red bell
    peppers, diced
¼ cup baby corn
2 tablespoons chopped
    chives*

Pumpkin Soup

This soup is packed with a triple play of fiber in the pumpkin, dried cranberries, and pumpkin seeds. Pumpkin is also one of the highest sources of vitamin A on the list.

Serves 4

Calories: 359.29
Protein: 13.30 grams
Carbohydrates: 34.26 grams
Fiber: 6.94 grams
Fat: 20.61 grams

½ cup chopped shallots
2 tablespoons chopped fresh sage
2 tablespoons olive oil
4 cups vegetable broth
2 cups canned pumpkin, peeled and chopped
½ cup plain yogurt
salt to taste
white pepper to taste
½ cup dried cranberries
½ cup roasted pumpkin seeds

1. Sauté shallots and sage in olive oil in a soup pot 5 minutes over medium heat. Add vegetable broth and pumpkin.

2. Bring to a boil, then simmer until pumpkin is cooked, about 45 minutes.

3. Purée soup in a blender until smooth.

4. Stir in yogurt and season with salt and white pepper.

5. Serve garnished with dried cranberries and roasted pumpkin seeds sprinkled on top.

Pepitas

Making your own toasted pumpkin seeds to snack on is noble, but you can buy pumpkin seeds that have already been roasted and shelled. They're called pepitas, and more and more supermarkets are carrying them. Just be sure the ones you buy shelled and roasted are not overloaded with sodium.

Cold Fennel Soup

*Cold soups like this one are refreshing to sip on a hot day,
especially with yogurt ice cubes. Fennel is wonderful cooked or raw,
with a sweet flavor that only intensifies when you cook it.*

1. Heat the olive oil in a soup pot. Sauté the chopped celery and onion over medium heat for 5 minutes. Sprinkle the fennel seeds, flour, salt, and pepper over the vegetables and continue cooking for 2 minutes.

2. Gradually add the vegetable broth and bring to a boil. Turn the heat down and simmer for about 15 minutes. Purée the soup in a blender.

3. Chill the soup completely.

4. Stir the diced fennel bulb, pear, and chopped fennel fronds with the liqueur.

5. Whisk the yogurt into the chilled soup and adjust the seasoning with salt and pepper. Serve it in coffee mugs garnished with the diced fennel mixture.

Serves 6

Calories: 110.69
Protein: 2.60 grams
Carbohydrates: 13.25 grams
Fiber: 2.98 grams
Fat: 5.61 grams

2 tablespoons olive oil
2 cups chopped celery
1 medium sweet onion, chopped
1 teaspoon fennel seeds
3 tablespoons flour
½ teaspoon salt
½ teaspoon pepper
3 cups vegetable broth
1 cup diced fennel bulb
½ cup diced pear
1 tablespoon chopped fennel fronds
1 tablespoon anise liqueur
½ cup plain yogurt

Southwest Tortilla Soup

Serves 6

Calories: 485.86
Protein: 14.30 grams
Carbohydrates: 59.82 grams
Fiber: 11.29 grams
Fat: 24.38 grams

1 small onion, diced
1 celery stalk, diced
2 tablespoons olive oil
2 garlic cloves, minced
1 cup corn kernels
4 cups chicken broth
*½ cup diced roasted red bell
    pepper*
1 cup diced, peeled tomatoes
½ cup tomato purée
*3 blue corn tortillas,
    cut in ¼" strips*
1 teaspoon ground cumin
1 tablespoon chili powder
*2 teaspoons puréed chipotle
    peppers in adobo sauce*
salt and pepper to taste
¼ cup chopped cilantro
2 avocados, diced
*1 cup crushed blue corn
    tortilla chips*
*1 cup shredded Monterey
    Jack cheese*

From corn to avocados, this soup is packed with fiber and flavor. Be sure to leave the "strings" on the celery for fiber, and always include the leaves.

1. Sauté the onion and celery in olive oil until translucent. Add the garlic, corn, chicken broth, bell pepper, tomatoes, and tomato purée.

2. Bring to a boil, add the tortilla strips, cumin, chili powder, and chipotle purée, and simmer for 30 minutes. Remove from heat.

3. Season the soup with salt, pepper, and cilantro.

4. Serve the soup hot garnished with diced avocado, blue corn tortilla chips, and cheese.

Creamy Tortilla Soup

This recipe is for a brothy version of tortilla soup. To transform this recipe into a creamy style of tortilla soup, simply purée the corn kernels before adding them. The starch in the puréed corn will thicken the soup into a creamy yellow version studded with a colorful confetti of vegetables.

Chapter 5
Healthy Sandwiches

Reuben on Pumpernickel

*This classic deli sandwich is a way to add fiber to a corned beef sandwich
by way of the addition of sauerkraut, which is made from cabbage.
Look for pumpernickel bread made with whole grains. If you are dieting,
substitute butter-flavored nonstick spray for butter.*

Serves 1

Calories: 685.41
Protein: 28.58 grams
Carbohydrates: 33.54 grams
Fiber: 5.58 grams
Fat: 48.55 grams

1 tablespoon butter
2 slices pumpernickel bread
1 slice Swiss cheese
3 ounces thinly sliced corned
    beef brisket
¼ cup drained sauerkraut
2 tablespoons Thousand
    Island salad dressing
1 garlic dill pickle spear

1. Butter one side of each slice of bread.

2. Layer one slice of bread, butter-side out, with cheese, corned beef, sauerkraut, and dressing. Top with the other slice of bread, butter-side out.

3. Grill sandwich in a skillet or on a griddle until toasted.

4. Cut in half and serve warm with a garlic dill pickle spear.

Avocado Bagel

*This sandwich is on an untoasted bagel, so be sure to use a fresh,
chewy bagel. You can also slice the bagel in thirds horizontally, adding a bit
more onion and slicing the avocado thinly.*

Serves 1

Calories: 671.55
Protein: 19.29 grams
Carbohydrates: 75.48 grams
Fiber: 16.42 grams
Fat: 36.96 grams

2 ounces whipped cream
    cheese
1 whole-wheat bagel, sliced
1 slice tomato
1 slice red onion
½ avocado, sliced
¼ cup alfalfa sprouts

1. Spread the cream cheese on both halves of the bagel.

2. Layer the tomato, red onion, avocado, and alfalfa sprouts on the bottom half of the bagel.

3. Top with the other half of the bagel and cut the sandwich in half.

Roasted Vegetable Sandwich

*The variety of vegetables in this sandwich provides a lot of fiber
with a lot of flavor. If you leave the skin on the eggplant, you'll have more fiber.
If you are grilling outdoors, add extra vegetables and use them
the next day on a sandwich. Try to find whole-grain Foccacia;
it's got loads more nutrition and fiber than white bread.*

1. Preheat the oven to 375°F.

2. Brush the eggplant, zucchini, summer squash, red onion, and fennel slices with the olive oil and sprinkle them with salt and pepper.

3. Place them on a baking pan lined with nonstick foil and roast them in the oven for about 35 minutes. Let cool.

4. Mix the mayonnaise and pesto and spread the mixture onto the inside of both the top and bottom pieces of Foccacia.

5. Layer the roasted vegetables, including the red bell pepper, on the bottom half of the Foccacia, and then top them with alfalfa sprouts. Place the top half of Foccacia on and cut the sandwich in half diagonally. Serve with carrot sticks.

Grilled Vegetables

From sandwich fillings to salads to side dishes, grilled vegetables are absolutely versatile. They are beautiful when dressed with a bit of sesame oil for an Asian flavor and served over brown rice. Add Mediterranean herbs, such as basil, oregano, and/or rosemary and toss them over an arugula salad. You'll get great flavor as well as plenty of fiber.

Yields 1 sandwich

Calories: 343.98
Protein: 7.46 grams
Carbohydrates: 39.83 grams
Fiber: 5.19 grams
Fat: 18.46 grams

½"-thick slice eggplant
2 ½"-thick slices zucchini
2 ½"-thick slices yellow
    summer squash
½"-thick slice red onion
½"-thick slice fennel bulb
2 teaspoons olive oil
½ teaspoon salt
¼ teaspoon pepper
1 teaspoon mayonnaise
1 teaspoon basil pesto
1 square Foccacia bread, split
    horizontally
1 large piece roasted red bell
    pepper
¼ cup alfalfa sprouts
carrot sticks

Peanut Butter–Banana Tortilla Wrap

Yields 1 wrap

Calories: 554.83
Protein: 18.02 grams
Carbohydrates: 62.21 grams
Fiber: 10.38 grams
Fat: 32.86 grams

1 large whole–wheat tortilla
2 tablespoons peanut butter
¼ cup sunflower seeds,
    shelled and roasted
1 banana, peeled

Bananas, which contain potassium and fiber, are a naturally sweet addition to any peanut butter sandwich—just ask Elvis.

1. Lay the tortilla out on a flat surface. Spread the peanut butter over most of the tortilla.

2. Sprinkle the sunflower seeds over the peanut butter. Lay the banana on the peanut butter and roll the tortilla around it like a carpet.

3. Cut the wrap in half diagonally.

Walnut Tarragon Chicken Salad on Raisin Foccacia

Serves 6

Calories: 648.40
Protein: 50.25
Carbohydrates: 30.05 grams
Fiber: 1.75 grams
Fat: 36.02 grams

1 oven-roasted chicken,
    bones and skin removed
½ cup mayonnaise
½ cup plain yogurt
1 tablespoon chopped
    tarragon
¼ cup diced celery
½ cup chopped walnuts
salt and pepper to taste
6 squares raisin Foccacia

This sandwich is prepared quickly when made from a convenient preroasted chicken from the supermarket. Make the recipe for Raisin Foccacia (page 243), but use golden raisins instead. To vary this, try almonds instead of walnuts and add a slice of Romaine lettuce.

1. Shred the chicken with your fingers.

2. Combine the mayonnaise, yogurt, and tarragon.

3. Add the shredded chicken, celery, and walnuts to the yogurt mixture.

4. Season with salt and pepper, taste, and adjust seasoning.

5. Slice the foccacia squares in half horizontally and make sandwiches with chicken salad.

Hummus Pita Sandwich

Use the freshest whole-wheat pita bread you can find for this crunchy, juicy, cool sandwich. Some fresh, chopped mint is an excellent addition.

Serves 1

Calories: 452.61
Protein: 15.55 grams
Carbohydrates: 63.36 grams
Fiber: 10.17 grams
Fat: 17.82 grams

1. Mix the yogurt and ranch dressing spices. Set aside in the refrigerator.

2. To make the hummus, purée the garlic and salt in a food processor. Add the garbanzo beans and purée to a paste. Add the tahini, lemon juice, olive oil, and cumin, and process until smooth, scraping down the sides of the bowl.

3. Spread the hummus on one side of the pita bread. Add carrots, tomatoes, cucumbers, and sprouts. Drizzle the yogurt sauce on and fold the pita in half like a taco.

¼ cup plain yogurt
¼ teaspoon ranch dressing spice mix
1 small clove garlic, peeled
pinch of salt
¼ cup canned garbanzo beans
1 tablespoon tahini
1 teaspoon lemon juice
1 teaspoon olive oil
pinch of ground cumin
1 whole-wheat pita bread round
¼ cup shredded carrots
¼ cup diced Roma tomatoes
5 slices cucumber
¼ cup alfalfa sprouts

Wrap It Up!

It seems that every culture has a way of putting savory and sweet mixtures into delectable wrappings. You can put sweet and savory together, as in a fruity, curried shrimp mixture. You can make your fillings rich in fiber and stuff them into a good, multigrain pita or hero roll. Just be creative and experiment to build a diet high in whole grains and fiber for yourself and your family.

Stone Fruit Slaw on Cornmeal Catfish Po'Boy

*Cornmeal, nectarine, plum, celery, and celery seed provide
enough fiber to indulge in a fried-fish po'boy and feel good about it.
You can also substitute a whole-grain baguette for the submarine sandwich
bun. That way, you'll get some vitamin B and extra fiber.*

Serves 1

Calories: 662.17
Protein: 27.97 grams
Carbohydrates: 67.30 grams
Fiber: 5.77 grams
Fat: 31.79 grams

1 catfish fillet, about ¼ pound
¼ cup yellow cornmeal
⅛ teaspoon salt
pinch cayenne pepper
¼ cup canola oil
½ nectarine, pit removed
½ plum, pit removed
1 teaspoon mayonnaise
2 teaspoons plain yogurt
1 teaspoon lemon juice
1 teaspoon grated lemon zest
1 teaspoon grated fresh
    ginger
1 teaspoon celery seeds
salt to taste
pepper to taste
1 tablespoon minced celery
6" submarine sandwich bun
¼ cup shredded lettuce

1. Rinse the catfish fillet and pat dry with a paper towel.

2. Mix the cornmeal, salt, and cayenne pepper together.

3. Heat the canola oil in a large skillet over medium-high heat. Dip the catfish fillet into the cornmeal mixture, then carefully place in the hot oil. Cook for 3 minutes, then turn it over and cook until catfish can be flaked with a fork, about 2 minutes. Drain catfish on paper towels.

4. Cut the nectarine and plum into matchstick strips. Mix the mayonnaise, yogurt, lemon juice, lemon zest, ginger, celery seeds, salt, and pepper together, then add the nectarine, plum, and celery and toss to combine.

5. Break the catfish into pieces and place them in the bun. Top the catfish with the slaw and lettuce.

Crunchy Tuna Salad Melt on Rye

*Tuna salad is made chunky with onions and celery, and seeded
rye bread boosts the fiber count, too. The addition of a minced
dill pickle or pickle spears on the side will add to the flavor and fiber.*

1. Combine tuna, onion, celery, cheese, and mayonnaise in a bowl.

2. Season with parsley, salt, and pepper.

3. Make sandwiches out of the tuna salad and grill on a griddle or in a skillet until golden and toasted.

Serves 4

Calories: 399.69
Protein: 21.55 grams
Carbohydrates: 31.58 grams
Fiber: 2.27 grams
Fat: 21.04 grams

*6-ounce can tuna packed in
   water, drained*
¼ cup onion, diced
2 tablespoons celery, diced
*¾ cup shredded Monterey
   Jack cheese*
¼ cup mayonnaise
1 tablespoon chopped parsley
salt to taste
pepper to taste
8 slices seeded rye bread
nonstick spray oil

Cashew Egg Salad Sandwich

*This recipe lends fiber to an egg salad sandwich with multigrain bread
and the addition of celery, onions, and cashews to the egg mixture.*

1. Peel and chop the hard-boiled eggs and put in a bowl with celery and green onions. Toss briefly to mix.

2. Add mayonnaise, yogurt, mustard, honey, and curry powder to the bowl and mix well.

3. Season with salt and pepper to taste.

4. Sprinkle the cashews over the egg salad and fold them into the mixture.

5. Make sandwiches with the egg salad, lettuce, and multigrain bread and cut into fours diagonally.

Serves 2

Calories: 564.24
Protein: 17.65 grams
Carbohydrates: 35.81 grams
Fiber: 7.10 grams
Fat: 41.61 grams

3 hard-boiled eggs
2 tablespoons diced celery
*1 tablespoon chopped green
   onions*
¼ cup mayonnaise
1 tablespoon plain yogurt
2 tablespoons Dijon mustard
2 teaspoons honey
¼ teaspoon curry powder
salt to taste
pepper to taste
¼ cup chopped toasted cashews
4 leaves red or green leaf lettuce
4 slices multigrain bread

Fish Taco with Purple Cabbage

Two tortillas are used for one hearty taco in this recipe to keep the taco walls together. Corn tortillas have a lot more flavor than white flour tortillas. They also tend to be thicker and heavier and loaded with healthful fiber. They can be blistered on the grill, pan toasted, or fried.

Serves 1

Calories: 341.81
Protein: 28.22 grams
Carbohydrates: 35.58 grams
Fiber: 4.29 grams
Fat: 10.51 grams

2 corn tortillas
¼ pound firm white fish such as halibut or snapper
1 teaspoon olive oil
pinch of salt and pepper
1 lemon wedge
¼ cup cooked corn kernels
1 teaspoon diced jalapeño pepper (optional)
¼ cup shredded purple cabbage
1 teaspoon tartar sauce

1. Wrap tortillas in a paper towel and warm in the microwave, then wrap in foil to keep warm.

2. Brush the fish with olive oil and sprinkle with salt and pepper. Grill for 4 minutes on each side. Break the cooked fish into smaller chunks.

3. Stack the two tortillas on top of each other and place the fish in the middle.

4. Squeeze the lemon wedge on the fish, then top with corn, jalapeño pepper, purple cabbage, and tartar sauce.

5. Fold the tortillas in half and eat with plenty of napkins.

Stuffing Tortillas

You can stuff a tortilla with any sort of sandwich filling. Try mixing cooked black beans, corn, chopped tomatoes, and some chipotle sauce in adobo and putting it into a tortilla. Shrimp and pineapple with a bit of mayonnaise and macadamia nuts will add fiber and a Hawaiian feeling.

Sunflower Veggie Burgers

Vary the herbs in this recipe for your own favorite flavors.
For a vegan version of the recipe, substitute vegetable broth for beef broth
and omit Worcestershire sauce, as it has a trace of anchovy flavoring.
You can serve these burgers with pesto, add cheese to melt on top,
and make some caramelized onions to add to the fiber.

1. Put broth, water, bulgur, and lentils in a saucepan. Bring to a simmer, cover, and turn to low for 30 minutes. Set aside.

2. In a large bowl, combine the mushrooms, shallot, herbs, spices, mustard, salt, sunflower seeds, and whole-wheat flour.

3. Stir the miso, soy sauce, and Worcestershire sauce into the warm bulgur mixture, then add the mixture to the mushroom mixture. Stir well, then stir in the bread crumbs.

4. Measure and mold the mixture into 7 or 8 portions on a wax paper–lined sheet pan. Press down the mounds with your hand to flatten them slightly into patties. Cover with plastic wrap and refrigerate 3 hours or overnight.

5. To cook the patties, brush both sides with olive oil and cook in a nonstick pan 2 minutes per side over medium-high heat. Serve hot on buns with condiments of your choice.

Veggie Burgers

These luscious treats, made with various legumes such as chickpeas, black beans, black-eyed peas, chickpeas, and soy are now available everywhere in frozen form. You can make your own using the recipes in this chapter for a fresher, more hands-on approach. They are a high-fiber, nutritious lunch, dinner, or snack.

Yields 7–8 burgers

Calories: 268.05
Protein: 10.60 grams
Carbohydrates: 28.97 grams
Fiber: 7.06 grams
Fat: 13.88 grams

1½ cups beef broth
½ cup water
¾ cup medium bulgur
⅓ cup dried red lentils
1½ cups chopped mushrooms
1 minced shallot
½ teaspoon celery salt
1½ teaspoons chopped fresh oregano
½ teaspoon chopped fresh thyme
1½ teaspoons chopped fresh sage
¼ teaspoon onion powder
¼ teaspoon paprika
1 teaspoon Dijon mustard
1 teaspoon kosher salt
1 cup sunflower seeds, shelled and roasted (no salt)
½ cup whole-wheat flour
2 teaspoons instant yellow miso
1 tablespoon soy sauce
1 tablespoon Worcestershire sauce
2 tablespoons bread crumbs
olive oil

Falafel Sandwich

This is a Middle Eastern classic. Stands are on every downtown street, as ubiquitous as McDonalds but much healthier.

Calories: 449.29
Protein: 12.55 grams
Carbohydrates: 51.72 grams
Fiber: 10.58 grams
Fat: 23.65 grams

1 cup dried garbanzo beans
½ cup chopped red onion
3 cloves garlic, peeled
1 teaspoon salt
1 teaspoon pepper
1 teaspoon ground cumin
pinch of cayenne pepper
1 teaspoon baking powder
3 tablespoons all-purpose flour
3 tablespoons whole-wheat flour
2 cups vegetable oil
3 rounds of pita bread
6 tablespoons hummus
1 cup chopped fresh tomatoes
1 cup shredded lettuce
½ cup chopped cucumbers
6 tablespoons plain yogurt
2 tablespoons chopped fresh parsley

1. Soak the garbanzo beans in 3 cups of water overnight.

2. Drain the garbanzo beans and put them in a food processor with the red onion, garlic, salt, pepper, cumin, and cayenne pepper. Pulse until everything is combined and the texture is fine but not a paste.

3. Sprinkle the baking powder and flours over the mixture and pulse again until well combined. Refrigerate for 3 hours.

4. Heat the oil in a deep fryer or large pot to 375°F. Shape falafel mixture into small balls and fry 4 to 5 at a time. Drain on paper towels.

5. Cut the pita rounds in half and open them to create a pocket bread out of each half. For each sandwich, spread the inside of a pita pocket with hummus, stuff a few falafel into it, and top with tomatoes, lettuce, and cucumbers. Drizzle yogurt over the top and sprinkle with parsley.

Meatless Meatloaf Sandwich

You may use vegetable broth instead of beef for a vegetarian dish. However, it would not be vegan because it still has animal products— egg, cheese, and Worcestershire sauce.

Serves 8

Calories: 396.68 grams
Protein: 13.45 grams
Carbohydrates: 40.72 grams
Fiber: 9.71 grams
Fat: 23.14 grams

1. Preheat oven to 350°F. Spray a loaf pan with oil.

2. Bring the beef broth to a boil in a saucepan and add the kasha. Cover, turn down the heat, and simmer for 15 minutes.

3. Add the olive oil to the sauté pan and sauté the carrots, onion, and celery in it for 5 minutes. Transfer them to a large bowl.

4. Add the Parmesan cheese, parsley, Dijon mustard, Worcestershire sauce, egg, salt, and pepper and mix together with a wooden spoon. Add the cooked kasha and pecans and combine thoroughly. Add a little beef broth if it seems too dry.

5. Press the mixture into the oiled loaf pan. Spread the tomato paste on top of the loaf, sprinkle the brown sugar over the tomato paste and scatter the red onions across and bake 30 minutes. Remove the meatless loaf from the loaf pan and cut into slices.

6. Per sandwich: Sprinkle 1 tablespoon Parmesan cheese on each meatless loaf slice and brown in a skillet, then sandwich it between 2 slices of bread. Add lettuce, mayonnaise, ketchup, or any other sandwich ingredients you like.

1 cup beef broth
¾ cup kasha
¼ cup olive oil
¾ cup shredded carrots
1 cup diced onion
½ cup diced celery
¼ cup grated Parmesan
    cheese
2 tablespoons chopped fresh
    parsley
1 tablespoon Dijon mustard
1 tablespoon Worcestershire
    sauce
1 egg, beaten
1 teaspoon salt
½ teaspoon pepper
1 cup finely chopped pecans,
    in a food processor
2 tablespoons tomato paste
1 tablespoon brown sugar
½ cup sliced red onions
1 tablespoon grated
    Parmesan cheese per
    sandwich
2 slices of bread per sandwich

Kasha Buckwheat Groats

Kasha is a term that means porridge, and can be made from grains such as wheat, buckwheat, and rice. It is often used to refer specifically to whole-grain buckwheat, or groats, in the United States. You can make a meaty meatloaf and add fiber with a few tablespoons of unflavored kasha.

Cranberry Turkey Salad Sandwich

*A whole-wheat croissant, celery, and dried cranberries add fiber
to a plain turkey sandwich in this recipe.*

1. Combine the smoked turkey, mayonnaise, celery, and cranberries.

2. Mix well and season with salt and pepper.

3. Cut the croissant in half horizontally, lay the lettuce on the bottom, and top it with the turkey salad. Put the top of the croissant on and cut the sandwich in half.

Open-Face Ham Salad Sandwich

*These gooey melted sandwiches are made on whole-grain English muffins,
with onions, celery, parsley, and celery seed bumping up the fiber content.
Cut each half muffin in quarters for neater eating.*

1. Preheat the broiler. Put the ham in a food processor with the cheese, onion, celery, parsley, celery seed, mustard, olive oil, and egg. Pulse to combine into a spreadable consistency.

2. Spread the mixture onto the muffin halves and set them on a broiler pan lined with nonstick foil.

3. Broil until brown and bubbly. Serve hot.

Chapter 6
Appealing Appetizers

Zinfandel Pears with Greens and Hazelnuts

The pears in this recipe are half red and half white from the cooking method. You may double the pears in this recipe to serve as a luncheon entrée salad with a whole pear each. To add protein to a pear salad entrée, sprinkle a tablespoon of crumbled Gorgonzola on each serving.

Serves 4
Serving Size ¼ recipe

Calories: 525.36
Protein: 3.56 grams
Carbohydrates: 46.15 grams
Fiber: 5.23 grams
Fat: 37.46 grams

¼ cup Zinfandel
2 tablespoons lemon juice
½ cup sugar
2 pears
1 strip lemon peel
2 tablespoons red wine
    vinegar
1 teaspoon minced shallot
½ teaspoon Dijon mustard
salt and pepper to taste
½ cup olive oil
4 cups mixed baby greens
½ cup toasted hazelnuts

1. Mix the Zinfandel, lemon juice, and sugar with 2 cups of water in a pot and bring to a boil. Peel the pears around the bottom but not up the shoulders and neck. Reduce the boiling liquid to a simmer, add the lemon peel and the half-peeled pears. Cook over medium-low heat for 45 minutes. Let pears cool, then peel, halve, and core them. Chill in the refrigerator.

2. Reduce the pear poaching liquid in a saucepan until it is syrupy, then chill it.

3. Mix the red wine vinegar, shallot, mustard, salt, and pepper together in a bowl with a whisk. Whisk in the olive oil.

4. Toss the mixed greens with the dressing and plate them. Cut the pear halves into slices and arrange the slices of one-half pear on each plate of greens. Drizzle some of the reduced poaching syrup over the pears.

5. Chop the toasted hazelnuts into large pieces and scatter them over the salads.

Going Nuts for Nuts

Nuts are a fine source of fiber and provide excellent nutritional value. If you toast the nuts before adding them to your salad, they will be even crunchier and tastier. Chopped nuts, mixed with cream cheese and spread on multigrain crackers, make an excellent side for soups or salads.

Artichokes with Aioli

Whole cooked artichokes are usually eaten leaf by delicious leaf, dipped in melted butter while still warm, or chilled like this recipe and dipped in aioli. This is a classic Italian antipasto dish that you can also serve with frozen, cooked baby artichoke hearts. Fresh ones are far better than canned and even taste more fibrous, not mushy!

Serves 4
Serving Size 1 artichoke

Calories: 411.84
Protein: 4.71 grams
Carbohydrates: 16.38 grams
Fiber: 6.75 grams
Fat: 36.44 grams

4 whole artichokes
1 lemon, cut in half
1½ cups water
½ cup dry white wine
1 clove garlic, minced
1 tablespoon olive oil
1 teaspoon fresh lemon juice
¾ cup mayonnaise

1. Prepare the artichokes by cutting the stems off the bottoms first. Rub the cut lemon on all the places of the artichokes you will cut to prevent browning. Next cut the top inch off each artichoke with a serrated knife and discard. Rub the lemon on the cut. Snip the thorny tips off the remaining leaves with kitchen scissors and rub the cut surface with the lemon.

2. Pull out the center leaves to expose the fuzzy choke in the center, and then scoop out the choke with a melon baller. Squeeze lemon juice into the center of each artichoke.

3. Pour the water and white wine into the bottom of a large pot. Place a steamer rack in the bottom of the pot and put the artichokes upside-down on the rack. Cover the pot with a tight fitting lid and simmer for 50 minutes or until a leaf can be pulled easily from an artichoke. Remove the artichokes and let them drain and cool upside-down. Turn them over and chill them in the refrigerator.

4. Combine the garlic, olive oil, lemon juice, and mayonnaise in a food processor while the artichokes chill. Chill this quick aioli until ready to serve.

5. Put each chilled artichoke on an appetizer plate, spoon the aioli into the middle of each artichoke, and serve.

Hummus Plate

Hummus is an essential component of the meze selection of appetizers served in Greece, Turkey, and the Middle East. The fiber content is classic, and the contrasting flavors of olives gives a delightful taste experience.

Serves 4

Calories: 525.29
Protein: 15.28 grams
Carbohydrates: 60.13 grams
Fiber: 8.37 grams
Fat: 26.31 grams

6 cloves garlic, peeled
½ teaspoon salt
1½ cups cooked garbanzo beans
⅓ cup tahini
2 tablespoons lemon juice
3 tablespoons olive oil
½ teaspoon ground cumin
4 pita bread rounds
1 cup assorted olives
1 cup cherry tomatoes

1. Purée the garlic and salt in a food processor. Drain and add the garbanzo beans and purée to a paste.

2. Add the tahini, lemon juice, 2 tablespoons olive oil, and cumin and process until smooth, scraping down the sides of the bowl.

3. Transfer the finished hummus to a bowl and drizzle the remaining tablespoon of olive oil over it.

4. Cut the pita bread into triangles and serve them on the side of the hummus with the olives and cherry tomatoes.

What If I Can't Find Tahini?

Tahini is a paste made from ground sesame seeds that is used in Middle Eastern cuisine. It has a nutty, malt flavor that pairs well with chickpeas in hummus. You may substitute peanut butter in a pinch, but try to use the real thing. You will find many uses for it other than in hummus.

White Bean Dip

This dip is similar to hummus, only it is made with white beans instead of garbanzo beans. Many Italian antipasti platters include this dip with toasted chunks of multigrain bread. You can vary the seasonings by adding fresh basil or oregano. Dot it on halved cherry tomatoes for a great cocktail snack.

1. Purée the garlic and salt in a food processor. Drain and add the white beans and purée to a paste.

2. Add the remaining ingredients and process until smooth, scraping down the sides of the bowl.

3. Transfer the finished purée to a bowl and serve with crackers or pita bread and carrot sticks.

Serves 4
Serving Size ½ cup

Calories: 281.06
Protein: 9.64 grams
Carbohydrates: 22.83 grams
Fiber: 8.01 grams
Fat: 18.04 grams

2 cloves garlic, peeled
½ teaspoon salt
1½ cups cooked white beans
⅓ cup tahini
2 tablespoons lemon juice
2 tablespoons olive oil
1 teaspoon thyme

Guacamole

This favorite from Mexican cuisine is packed with fiber since it is composed mostly of avocado and served on toasted corn chips. For extra fiber, add ¼ cup of minced white onion. You can also add a bit of minced jalapeño pepper for heat.

Serves 4
Serving Size 1 cup

Calories: 328.88
Protein: 4.1 grams
Carbohydrates: 16.49 grams
Fiber: 10.13 grams
Fat: 30.81 grams

4 ripe avocados
1 clove garlic, minced
¼ cup lime juice
salt to taste

1. Cut the avocados in half, remove the pits, and scoop out the flesh into a bowl. Mash it up with a potato masher.

2. Stir in the garlic and lime juice.

3. Season to taste with salt.

Black Bean Nachos with Corn Tomato Salsa

Black beans, cornmeal tortilla chips, tomatoes, and corn all boost the fiber content higher than nacho chips with plain salsa.

Serves 4

Calories: 581.61
Protein: 22.59 grams
Carbohydrates: 40.54 grams
Fiber: 8.26 grams
Fat: 37.51 grams

4 cups corn tortilla chips
1 cup cooked black beans
½ cup sour cream
2 cups shredded cheddar cheese
½ cup corn kernels
1 ripe tomato, diced
2 tablespoons chopped fresh cilantro
¼ cup diced red onion
1 tablespoon diced jalapeño pepper
¼ cup fresh lime juice
½ cup guacamole
2 tablespoons sliced black olives
1 tablespoon sliced green onions

1. Preheat the oven to 350°F.

2. Scatter the tortilla chips on an ovenproof platter and set aside.

3. Mash the black beans with half of the sour cream and put spoonfuls of the bean mixture all over the tortilla chips. Sprinkle the cheddar cheese over the tortilla chips and bake until the cheese melts, about 10 minutes.

4. Combine the corn kernels, tomato, cilantro, red onion, jalapeño pepper, and lime juice in a bowl. Remove the nachos from the oven and top them with the corn salsa, guacamole, olives, green onions, and the remaining sour cream. Serve immediately.

Crudités with Radish Dip

Crudités, otherwise known as assorted raw vegetables, are all about fiber, and so is this radish dip that accompanies them.

1. Combine the cottage cheese and yogurt in a blender or food processor.

2. Add the parsnip, radish, parsley, dill, turmeric, cayenne, and salt and purée until smooth.

3. Put the dip in a bowl on a platter and surround it with assorted raw vegetables for dipping.

Serves 8
Serving Size ¼ cup

Calories: 75.58
Protein: 3.97 grams
Carbohydrates: 14.54 grams
Fiber: 3.66 grams
Fat: 1.38 grams

¾ cup cottage cheese
¼ cup plain yogurt
1 tablespoon grated parsnip
4 tablespoons grated radish
1 tablespoon chopped parsley
1 tablespoon chopped dill
pinch of turmeric
pinch of cayenne pepper
½ teaspoon salt
raw vegetables for dipping

Pear, Roquefort, and Walnuts on Endive

This appetizer gets fiber from the endive lettuce petals, pears, and walnuts, which are partnered with blue cheese in a classic combination of flavors.

1. Separate the leaves of the endive and trim the stem ends. Lay the leaves out on a tray.

2. Core and slice the pears and lay a slice on each endive leaf.

3. Crumble a little Roquefort cheese onto the pear slices and sprinkle them with walnuts. Serve immediately.

Serves 6
Serving Size 4 leaves

Calories: 102.89
Protein: 3.77 grams
Carbohydrates: 9.93 grams
Fiber: 2.15 grams
Fat: 6.06 grams

2 heads Belgian endive
2 ripe pears
2 ounces Roquefort cheese
¼ cup chopped walnuts

Edamame

Edamame are fresh soybeans. They are the base of soy sauce, tofu, and soy-milk. You can eat them as a snack before sushi or as part of a crudités platter. Edamame are also an excellent addition to salads, soups, and rice dishes.

Serves 6
Serving Size 1/6 pound

Calories: 111.13
Protein: 9.79 grams
Carbohydrates: 8.35 grams
Fiber: 3.18 grams
Fat: 5.14 grams

6 cups of water
½ teaspoon salt
1 pound frozen edamame
*   in pods*

1. Bring the water and the salt to a boil in a saucepan.

2. Add the edamame and let the water come back to a boil.

3. Cook on medium-high for 5 minutes.

4. Drain the edamame and rinse with cold water.

5. Drain again and serve either warm or cool.

Snacks Should Be Healthful and Fun

Tastes are formed early. If your kids don't try something, don't make an issue, but keep presenting the food and see what happens. If you have a few kids in the house, have a "crunch contest"! Whose bite of celery or carrot or cucumber makes the loudest crunch? Everybody wins!

Eggplant Crostini

*Eggplant is a most versatile and delicious vegetable. You
don't have to salt or soak the Japanese eggplants to get the
bitterness out as you do with their larger relatives.*

1. Preheat the oven to 350°F. Slice the baguette into ¼"-thick rounds and lay them out on a cookie sheet. Brush both sides with olive oil, then toast them in the oven for about 5 minutes. Turn them over and toast the other side.

2. Remove from oven, rub one side of each toast with garlic clove, and set aside.

3. Slice the eggplants into ¼"-thick slices, brush them with olive oil, and sprinkle them with salt.

4. Grill the eggplant rounds on both sides for about 10 minutes total.

5. Top each toast with a grilled eggplant round, sprinkle the pecorino Romano cheese over the eggplant, and garnish each with the roasted red bell pepper.

Serves 4
Serving Size 4 slices

Calories: 406.36
Protein: 7.45 grams
Carbohydrates: 22.99 grams
Fiber: 6.54 grams
Fat: 32.74 grams

1 baguette loaf of bread
½ cup olive oil, divided
6 cloves garlic, peeled
2 Japanese eggplants
1 teaspoon salt
*½ cup grated pecorino
    Romano cheese*
*¼ cup diced roasted red bell
    pepper*

Stuffed Snow Peas

Snow peas are the immature pods of peas, with tiny peas inside. They make a unique and fanciful treat—stuffed snow pea pods for fibrous cocktail snacks!

Calories: 155.01
Protein: 5.4 grams
Carbohydrates: 3.27 grams
Fiber: 2.31 grams
Fat: 13.69 grams

8 ounces cream cheese
1 tablespoon fresh lemon juice
1 teaspoon grated lemon zest
¼ cup chopped smoked salmon
2 cups snow pea pods
½ cup chopped parsley
¼ cup chopped chives

1. Purée the cream cheese in a food processor. Add the lemon juice, lemon zest, and smoked salmon, and purée until smooth again. Scrape down the sides when necessary.

2. Put this cream cheese mousse into a large freezer bag and refrigerate.

3. Snap the stems and zip the strings off the snow pea pods and blanch them in boiling water for 3 minutes. Plunge them into ice water to cool, then drain completely on paper towels. Split the pods open on one side. Combine the chopped parsley and chives and set aside.

4. Remove the cream cheese mousse from the refrigerator and press the contents down into one corner of the bag. Snip the tip off the bag and pipe a row of the cream cheese mousse into each snow pea pod.

5. Squeeze the filling into each pea pod, so it sticks out of the side like a ruffle, and dip the tip of the ruffle in the chopped parsley and chives. Place the stuffed pea pods on a serving tray. Serve or wrap and refrigerate.

Stuffed Vegetables

Stuffed vegetables can combine many different ingredients and turn your next cocktail party into a roaring success that's also full of healthful fiber and gratuitous protein! Think about making a cup of shrimp or crabmeat salad and stuffing it into halved Italian or jalapeño peppers.

Pea Salad Parfait

This pretty layered salad makes a lovely appetizer for a picnic-style dinner or a light lunch of soup and bread. Baby peas have the sweetness of the early crop, even in midwinter.

1. Place half of the peas in a clear glass trifle bowl.

2. Top the peas with a layer of red onion and half of the cheddar cheese. Top the cheese with a layer of celery and red bell pepper.

3. Layer the remaining peas on top of the pepper, followed by the peanuts, and topped with the remaining cheese.

4. Combine the sour cream, mayonnaise, lemon juice, salt, and pepper, and "frost" the top of the salad with it. Cover and refrigerate for 60 minutes.

5. Sprinkle crumbled bacon over the top before serving. Toss all the layers together at the table with serving spoons.

Serves 4
Serving Size 1 cup

Calories: 574.44
Protein: 17.65 grams
Carbohydrates: 16.96 grams
Fiber: 5.6 grams
Fat: 49.61 grams

2 cups fresh or thawed frozen baby peas
½ cup diced red onion
1 cup shredded cheddar cheese
½ cup chopped celery
1 tablespoon diced red bell pepper
½ cup chopped peanuts
¼ cup sour cream
½ cup mayonnaise
1 teaspoon lemon juice
salt and pepper to taste
¼ cup crumbled bacon

Caponata

This is an Italian country classic. Caponata is excellent stuffed into endive petals, small Romaine lettuce wraps, and fabulous tortilla wraps. You can spread it over grilled fish or chicken.

Serves 8
Serving Size ¾ cup

Calories: 69.35
Protein: 1.26 grams
Carbohydrates: 8.04 grams
Fiber: 2.4 grams
Fat: 4.1 grams

1 eggplant
1 teaspoon kosher salt
4–6 stalks of celery
¼ large onion
¼ cup green olives
2 tablespoons olive oil
1½ cups canned diced
*   tomatoes*
1 tablespoon capers
3 tablespoons red wine
*   vinegar*
2 teaspoons sugar
1 tablespoon tomato paste
salt and pepper to taste

1. Cut the eggplant in cubes and put them in a colander in the sink or over a larger bowl. Sprinkle them with salt and let them drain for 15 to 60 minutes, depending on your time constraints.

2. Dice the celery and onion, and chop the green olives.

3. Sauté the celery and onion in 1 tablespoon of olive oil for 15 minutes over medium heat in a 6-quart pot. Transfer to a bowl and reserve.

4. Sauté the eggplant in the pot for 10 minutes in the remaining olive oil. Return the sautéed celery and onions to the pot and add the remaining ingredients. Simmer for 20 minutes, stirring occasionally.

5. Add salt and pepper to taste. Refrigerate.

Salt and Eggplant
Salting eggplant reduces the bitterness of the eggplant. Be sure to place the eggplant in a colander so that as the salt draws the liquid out of the eggplant, the liquid can easily drain away. The longer you can let the salt work its magic, the less bitter your eggplant will be. Also consider the size of your eggplant; larger eggplants tend to be more bitter than smaller ones.

Fresh Fruit Pizza Bites

*Fresh fruit is the best fiber-rich diet dessert to have every day,
and this pizza dresses it up for a party. You can use other fruits as they come
into season, including nectarines, peaches, pears, and melons. Toss a few
roasted nuts on top for an extra crunch and more fiber.*

Serves 6
Serving Size 1 wedge

Calories: 516.99
Protein: 5.70 grams
Carbohydrates: 68.10 grams
Fiber: 2.22 grams
Fat: 25.14 grams

1 pound sugar cookie dough
*8 ounces cream cheese,
    softened*
½ cup powdered sugar
6 sliced strawberries
½ mango, cut in slices
1 sliced banana
¼ cup blueberries
¼ cup apple jelly

1. Preheat oven to 350°F. Press the sugar cookie dough out onto a 12" pizza pan.

2. Bake the cookie dough for 20 minutes, then let cool on a rack.

3. Whip the cream cheese. Add the powdered sugar and mix well.

4. Spread the cookie dough with the cream cheese mixture.

5. Arrange the fruit on top of the cream cheese, glaze the fruit with warm apple jelly, and chill for 10 minutes. Cut into wedges to serve.

Pita Snacks

When you put cheese or hummus and mixed vegetables into the pocket of a whole-wheat pita, give it a quick run under the broiler for a perfect snack. Fill whole-wheat pitas with cream cheese, nuts, and prosciutto ham. Try tucking in some caramelized onions, Monterey Jack cheese, and smoked turkey. Tart apple, grated cheddar cheese, and a couple of pecan halves also make great fillings. Just keep adding fiber to the whole wheat and you can't go wrong.

Broccoli Calzones

*These are little turnovers baked with a filling of broccoli and cheese.
Serve them as appetizers or snacks. If you use frozen spinach, be sure to thaw
it completely and then squeeze all of the moisture out of it. These yummy
minis can be filled with all sorts of goodies to add fiber.*

Serves 4

Calories: 508.93
Protein: 29.51 grams
Carbohydrates: 65.75 grams
Fiber: 22.76 grams
Fat: 19.66 grams

*16 frozen dinner rolls,
    unbaked dough
2 cups chopped cooked
    broccoli
¼ cup diced ham
1 cup grated cheddar cheese
½ cup grated Parmesan
    cheese*

1. Spray a sheet of plastic wrap with vegetable oil. Lay the frozen dinner roll dough out on a plastic-lined baking sheet and cover with the plastic wrap. Let thaw in the refrigerator overnight.

2. Mix the broccoli, ham, and cheeses together in a bowl. Press each roll flat and put a spoonful of the broccoli mixture in the center of each one.

3. Fold each dough circle in half over the filling and press down to make a half-circle. Use a fork to crimp the edges.

4. Preheat the oven to 375°F.

5. Bake the calzones for 15–20 minutes and serve warm.

Chapter 7
Eat Your Vegetables

Sesame Green Beans

*Crunchy green beans and sesame are seasoned with
sesame oil for this vegetarian side dish. Leftovers will stand up
with a shot of lemon juice or vinegar.*

Serves 4
Serving Size ¼ pound

Calories: 119.22
Protein: 3.66 grams
Carbohydrates: 10.21 grams
Fiber: 4.92 grams
Fat: 8.11 grams

1 pound fresh green beans
1 tablespoon sesame oil
1 teaspoon salt
¼ teaspoon pepper
¼ cup sesame seeds

1. Trim the stem ends off the green beans.

2. Add the green beans to boiling water and cook them for 5 minutes.

3. Drain the beans and plunge them into ice water. Drain them again.

4. Heat a sauté pan over medium heat and add the sesame oil to it. Sauté the beans in the sesame oil for 3 minutes.

5. Season the beans with salt and pepper and sprinkle the sesame seeds over them. Serve hot.

Sesame Asparagus

Take a bunch of asparagus and trim about 2 inches off the bottom. Blanch them in boiling water and shock them in cold water like the green beans. Cut the asparagus on the diagonal into ½-inch pieces and sauté them in sesame oil. Season them and sprinkle them with sesame seeds.

Stuffed Onions

Onions can be turned into vessels for soufflés or stuffings.
Onions have special phytochemicals that provide protection against disease.

Serves 4
Serving Size ½ onion

Calories: 235.76
Protein: 11.3 grams
Carbohydrates: 17.63 grams
Fiber: 2.88 grams
Fat: 14.01 grams

1. Preheat the oven to 350°F. Cut the onions in half horizontally and peel them.

2. Bring a pot of salted water to boil and cook the onions for 12 minutes. Drain and take out the center of each onion, creating four onion cups. Put the cups in a baking dish that has been brushed with olive oil. Set aside.

3. Chop the centers of the onions and sauté them in olive oil. Transfer them to a bowl and add the sausage, cheese, bread crumbs, herbs, green chilies, salt, and pepper. Mix well, add the egg, and mix again.

4. Make four balls out of the stuffing and put one in each onion cup.

5. Cover and bake for 20 minutes. Uncover and bake for 10 more minutes. Serve hot with enchilada or tomato sauce spooned on top.

2 large sweet onions
1 tablespoon olive oil
2 ounces cooked and
*   crumbled breakfast*
*   sausage*
2 ounces shredded Monterey
*   Jack cheese*
3 tablespoons bread crumbs
1 tablespoon chopped fresh
*   herbs*
2 tablespoons chopped green
*   chilies*
salt and pepper to taste
1 egg, beaten
1 cup enchilada or tomato
*   sauce, warmed*

Herbs and Crumbs

For toppings of broiled, grilled, or baked vegetables, herbs and crumbs are absolutely the most interesting and versatile ways to turn ho-hum into mouthwateringly delicious. Take some leftover whole-grain bread and put it in the food processor with seasoned salt, oregano, and Parmesan cheese, and let it grind away. Sprinkle over grilled vegetables.

Colcannon

The combination of cabbage and mashed potatoes is classic Irish fare.
Potatoes have long been a fibrous staple in the Irish diet.

Serves 6
Serving Size 1 cup

Calories: 312.3
Protein: 7.42 grams
Carbohydrates: 37.32 grams
Fiber: 4.55 grams
Fat: 16.62 grams

1 pound kale
1 tablespoon olive oil
3 large potatoes, about
    3 pounds
2 teaspoons kosher salt
4 tablespoons butter
⅓ cup milk
½ teaspoon white pepper

1. Pull the stems of the kale and discard. Chop the greens and sauté them in olive oil over medium heat for 15 minutes. Take them off the heat and reserve.

2. Peel potatoes and cut them into 2" pieces. Put potato pieces in a pot with cold water to cover and 1 teaspoon salt.

3. Turn heat to medium-high and bring potatoes and water to a boil. Turn down to a simmer and cook until the potatoes can be easily pierced with a fork, about 15 minutes.

4. Drain potatoes in a colander, then put them in a bowl and mash them with a potato masher, or put them through a ricer. Add butter and milk and mix to a creamy consistency. Season with 1 teaspoon salt and the white pepper.

5. Add the sautéed kale to the mashed potatoes and fold it in. Serve hot.

Peas with Butter Lettuce

Sweet peas and butter lettuce provide a double dose of fiber in one dish.

1. Cook the peas in boiling water until tender.

2. Cut the butter lettuce into shreds and sauté it in the butter until limp.

3. Add the peas to the lettuce and season with salt and pepper.

Serves 4
Serving Size 1 cup

Calories: 111.05
Protein: 4.13 grams
Carbohydrates: 10.75 grams
Fiber: 3.81 grams
Fat: 6.07 grams

*2 cups fresh or frozen
    baby peas*
6 butter lettuce leaves
2 tablespoons butter
salt to taste
¼ teaspoon white pepper

Roasted Garlic Spinach

*This spinach dish is good with steak, roast chicken, lasagna, fish, and much
more. You can use fresh baby arugula if you can't find fresh spinach.*

1. Preheat oven to 400°F. Toss the garlic cloves in olive oil. Put them on a
   piece of foil in a baking dish and roast in the oven for about 30 minutes.

2. When the garlic is done, melt the butter in a sauté pan and add the spinach. Sauté the spinach in the butter for about 10 minutes over medium-
   high heat.

3. Add the roasted garlic cloves to the spinach and season with salt, pepper, and nutmeg. Serve hot.

Serves 4
Serving Size ¼ cup

Calories: 99.96 grams
Protein: 1.46 grams
Carbohydrates: 3.87 grams
Fiber: 0.99 grams
Fat: 9.28 grams

¼ cup peeled garlic cloves
1 tablespoon olive oil
2 tablespoons butter
*4 cups fresh baby spinach
    leaves*
1 teaspoon salt
¼ teaspoon pepper
pinch of nutmeg

Sweet and Sour Red Cabbage

Sweet and sour red cabbage is a nice bed for chicken, roast pork, or rabbit. Sweet, tangy, slightly sour, and crunchy, cabbage is a great accompaniment to sausages, duck, and spaetzle or noodles.

Serves 4
Serving Size 1 cup

Calories: 206.54
Protein: 3.76 grams
Carbohydrates: 37.39 grams
Fiber: 6.07 grams
Fat: 6.57 grams

1 red cabbage, shredded
1 large onion, sliced
2 peeled apples, sliced
2 tablespoons bacon fat
1 tablespoon sugar
1 cup apple juice
1 cup red wine vinegar
2 teaspoons salt
1 teaspoon pepper

1. Preheat oven to 350°F.

2. Layer cabbage, onion, and apples in a baking dish.

3. Heat bacon fat, sugar, juice, and vinegar in a saucepan to a simmer.

4. Pour hot liquid over cabbage; then sprinkle cabbage with salt and pepper. Toss to combine.

5. Cover and bake cabbage in oven for 2 hours, until tender.

Prosciutto-Wrapped Asparagus

Some diners prefer the fat asparagus, and that's fine—thin or thick, they all have the same amount of fiber per ounce.

Serves 4
Serving Size 2 bundles

Calories: 185.85
Protein: 9.59 grams
Carbohydrates: 4.8 grams
Fiber: 2.4 grams
Fat: 14 grams

1 bunch fresh asparagus
2 tablespoons olive oil
1 teaspoon kosher salt
½ teaspoon pepper
8 thin slices prosciutto ham

1. Bend one asparagus stalk near the cut end until it snaps. This will find the natural breaking point of the asparagus. You can discard the fibrous ends or use them for soup.

2. Using the snapped asparagus as a guide, measure and cut the other stalks at the same place and discard the woody ends. Toss asparagus with oil, salt, and pepper. Grill for about 5 minutes, until tender and tips are crispy. Set aside to cool.

3. Wrap a slice of prosciutto around three asparagus into a bundle. Repeat with remaining asparagus and prosciutto and serve warm.

Prosciutto Ham and Vegetables

It's amazing how such a paper-thin slice of Italian ham can change an ordinary vegetable dish into something extraordinary. It adds only flavor and a bit of protein and has no fiber, but it enhances the taste of certain fibrous vegetables.

Summer Swiss Chard

Both stalks and leaves are edible parts of the chard plant,
and the stems can be separated and cooked separately for a different dish.
Chard adds a bit of spice to any dish.

Serves 4
Serving Size ½ cup

Calories: 132.16
Protein: 2.54 grams
Carbohydrates: 7.87 grams
Fiber: 2.61 grams
Fat: 10.81 grams

1 pound Swiss chard
3 tablespoons olive oil
1 cup diced onion
½ teaspoon oregano
3 tablespoons red wine
*   vinegar*
salt and pepper to taste

1. Chop the chard and set aside.

2. Heat the olive oil in a skillet over medium heat.

3. Add the diced onion, a pinch of salt, and oregano and cook until the onions are tender.

4. Add the chopped chard and sauté for a few minutes and then remove from heat.

5. Stir in the vinegar and season with salt and pepper.

Roasted Corn on the Cob

Forget shucking and boiling corn on the cob. Roast your corn in the oven, as in this recipe, or on the grill if you prefer. This side/snack will give your family a delicious dose of both soluble and insoluble fiber.

Serves 8
Serving Size 1 ear

Calories: 249.64
Protein: 5.44 grams
Carbohydrates: 35.46 grams
Fiber: 2.74 grams
Fat: 13.26 grams

8 ears of fresh sweet corn, unshucked
¼ teaspoon garlic salt
pinch of lemon pepper seasoning
pinch of seasoned salt
pinch of chili powder
pinch of dried mixed herbs
½ cup melted butter
¼ cup kosher salt

1. Pull the corn silk out of the tops of the corn and then peel the husks down far enough to clean the rest of the silk, but leave the husks attached. Pull the husks back up around the corn. Put them in a roasting pan and fill it with water. Let the corn soak for 10 minutes so the husks won't burn in the oven. The moisture will also help create steam.

2. Preheat the oven to 400°F.

3. Drain the water from the corn and put it in a single layer on cookie sheets.

4. Roast the corn in the oven for 45 minutes. Remove from the oven and peel the husks back from the cobs to make a handle at the bottom.

5. Add the garlic salt, lemon pepper, seasoned salt, chili powder, and mixed herbs to the melted butter. Brush the corn with butter-spice mixture and place on a platter. Serve hot with kosher salt for sprinkling.

Corn Trivia

Corn combines soluble and insoluble fiber, and it can be added to many satisfying creations. Try stuffing a tomato with corn and bake it, melting some cheddar cheese on top and into the corn filling. Make corn relish with vinegar, honey, and spices. You can easily add this special fiber to your diet regularly.

Ratatouille

This is a mélange of summertime vegetables with herbs from the south of France, mixed with fruity olive oil. The dish has been popular for years as a sandwich spread on crusty French bread.

Serves 4
Serving Size ½ cup

Calories: 145.94
Protein: 0.88 grams
Carbohydrates: 4.37 grams
Fiber: 1.35 grams
Fat: 14.11 grams

¼ cup diced onion
2 tablespoons diced red bell pepper
2 tablespoons diced green bell pepper
2 cloves minced garlic
¼ cup olive oil
1 cup diced eggplant
½ cup diced zucchini
¼ cup diced tomatoes, fresh or canned
1 tablespoon fresh thyme, chopped
salt to taste
pepper to taste

1. Sauté the onion, peppers, and minced garlic in olive oil for 5 minutes.

2. Add the eggplant and zucchini, toss with oil to coat, and add the fresh tomatoes and thyme.

3. Cover and simmer for 30 minutes, stirring occasionally. Season with salt and pepper.

Yams with Coconut Milk

This vegetable dish has an Afro-Caribbean flavor and is perfect with a fish or beef curry. The nuts add fat, fiber, and a bit of protein.

1. Preheat the oven to 350°F.

2. Peel sweet potatoes and slice them into ½"-thick rounds.

3. Overlap the sweet potato slices in one layer in a baking dish.

4. Pour the coconut milk over the sweet potatoes, then sprinkle them with coconut and macadamia nuts.

5. Bake them uncovered for 60 minutes.

Yams vs. Sweet Potatoes

Yams and sweet potatoes are so close that they can be used interchangeably in cooking. Sweet potatoes are a rich orange inside and have a deeper brown skin. They're also by far the sweeter of the two. Both tubers are very high in soluble fiber. To add extra fiber, sprinkle them with nuts, cook them with apples, and mix them with sweet green peas.

Serves 4
Serving Size 1 cup

Calories: 262.64
Protein: 3.49 grams
Carbohydrates: 31.32 grams
Fiber: 3.83 grams
Fat: 15 grams

3 pounds sweet potatoes
1 cup coconut milk
¼ cup shredded coconut
½ cup chopped macadamia nuts

Beets with Beet Greens

This recipe takes the whole beet and transforms it into a combination vegetable side dish. It's full of soluble and insoluble fiber; the greens provide roughage and the beets themselves are loaded with soluble fiber and vitamins.

Serves 4
Serving Size 4 beets

Calories: 238.46
Protein: 9.72 grams
Carbohydrates: 41.22 grams
Fiber: 18.08 grams
Fat: 6.46 grams

16 baby beets, greens attached
2 tablespoons butter
1 tablespoon fresh lemon juice
½ teaspoon salt

1. Wash beets but don't peel them.

2. Bring about 3 inches of water to a boil and then put the beets, root down, into the boiling water. The beet roots will be in the water and the greens will cook in the steam above the water.

3. Cover and cook for 12 minutes. Drain and cut the greens off the roots.

4. Chop the greens and peel the roots. The skin will slip off easily.

5. Put the beets, greens, and roots in a saucepan and add butter, lemon juice, and salt. Warm them over low heat and serve hot.

Baked Fennel

Fennel has the texture of crisp celery crossed with onion and is subtly scented and flavored with anise, or licorice. When fennel is cooked, it develops greater, more intense sweetness and anise flavor.

1. Cut the fennel bulbs in half lengthwise through the root end.

2. Put the fennel cut-side down in a skillet and add the chicken broth. Cover and simmer for 20 minutes.

3. Preheat oven to 375°F. Place cooked fennel bulbs in a baking dish, cut-sides up.

4. Mix the gorgonzola with the bread crumbs and divide the mixture evenly on the top of each fennel bulb.

5. Bake for 25 minutes, season with salt and pepper, and serve hot.

Serves 6
Serving Size ½ fennel bulb

Calories: 74.6
Protein: 3.28 grams
Carbohydrates: 12.2 grams
Fiber: 4.13 grams
Fat: 1.9 grams

3 fennel bulbs
1 cup chicken broth
¼ cup crumbled Gorgonzola cheese
¼ cup panko bread crumbs
salt and pepper to taste

Eggplant with Romesco Sauce

This dish gets its Catalonian flavor from grilled eggplant slices, puréed roasted red bell peppers, and ground almonds. To add protein, you can sprinkle some grated Manchego cheese on top or add more fiber with snipped fresh herbs, such as parsley or oregano.

Serves 4
Serving Size 3 slices

Calories: 335.76
Protein: 3.12 grams
Carbohydrates: 11.16 grams
Fiber: 4.03 grams
Fat: 31.55 grams

1 eggplant
3 tablespoons kosher salt
6 ounces roasted red bell pepper
¼ cup toasted sliced almonds
1 clove peeled garlic
1½ teaspoons red wine vinegar
1½ teaspoons paprika
¼ teaspoon cayenne pepper
½ teaspoon salt
½ cup olive oil, divided use

1. Slice the eggplant into ½"-thick rounds and place them in a colander over a bowl or in the sink. Sprinkle kosher salt over the eggplant and let sit for 30 minutes.

2. Meanwhile, make the romesco sauce by putting the roasted red bell peppers in a food processor with the almonds, garlic, vinegar, paprika, cayenne, and salt. Purée and then add ¼ cup olive oil while the motor is running.

3. Rinse the eggplant rounds and drain them on paper towels. Blot them dry and brush them with remaining olive oil.

4. Grill the eggplant on a preheated grill or grill pan for about 5 minutes per side.

5. Place half of the grilled eggplant on a platter and spoon half of the sauce over it. Top with the remaining eggplant rounds and spoon the remaining sauce over the top.

Eggplant Facts

Any big eggplant will do for frying or baking. Most cooks today find the tiny eggplants and their wonderful range of colors easier to deal with because they don't need soaking to reduce the bitterness of large eggplants. Smaller versions don't need peeling, and you get added fiber by eating the tender skins.

Chapter 8
On the Side

Baked Beans

Serves 6
Serving Size 1 cup

Calories: 357.49
Protein: 13.52 grams
Carbohydrates: 69.82 grams
Fiber: 12.85 grams
Fat: 3.65 grams

4 cups cooked white beans
1 cup sliced onion
4 slices bacon, chopped
1 teaspoon dry mustard
½ cup brown sugar
½ cup maple syrup
2 tablespoons ketchup
½ teaspoon salt
1 teaspoon pepper
1½ cups water

Baked beans are an example of picnic food being a sort of "health" food and not a junk food like the fried chips, French fries, and sugary snacks they often accompany. Depending on their preparation, hot dogs, fried chicken, and deviled eggs can be healthful if accompanied by crudités, served with whole-grain buns, and high-fiber beans.

1. Preheat oven to 350°F.

2. Drain the beans and layer them with the onions and bacon in a casserole dish.

3. Combine the dry mustard, brown sugar, maple syrup, ketchup, salt, pepper, and water, and pour the mixture over the beans.

4. Cover and bake the beans for 2 hours.

5. Uncover and bake for 15 minutes more.

Black Beans

You can increase the flavor and fiber by adding chopped fresh apples or oranges. Garnish the beans with fresh chopped parsley, minced celery, carrots, and chives.

1. Cover the beans with boiling water for 10 minutes. Reserve the beans and discard the water.

2. Sweat the onion in a pot with the bacon for 5 minutes, then add the beans. Add 5 quarts water.

3. Add the cumin, salt, honey, and chili powder and bring to a simmer.

4. Simmer slowly for 90 minutes, stirring occasionally.

5. Test a few beans in a small spoon for doneness by blowing on them. The skin will crack if they're done.

Beans for Your Budget

The variety of dried beans numbers in the hundreds. They are packed with flavor, protein, and both soluble and insoluble fiber. Very little, if any, meat is necessary when beans are combined with onions, garlic, carrots, and tomatoes. They marry happily with parsley, cilantro, rosemary, basil, and tarragon. Plus, they should be the basis of a very high-fiber diet.

Serves 6
Serving Size ¾ cup

Calories: 301.60
Protein: 17.13 grams
Carbohydrates: 52.09 grams
Fiber: 12.39 grams
Fat: 3.62 grams

1 pound black beans
½ onion, diced
1 slice bacon
1 tablespoon cumin
1 tablespoon salt
1 tablespoon honey
2 teaspoons chili powder

Refried Pinto Beans

*You can give refried beans added crunch and flavor
by sprinkling a mixture of minced carrots, celery, chives, peanuts, or pepitas
over the top. Either cilantro or parsley will add a bright green note.*

Serves 4
Serving Size ¾ cup

Calories: 188.85
Protein: 7.30 grams
Carbohydrates: 23.90 grams
Fiber: 7.73 grams
Fat: 7.48 grams

*½ cup diced onion
1 clove minced garlic
2 tablespoons olive oil
2 cups cooked pinto beans,
     with liquid
1 cup water
1 teaspoon salt*

1. Sauté onion and garlic in olive oil until translucent.

2. Mash beans and stir half of them into the onion mixture over medium heat.

3. Stir in half the water and then the remaining beans.

4. Stir in the rest of the water and the salt and cook for 10 minutes, stirring often.

Black-Eyed Peas

*These lucky legumes are supposed to bestow good fortune
on those who eat them on New Year's Day. Don't forget to add
plenty of freshly ground black pepper to taste.*

Serves 4
Serving Size ¾ cup

Calories: 305.75
Protein: 22.35 grams
Carbohydrates: 52.57 grams
Fiber: 9.47 grams
Fat: 1.53 grams

*2 cups black-eyed peas
½ cup diced celery
½ cup diced onion
¼ cup diced smoked ham
salt and pepper to taste*

1. Soak the black-eyed peas in water for 4 hours. Drain and put in a pot with 4 cups water.

2. Add the celery, onion, and ham and bring the water to a simmer. Simmer for 30 minutes and then drain off any liquid that's left.

3. Season with salt and pepper and serve hot.

Brown Rice

Brown rice makes an excellent oatmeal substrate for those with gluten intolerance. It's wonderful with fresh or dried fruits and berries.

1. Preheat oven to 375°F.

2. Combine the water, salt, and olive oil in a saucepan and bring to a boil.

3. Put the brown rice in a 2-quart baking dish and pour the boiling water mixture over it. Stir, cover with foil, and bake for 60 minutes. Fluff with a fork and serve hot.

Serves 4
Serving Size 1 cup

Calories: 249.9
Protein: 4.52 grams
Carbohydrates: 45.84 grams
Fiber: 3.51 grams
Fat: 5.12 grams

2½ cups water
1 teaspoon salt
1 tablespoon olive oil
1½ cups uncooked brown rice

Bulgur Wheat

You can stuff the cooked bulgur into red or yellow tomatoes for baking. It's also an excellent stuffing for red, yellow, or green peppers, adding flavor and fiber.

1. Heat the olive oil in a skillet over medium-high heat and cook the bulgur in it for 1 minute; then add the green onions.

2. Sauté for another minute and add the chicken broth.

3. Add the seasonings and stir. Cover with a lid and turn the heat to low.

4. Simmer for 20 minutes.

Serves 4
Serving Size ¾ cup

Calories: 193.66
Protein: 5.04 grams
Carbohydrates: 28.53 grams
Fiber: 7.27 grams
Fat: 7.5 grams

2 tablespoons olive oil
1 cup medium bulgur wheat
3 chopped green onions
2 cups chicken broth
¼ teaspoon oregano
1 teaspoon salt
½ teaspoon pepper

Lentils

This legume dish can be puréed to make more of a "refried bean" texture if desired. Add color and fiber to this dish with diced sweet potatoes, hot or sweet red peppers, minced carrots, and lots of chives.

1. Soak lentils in the chicken broth and water for 3 hours. Bring to a simmer and cook over medium-low heat for 60 minutes.

2. Preheat the oven to 325°F. Mix the onions, olive oil, sesame oil, and salt in the lentils and pour them out into a baking pan.

3. Bake for 60 minutes.

Serves 8
Serving Size ¾ cup

Calories: 227.11
Protein: 13.95 grams
Carbohydrates: 29.63 grams
Fiber: 15.25 grams
Fat: 6.44 grams

2 cups lentils
2 cups chicken broth
2 cups water
1 cup diced onions
3 tablespoons olive oil
1 teaspoon sesame oil
1 teaspoon salt

Lima Bean Succotash

This was originally a Native American dish made with broth from fowl, venison, and other game instead of cream. It contributes to a high-fiber diet.

1. Heat the cream in a saucepan over medium-high heat and reduce by half.

2. Add the lima beans and corn and turn the heat to low.

3. Cover and cook for 10 minutes.

4. Stir in butter and season to taste with salt and pepper.

5. Remove from heat and serve hot.

Serves 4
Serving Size ¾ cup

Calories: 248.44
Protein: 6.17 grams
Carbohydrates: 25.76 grams
Fiber: 4.42 grams
Fat: 15 grams

¾ cup cream
1 cup frozen cooked baby
    lima beans
1½ cups corn kernels
1 tablespoon butter
salt and pepper to taste

Millet

This grain side dish is often mixed with ground corn, buckwheat, and other grains for added fiber and flavor. It mixes well with fruit for breakfast and is excellent for people with gluten intolerance.

1. Heat the chicken broth to boiling.

2. Sauté millet in butter for a few minutes; then add boiling chicken broth and salt. Stir and cover.

3. Turn heat to low and simmer 25 minutes. Turn off heat and let stand, covered, for 5 minutes.

Serves 4
Serving Size ¾ cup

Calories: 252.36
Protein: 6.2 grams
Carbohydrates: 37.68 grams
Fiber: 4.88 grams
Fat: 8.18 grams

2½ cups chicken broth
1 cup millet
2 tablespoons butter
½ teaspoon salt

Couscous Tabouli

For a Moroccan touch add Harrissa, a very hot condiment.
If you can't find that, use Tabasco sauce.

1. Bring the water to a boil in a saucepan, add the couscous, cover, remove from heat, and let sit 5 minutes to absorb the liquid.

2. Fluff the couscous with a fork and put it in a large bowl to let it cool.

3. Add the remaining ingredients to the couscous and mix well.

4. Let sit at room temperature for 60 minutes or refrigerate overnight.

5. Serve chilled or at room temperature.

Serves 4
Serving Size 1 cup

Calories: 327.93
Protein: 7.3 grams
Carbohydrates: 42.57 grams
Fiber: 4.29 grams
Fat: 14.76 grams

1½ cups water
1 cup couscous
⅓ cup lemon juice
2 tablespoons chopped
    fresh mint
1 teaspoon salt
1 teaspoon pepper
¼ cup extra-virgin olive oil
1 cup chopped fresh parsley
½ cup chopped green onions
2 large tomatoes, diced
½ cup diced cucumber
1 tablespoon minced garlic

Baked Sweet Potatoes

*Top these bakers with anything from sweet to savory,
like cinnamon sugar and pecans, whipped butter and mini marsh-
mallows, bacon and brown sugar, or sour cream and green onions.
You can also make a delicious herb butter, incorporating basil, thyme,
chives, and rosemary into whipped butter to melt into the potatoes.*

Serves 4

Calories: 441.36
Protein: 6.67 grams
Carbohydrates: 37.17 grams
Fiber: 5.61 grams
Fat: 32.08 grams

4 medium sweet potatoes
4 ounces soft unsalted butter
½ teaspoon salt
¼ teaspoon white pepper
¼ teaspoon cinnamon
½ cup chopped peanuts
¼ cup chopped chives

1. Preheat oven to 400°F. Scrub the sweet potatoes and poke them all over with a fork or paring knife. Bake directly on the oven rack for 45–60 minutes.

2. Mix the soft butter with the salt, white pepper, and cinnamon.

3. Split the baked potatoes and top with the butter, peanuts, and chives.

Roasted Red Potatoes

*The skin of the potatoes is delicious. You can use seasoned salt
and hot red pepper flakes to enhance the flavor.*

Serves 4
Serving Size 1 cup

Calories: 263.75
Protein: 3.35 grams
Carbohydrates: 37.21 grams
Fiber: 3.45 grams
Fat: 7.01 grams

3 pounds small red potatoes
2 tablespoons olive oil
1 teaspoon salt
½ teaspoon pepper
½ teaspoon dried thyme

1. Preheat the oven to 350°F.

2. Quarter the potatoes and toss them with oil and seasonings.

3. Spread the potatoes out on a sheet pan and roast uncovered for 45 minutes.

Kasha–Buckwheat Groats

Kasha is toasted buckwheat kernels that can be purchased whole, cracked, or ground. Use whole buckwheat groats in salads, soups, and stews.

1. Heat the olive oil in a skillet over medium-high heat and sauté the kasha in it for 3 minutes.

2. Add the chicken broth and salt and bring to a boil. Cover, turn heat to low, and simmer for 15 minutes.

3. Take the pan off the heat and let it sit with the cover on for 10 minutes. Serve warm.

Serves 4
Serving Size ¾ cup

Calories: 183.36
Protein: 5.31 grams
Carbohydrates: 31.73 grams
Fiber: 4.72 grams
Fat: 4.86 grams

1 tablespoon olive oil
1 cup whole kasha
2 cups chicken broth
½ teaspoon salt

Red Beans and Rice

Another marriage of legume and grain, like succotash, this is a Caribbean favorite that will fill up a family without leaving anyone hungry. You can substitute brown rice for extra fiber.

1. Sauté celery, onion, green bell pepper, and garlic in olive oil.

2. Add ham, beans, thyme, cayenne pepper, water, and salt.

3. Simmer for 45 minutes. Adjust seasoning and serve over rice.

Serves 4
Serving Size 1 cup

Calories: 302.55
Protein: 13.05 grams
Carbohydrates: 48.6 grams
Fiber: 9.14 grams
Fat: 6.17 grams

¼ cup diced celery
¼ cup diced onion
¼ cup diced green bell pepper
1 clove garlic, minced
1 tablespoon olive oil
¼ cup diced ham
2 cups cooked red beans
½ teaspoon dried thyme
¼ teaspoon cayenne pepper
¾ cup water
salt to taste
2 cups cooked white rice

Chapter 9
Pizza and Pasta

Whole-Wheat Biscuit Pizza

*If you have premade Whole-Wheat Biscuits (page 273)
you can use them to make your pizzas more quickly.
The whole wheat in the biscuits adds fiber and B-vitamins to the dish.*

Serves 6

Calories: 489.65
Protein: 16.01 grams
Carbohydrates: 62.75 grams
Fiber: 10.76 grams
Fat: 21.86 grams

*12 unbaked Whole-Wheat
Biscuits (page 273)*
¼ cup pizza sauce
*½ cup shredded mozzarella
cheese*
¼ cup sliced black olives
¼ cup diced green peppers

1. Preheat oven to 375°F.

2. Lay the individual biscuits out on a sheet pan and press them down to make flat rounds.

3. Spoon pizza sauce over the rounds and sprinkle them with mozzarella cheese.

4. Top the pizzas with black olives and green peppers.

5. Bake for 15–20 minutes. Serve immediately.

Arugula and Grilled Radicchio Pizza

Whether using all-purpose flour or whole wheat, this pizza has plenty of fiber already in the greens and reds. For added protein, you can sprinkle it with Parmesan cheese and/or spoon ricotta cheese over the dough before adding the vegetables.

Serves 4
Serving Size ¼ pizza

Calories: 265.25
Protein: 5.13 grams
Carbohydrates: 33.24 grams
Fiber: 1.87 grams
Fat: 12.51 grams

½ package yeast
3 tablespoons warm water
¼ teaspoon sugar
1¼ cups whole-wheat flour,
    plus more for kneading
1 tablespoon olive oil
¼ cup cool water
¾ teaspoon salt
3 tablespoons butter
½ onion, peeled
pinch of kosher salt
fresh ground black pepper
    to taste
1 head radicchio lettuce
1 cup arugula

1. Combine yeast with the warm water, sugar, and ¼ cup flour. Let sit 10 minutes. Add olive oil, cool water, salt, and ½ cup flour and combine with a wooden spoon. Add remaining flour and mix to form dough.

2. Knead dough on a floured board for 5 minutes, adding flour as needed to prevent sticking. Cover the dough and let it rise in an oiled bowl for 60 minutes in a warm place. Punch down dough and roll it into a tight ball. Cover and let rise for 60 minutes.

3. Meanwhile, melt the butter in a large skillet. Thinly slice the onion and cook slowly in the butter over medium-low heat until tender, about 15 minutes. Add salt and pepper.

4. Quarter the radicchio, brush with olive oil, and grill 3 minutes. Remove from grill and chop coarsely.

5. Preheat oven to 450°F. Roll or stretch the dough into a 12" round on a lightly floured surface. Place the dough onto a cornmeal-dusted baking sheet and let rest 15 minutes.

6. Spread the cooked onions over the dough round and arrange the grilled radicchio on top. Bake for 15 minutes, until crisp. Top with arugula and cut into wedges.

The Amazing Pizza

You can create literally hundreds of combinations to top pizza that are delicious and very, very good for you. Sneak spinach under the sauce and cheese and experiment with exotic combinations such as sliced fresh figs and goat cheese. You'll get whole grains and fiber painlessly.

Hummus Tomato Salad Pita Pizza

Serves 2
Serving Size ½ pizza

Calories: 371.04
Protein: 12.78 grams
Carbohydrates: 31.60 grams
Fiber: 6.83 grams
Fat: 23 grams

½ cup hummus
1 pita round
1 small tomato, diced
1 tablespoon diced red onion
1 tablespoon diced cucumber
2 ounces feta cheese
6 pitted ripe olives
1 tablespoon olive oil

This is a nacho-style cold pizza appetizer. It combines the base of a hummus plate with the ingredients of a Greek salad served on top. Substituting a whole-wheat pita for a regular one boosts the fiber.

1. Spread the hummus around on the pita bread, leaving a small border around the edges.

2. Scatter the tomato, red onion, and cucumber over the hummus.

3. Crumble the feta cheese over the pizza. Scatter the olives over the cheese.

4. Drizzle the olive oil over the pizza.

5. Cut the pizza into wedges and serve.

Penne Primavera

Spring vegetables are full of fiber and their crunchy texture goes well with the chewy pasta. You can also spike your primavera with a garnish of chopped Italian flat-leaf parsley, a few tiny grape or currant tomatoes, a bit of hot red pepper flakes, and toasted walnuts. The walnuts add extra crunch, fiber, and protein.

1. Sauté onions, carrots, and red bell pepper in oil until tender.

2. Add chicken broth, asparagus and broccoli and simmer for 5 minutes.

3. Add cream and peas and simmer for 5 minutes.

4. Stir in Parmesan cheese and remove from heat.

5. Season with salt and pepper and serve sauce over cooked penne pasta.

Primavera

In Italian, primavera *means spring. Thus, it's appropriate to use young baby vegetables in this dish. You can use frozen baby peas, but sugar snaps are excellent and a fine source of fresh great-tasting fiber, too. Some primavera recipes also call for bits of chicken or chopped shrimp—all delicious.*

Serves 4
Serving Size 2 cups

Calories: 401.46
Protein: 15.65 grams
Carbohydrates: 40.61 grams
Fiber: 5.82 grams
Fat: 19.62 grams

½ cup diced onion
½ cup diced carrot
¼ cup diced red bell pepper
2 tablespoons olive oil
½ cup chicken broth
1 cup asparagus tips
1 cup broccoli florets
½ cup cream
½ cup peas
½ cup grated Parmesan cheese
salt and pepper to taste
4 cups cooked penne pasta

Asparagus Ravioli Lasagna

This is an exotic concoction whose sum is more than its parts combined.

Serves 4
Serving Size ¼ recipe

Calories: 738.46
Protein: 37.94 grams
Carbohydrates: 45.46 grams
Fiber: 5.10 grams
Fat: 45.27 grams

2 cups sliced asparagus,
　　¼"-diagonal slices
1 cup cream
4 cups cooked cheese ravioli
½ cup grated Parmesan
　　cheese
1 egg, beaten
1 cup ricotta cheese
1½ cups mozzarella cheese
1 tablespoon chopped
　　parsley
salt and pepper

1. Preheat oven to 350°F. Blanch the asparagus for 3 minutes and then set aside. Oil a baking pan and pour half of the cream on the bottom. Cover the cream with a layer of cooked ravioli, half of the asparagus, and half of the Parmesan cheese.

2. Combine the egg, ricotta, and half of the mozzarella cheese until well blended. Stir in the parsley, salt, and pepper.

3. Spread half of the ricotta mixture into the pan, then top it with another layer of ravioli.

4. Add the second half of the asparagus and Parmesan cheese to the ravioli. Cover the top with the remaining mozzarella cheese.

5. Pour the remaining cream over the top and bake uncovered for 45 to 60 minutes.

Lasagna Florentine

The term Florentine *is used in classic French and Italian cuisine to refer to a dish containing spinach. Seasonings such as nutmeg, lemon juice, and lemon zest all marry well with spinach.*

Serves 8

Calories: 473.19
Protein: 25.43 grams
Carbohydrates: 52.25 grams
Fiber: 4.20 grams
Fat: 18.36 grams

5 cups tomato sauce
1 pound box whole-wheat lasagna noodles, cooked
3 eggs
16 ounces ricotta cheese
2 cups mozzarella cheese, shredded
2 cups chopped cooked spinach
½ cup chopped fresh parsley
salt and pepper to taste
½ cup grated Parmesan cheese

1. Preheat oven to 350°F. Oil a baking dish and spread 1 cup tomato sauce on the bottom. Cover the sauce with a layer of cooked noodles.

2. In a bowl combine the eggs, ricotta, and 1 cup mozzarella cheese until well blended. Stir in the spinach, parsley, salt, and pepper.

3. Spread half of the ricotta mixture over the noodles in the pan, then top the ricotta with a layer of noodles. Ladle 2 cups of the tomato sauce over the noodles and top with another layer of noodles.

4. Spread the remaining ricotta mixture over the noodles. Top with another layer of noodles. Ladle the remaining tomato sauce over the noodles.

5. Scatter the remaining mozzarella cheese over the sauce, then sprinkle the Parmesan cheese over it. Bake for 75 minutes.

Spinach and Florentine

The cheeses and spinach are a high-protein and high-fiber combination. Fresh baby spinach is delicious and easy to deal with in the kitchen. You can also substitute arugula for spinach. If you want to get very aromatic, try adding some chopped watercress to the spinach.

Round Pumpkin Ravioli

The recipe for these easy-to-make ravioli uses potsticker wrappers.
Use precooked, canned pumpkin purée for easier, cleaner, and quicker
prep time. This recipe is loaded with fiber and vitamin A.

Serves 2
Serving Size 6 ravioli

Calories: 522.44
Protein: 22.67 grams
Carbohydrates: 72.20 grams
Fiber: 5.04 grams
Fat: 15.02 grams

½ cup cooked pumpkin purée
1 egg, beaten
pinch of pumpkin pie spice
2 tablespoons bread crumbs
2 tablespoon grated
    Parmesan cheese
1 tablespoon chopped dried
    cherries
2 tablespoons ground
    almonds
salt and pepper to taste
24 round potsticker wrappers
1 egg white, beaten with
    1 tablespoon water
¼ cup Alfredo sauce
pinch of nutmeg
1 teaspoon chopped parsley

1. Combine the pumpkin purée with 1 beaten egg, pumpkin pie spice, bread crumbs, Parmesan cheese, dried cherries, and ground almonds. Season to taste with salt and pepper.

2. Put one spoonful of filling in the middle of 12 potsticker wrappers. Brush the edges of the wrappers with the egg white–water combination and put the remaining wrappers on top of the filling. Press the edges down to seal.

3. Bring a large pot of salted water to a boil, add the ravioli, and cook for about 3 minutes. Drain the ravioli.

4. Heat the Alfredo sauce with the nutmeg and add the ravioli to it.

5. Serve hot sprinkled with parsley.

Whole-Wheat Fettuccine Carbonara

Whole-wheat pasta has more fiber and vitamins than plain white spaghetti products. The parsley also helps with the fiber, and you can increase it to a half-cup for color and flavor.

1. Cook the bacon in a sauté pan until crispy. Add 1 cup cream and turn off the heat.

2. Whisk egg yolks, ½ cup cream, and Parmesan cheese in a bowl.

3. Ladle about ½ cup of the warm cream from the pan into the egg yolk mixture so the yolks will not curdle when you add them to the pan.

4. Pour the yolk mixture into the pan with the bacon and cream; stir to combine. Cook for a few minutes while stirring over medium-low heat, then add cooked fettuccine and toss to coat with sauce.

5. Remove from heat, season with salt and pepper, and toss in chopped parsley.

New Pasta Products

Manufacturers of Italian-style pastas have awakened to the nutritional needs of human beings old and young. Today, pasta is being manufactured with whole grains and chickpea flour. These pastas may cost a bit more than the old-fashioned ones and they may take a bit longer to cook, but they are worth the cost and trouble.

Serves 4
Serving Size 1½ cups

Calories: 755.38
Protein: 25.85 grams
Carbohydrates: 41.65 grams
Fiber: 3.98 grams
Fat: 55.37 grams

6 slices bacon, chopped
1½ cups cream
4 egg yolks
1 cup Parmesan cheese
4 cups cooked whole-wheat
    fettuccine noodles
salt and pepper to taste
2 tablespoons chopped fresh
    parsley

Pasta Fagioli

The ham in this dish makes it high in sodium, so consult your dietician before including it in your menu plan if you are on a salt-restricted diet.

Serves 8

Calories: 380.19
Protein: 20.37grams
Carbohydrates: 57.48 grams
Fiber: 6.25 grams
Fat: 7.52 grams

16-ounce package ziti pasta
2 tablespoons olive oil
2 cloves garlic, minced
1½ cups sugar snap peas
1½ cups diced cooked extra-
    lean ham
1 cup cooked navy beans
¼ cup sun-dried tomatoes
    packed in oil, drained and
    chopped
1½ cups low-fat, reduced-
    sodium chicken broth
½ teaspoon kosher or sea salt
¼ teaspoon cracked black
    pepper
¼ cup grated Parmesan
    cheese

1. Cook the pasta according to package directions.

2. Meanwhile, heat a large skillet over medium heat and add the olive oil. Sauté the garlic for 2 minutes, being careful not to burn it. Add the peas and stir-fry for about 3 minutes. Stir in the ham, beans, tomatoes, broth, salt, and pepper and simmer for 5 minutes.

3. Toss the stir-fried bean mixture with the pasta and Parmesan cheese.

Little Bits

Don't waste the unused tomato paste left in the can. Spoon out tablespoon-size portions and place them on plastic wrap or in sandwich baggies. Seal the packages and store in the freezer. When you need tomato paste in a recipe, add the frozen paste directly to the sauce; there is no need to defrost it.

Whole-Wheat Pasta in Blue Cheese Sauce

Blue cheese and pasta are an unexpected combination, but their flavors complement each other. Add the walnuts for extra fiber.

1. Heat the olive oil in a large nonstick skillet. Add the garlic and sauté for 1 minute. Lower the heat, stir in the cottage cheese, and bring it to temperature. Add the blue cheese and stir to combine; thin the sauce with a little skim milk, if necessary.

2. Toss with the pasta and divide into 4 equal servings. Top each serving with 1 tablespoon of the Parmesan cheese, freshly ground black pepper to taste, and toasted walnuts.

Serves 4

Calories: 309.56
Protein: 16.32 grams
Carbohydrates: 38.55 grams
Fiber: 6.33 grams
Fat: 11.29 grams

4 teaspoons olive oil
2 cloves garlic, minced
½ cup nonfat cottage cheese
2 ounces crumbled blue
    cheese
skim milk, as needed
    (optional)
4 cups cooked whole-wheat
    pasta
¼ cup freshly grated
    Parmesan cheese
freshly ground black pepper
dry-toasted chopped walnuts
    (optional)

Easy Chicken Lo Mein

If you prefer to serve the stir-fry over brown rice—or another grain, like quinoa—simply add some lemon juice and mustard powder to the cooking water instead of the salt suggested on the package.

Serves 4

Calories: 406.19
Protein: 44.06 grams
Carbohydrates: 45.37 grams
Fiber: 5.27 grams
Fat: 5.38 grams

⅛ teaspoon Minor's Low
  Sodium Chicken Base
½ cup water
2 (10-ounce) packages
  Cascadian Farm Organic
  Frozen Chinese Stir-Fry
  Vegetables
1 tablespoon freeze-dried
  shallots
1 pound cooked dark and
  light meat chicken
⅛ cup or to taste Mr. Spice
  Ginger Stir-Fry Sauce
1 pound no-salt-added oat
  bran pasta
1 teaspoon lemon juice
⅛ teaspoon mustard powder
1 teaspoon cornstarch
¼ teaspoon toasted sesame
  oil
4 thinly sliced scallions
  (optional)
low-sodium soy sauce
  (optional)

1. Add the chicken base and water to a large microwave-safe bowl; microwave on high for 30 seconds. Stir to dissolve the base into the water. Add the vegetables and freeze-dried shallots; microwave on high for 3 to 5 minutes, depending on how you prefer your vegetables cooked. (Keep in mind that the vegetables will continue to steam for a minute or so while the cover remains on the dish.) Drain some of the broth into a small nonstick sauté pan and set aside. Add the chicken and stir-fry sauce to the vegetables; stir well. Cover and set aside.

2. Consult the package for the pasta. In a large pot, bring the noted amount of water to a boil, but omit the salt. Add the pasta, lemon juice, and mustard powder.

3. While the pasta cooks, in a small cup or bowl, add a tablespoon of water to the cornstarch and whisk to make a slurry. Bring the reserved broth in the sauté pan to a boil over medium-high heat. Whisk in the slurry; cook for at least 1 minute (to remove the raw cornstarch taste), stirring constantly.

4. Once the mixture thickens, remove from heat; add the toasted sesame oil to the broth mixture, then whisk again. Pour the thickened broth mixture over the vegetables and chicken; toss to mix. Cover and microwave the chicken-vegetable mixture at 70 percent power for 2 minutes or until the chicken is heated through.

5. Drain the pasta; add it to the chicken-vegetable mixture and stir to combine. Divide among 4 plates. Garnish with chopped scallion and serve with the low-sodium soy sauce at the table, if desired.

Chapter 10
Enticing Entrées

Cabbage Rolls

Also known as stuffed cabbage depending upon where you come from, high-fiber cabbage is stuffed with lean meat, with more fiber in the whole grains and brown rice.

Serves 4
Serving Size 3 rolls

Calories: 658.37
Protein: 30.56 grams
Carbohydrates: 32.05 grams
Fiber: 6.55 grams
Fat: 46.48 grams

12 large cabbage leaves
1 cup cooked brown rice
¼ cup currants
¼ cup toasted hazelnuts
¼ cup minced onion
¾ teaspoon salt
pepper to taste
½ pound ground beef
¾ pound ground pork
1 tablespoon olive oil
2 cups tomato sauce
2 garlic cloves, finely minced
1 tablespoon brown sugar

1. Blanch the cabbage leaves in boiling water for 4 minutes. Remove and lay flat on a tray. Chill in the refrigerator.

2. Combine the cooked brown rice, currants, hazelnuts, onion, salt, and pepper in a bowl. Add ground pork and beef and mix well. Remove cabbage leaves from the refrigerator and blot with paper towels. Place about ¼ cup meat mixture on each cabbage leaf. Fold in sides and then roll up leaf to completely enclose filling.

3. Heat the olive oil in a skillet. Add the tomato sauce, garlic, and brown sugar and stir to combine.

4. Place the cabbage rolls in the tomato sauce, seam sides down. Spoon some of the sauce over the rolls, cover, and cook over medium-low heat for 60 minutes. Reduce heat to low and simmer for an additional 20 minutes, adding a little water if needed. Serve hot.

Vegetarian Cabbage Rolls

For a meatless version, substitute chopped mushrooms for the ground beef and pork. You will also have to double the quantity of rice, add extra currants, and perhaps toss in some chopped celery and nuts. You can also up the amount of onions in this recipe for a vegetarian version. Heighten the protein by adding an egg or two to the filling.

Stuffed Bell Peppers

Similar to the cabbage rolls, stuffed peppers offer lean meat, vegetables, and whole grain fiber in the casing and the stuffing. For the extra nutrition-conscious cook, red and yellow peppers have far more vitamin C in them than the green ones.

1. Preheat oven to 350°F.

2. Cut peppers in half through the stem and discard seeds, stem, and membrane. Lay pepper cups in a casserole dish.

3. Mix together the meat, cereal, rice, onion, carrots, celery, and ½ cup tomato sauce. Season mixture with salt and pepper.

4. Stuff each pepper half with a ball of meat mixture, mounding it on top.

5. Pour tomato sauce over tops of stuffed peppers, cover with foil and bake 45–60 minutes.

Serves 6

Calories: 327.63
Protein: 20.70 grams
Carbohydrates: 22.74 grams
Fiber: 4.44 grams
Fat: 17.62 grams

2 large green bell peppers
2 large red bell peppers
2 large yellow bell peppers
1 pound ground beef
¼ pound ground pork
¼ cup Grape Nuts cereal
½ cup cooked brown rice
½ cup diced onion
¼ cup diced carrots
¼ cup diced celery
2 cups tomato sauce
salt and pepper

Cranberry Pecan Savory Bread Pudding

*This is a perfect solution to postholiday leftover turkey. It also freezes
beautifully. Use whole-grain bread and a cup more nuts and dried fruits
in this tribute to Thanksgiving dinner in a stuffing-style casserole.*

Serves 8

Calories: 812.51
Protein: 23.85 grams
Carbohydrates: 42.60 grams
Fiber: 4.72 grams
Fat: 61.39 grams

10 cups stale whole-wheat
    bread cubes
1 tablespoon soft butter
½ cup diced celery
½ cup diced sweet onion
1½ cups diced cooked turkey
1 cup chopped toasted
    pecans
½ cup dried cranberries
5 egg yolks
7 whole eggs
2½ cups chicken broth
3½ cups cream
½ teaspoon sage
½ teaspoon thyme
¼ teaspoon ground black
    pepper
1 teaspoon kosher salt
½ cup melted butter
1 cup turkey gravy

1. Preheat oven to 350°F. Generously butter a 9" × 13" baking dish.

2. Put the bread cubes in the buttered dish. Sprinkle the celery, onion, turkey, pecans, and cranberries over the bread cubes and toss them together lightly with your hands. Set aside.

3. Mix together the egg yolks, eggs, chicken broth, cream, sage, thyme, pepper, and salt. Pour evenly over the bread cubes. Press down the bread cubes to submerge them.

4. Drizzle the melted butter over the top of the bread-custard mixture.

5. Bake for about 60 minutes or until the liquid is set. Serve with gravy.

Pork Loin with Brandied Prunes

Dried plums, also known as prunes, are one of the best sources of fiber.
They also are excellent when paired with nuts, meat, and poultry.

Serves 6
Serving Size 8 ounces

Calories: 575.29
Protein: 67.37 grams
Carbohydrates: 11.31 grams
Fiber: 1.02 grams
Fat: 24.54 grams

1. Preheat oven to 450°F.

2. Coat the pork loin with rosemary, tarragon, thyme, kosher salt, and black pepper. Rub the olive oil over the meat.

3. Put the shallots in the bottom of a roasting pan to make a bed for the roast. Sprinkle the garlic powder over the onion and lay the pork loin on top. Roast for 15 minutes.

4. Turn the oven down to 300°F and roast for 1 hour and 15 minutes. Remove the meat from the roasting pan and keep warm on a platter with a tent of foil over the roast.

5. Add the brandy to the roasting pan and scrape up any browned bits. Add the chicken broth and then pour the contents of the roasting pan into a saucepan. Skim grease off the top. Simmer until reduced by half.

6. Strain the sauce and return it to the pan. Add the prunes and any juices; simmer until the prunes plump, about 10 minutes. Mix the cornstarch into the cream; add to the sauce. Simmer until sauce thickens slightly. Add salt and pepper if necessary.

7. Slice the pork roast, arrange the slices on a platter, and spoon the brandied prune sauce over them.

4-pound boneless pork loin
2 tablespoons finely chopped
*   fresh rosemary*
1 tablespoon crumbled dried
*   tarragon*
1 teaspoon thyme
1 tablespoon kosher salt
1 teaspoon ground black
*   pepper*
2 tablespoons olive oil
1 cup coarse chopped
*   shallots*
½ teaspoon garlic powder
¼ cup brandy
1 cup chicken broth
1 cup pitted prunes, cut in
*   quarters*
1 tablespoon cornstarch
¼ cup heavy cream
additional salt and pepper

Dried Plums: The New Prunes?

Suddenly, instead of good old prunes, we can buy dried plums—which are the same thing! This is a marketing ploy to change the image of prunes. Because of their extreme sweetness, they are fabulous when paired with savory dishes. They like parsley, sage, rosemary, and thyme, as well as lemon zest and nuts, especially high-fiber chestnuts. Put them in stuffing for game, turkey, and chicken.

Pork Tenderloin with Blackberry Gastrique

Serves 4
Serving Size 6 ounces

Calories: 384.84
Protein: 35.45 grams
Carbohydrates: 30.57 grams
Fiber: 2.45 grams
Fat: 12.83 grams

1 tablespoon olive oil
1 tablespoon coarse grain
    mustard
1½-pound pork tenderloin
1 tablespoon kosher salt
1 teaspoon ground black
    pepper
1 shallot, minced
½ cup blackberries, fresh or
    frozen
1 tablespoon balsamic
    vinegar
½ cup blackberry preserves

*This grilled pork tenderloin is glazed with whole-grain
mustard and served with a tangy blackberry sauce.
Serve it with delicious brown rice or couscous to sop up the flavors
with healthy fiber. Garnish the roast with fresh mint leaves.*

1. Preheat a grill or grill-pan over high heat.

2. Rub 1 teaspoon olive oil and coarse grain mustard on the tenderloin, then sprinkle the kosher salt and black pepper on it.

3. Grill the tenderloin on all sides, for a total of about 10 minutes. Set the tenderloin aside, cover it with foil, and let it rest at least 10 minutes before slicing.

4. Sauté the shallots until tender in remaining olive oil. Remove from heat and stir in the blackberries, balsamic vinegar, and blackberry preserves.

5. Cut the tenderloin in ½"-thick slices, arrange the slices on a platter, and spoon the blackberry sauce over them.

Temperature Tip

The internal temperature of the tenderloin will go up about 5 degrees after it has been removed from the heat. It should be 155°F when done. The roast should be allowed to stand, prior to cutting, covered with a kitchen towel. This practice keeps the juices in the meat and makes it more succulent. Cutting the meat instantly makes the juices run out, leaving the meat dry.

Pork Chops and Fruited Veggies Bake

These homemade pork chops are tender and juicy.
They are easy to cook, and they pack a ton of fiber.

Serves 4

Calories: 682.32
Protein: 42.69 grams
Carbohydrates: 96.35 grams
Fiber: 10.49 grams
Fat: 14.66 grams

1. Preheat oven to 425°F. Treat a large roasting pan or jelly roll pan with nonstick spray.

2. Place the carrots, peaches, brown sugar, cinnamon, and cloves in a medium-size bowl; stir to mix. Set aside.

3. Mix the pepper, thyme, rosemary, oregano, and lemon granules together and use a mortar and pestle or the back of a spoon to crush them.

4. Rub the pork chops with the garlic. Evenly spread the sliced potatoes and green beans across the prepared baking pan. Place the garlic cloves and pork chops atop the vegetables. Spray lightly with the spray oil. Sprinkle with the herb mixture.

5. Spread the carrot and peach mixture atop the pork chops and vegetables.

6. Bake for 30 minutes or until the meat is tender and the potatoes and carrots are tender.

Fruit Swaps

You can substitute 4 peeled and sliced apples or pears for the peaches in the Pork Chops and Fruited Veggies Bake recipe. If you do, toss the slices with 1 tablespoon of lemon juice before mixing them with the brown sugar, cinnamon, and cloves.

1 cup baby carrots, washed and peeled
10-ounce package frozen organic sliced peaches, thawed
2 teaspoons brown sugar
¼ teaspoon ground cinnamon
pinch ground cloves
¼ teaspoon freshly ground black pepper
¼ teaspoon dried thyme
¼ teaspoon dried rosemary
⅛ teaspoon dried oregano
½ teaspoon dried lemon granules
4 (6-ounce) bone-in pork loin chops
8 cloves garlic, crushed
4 large Yukon gold potatoes, washed and sliced
10-ounce package frozen whole green beans, thawed
Extra-virgin olive spray oil

Veal Roast with Agro Dolce

Agro dolce is a classic Italian sauce, balancing the flavors of sweet, bitter, and sour. Use it on meat and poultry to add tasty fiber and excitement. It can be used on the side of an antipasto of cold vegetables and cheeses.

Serves 10
Serving Size ¼ cup

Calories: 308.89
Protein: 41.89 grams
Carbohydrates: 10.67 grams
Fiber: 0.34 grams
Fat: 9.28 grams

5-pound rolled boneless veal shoulder roast
3 tablespoons sugar
¼ cup vinegar
3 shallots, minced
½ cup golden raisins
2 teaspoons capers
½ cup white wine
1 tablespoon canned beef consommé
salt and pepper to taste

1. Preheat the oven to 325°F. Place the meat in a roasting pan and set in the oven. Roast the meat for 3 hours or until meat thermometer registers 170°F. Transfer the meat to a serving platter. Remove string and let stand 15 minutes before serving.

2. While roast cools, make agro dolce sauce. Mix the sugar and vinegar together in a saucepan and cook over low heat, stirring constantly, until sugar has caramelized.

3. Add the shallots, raisins, capers, wine, and consommé. Simmer, stirring occasionally, until everything is melded together, about 5 minutes.

4. Season to taste with salt and pepper if necessary.

5. Serve warm with sliced roast veal.

Artichoke and Butternut Squash Risotto

Diced artichokes and butternut squash are combined in this short-grain rice specialty from Italy. The veggies are a perfect foil for the rice.

1. Preheat the oven to 400°F. Put the diced squash and artichoke bottoms in a baking dish with ¼ cup water. Cover and bake until tender, about 45 minutes.

2. Heat the chicken broth and 3 cups water and set aside.

3. Sauté the onion in the butter until translucent, about 5 minutes. Add rice to onion and sauté for 3 minutes.

4. Add ½ cup broth, stirring constantly over medium-high heat until most of the liquid evaporates. Repeat with the rest of the broth in ½-cup increments. It will take about 20 minutes.

5. Remove from heat and stir in the Parmesan cheese, pepper, and salt. Fold in the cooked squash and artichoke.

Serves 4
Serving Size 2½ cups

Calories: 740.45
Protein: 14.45 grams
Carbohydrates: 105.95 grams
Fiber: 5.26 grams
Fat: 26.29 grams

1 cup diced butternut squash, cooked
1 cup diced artichoke bottoms, cooked
3¼ cups water
3 cups chicken broth
1 cup diced onion
½ cup butter
2 cups arborio rice
6 tablespoons Parmesan cheese
¼ teaspoon pepper
salt to taste

Spinach and Garbanzo Bean Pie

This can be made crust-less by greasing a 9" cake pan and beating ½ cup of flour into the egg mixture. However, the whole-grain crust, beans, leeks, and spinach add fiber.

Serves 6
Serving Size 1 slice

Calories: 637.17
Protein: 32.33 grams
Carbohydrates: 33.53 grams
Fiber: 5.30 grams
Fat: 42.26 grams

1 Whole-Wheat Pie Dough
    round (page 282)
½ cup diced leeks, white part
    only
1 tablespoon olive oil
1 cup cooked garbanzo beans
1 cup shredded smoked
    Gouda cheese
1 cup baby spinach leaves,
    washed and shredded
3 eggs
1½ cups cream
1⁄16 teaspoon nutmeg
½ teaspoon salt
¼ teaspoon white pepper
2 tablespoons chopped
    chives

1. Preheat oven to 375°F. Line a greased 9" fluted tart pan with removable bottom with the pie dough. To keep the dough from puffing up, weigh it down by lining it with foil and covering the foil with dried beans. Bake for 20 minutes. Remove from the oven and discard the dried beans and foil. Return to the oven for 3 minutes.

2. Sauté leeks in olive oil until tender. Spread them on the bottom of the prebaked pastry shell. Sprinkle garbanzo beans and cheese on top of leeks. Tuck spinach leaves here and there in the cheese.

3. Combine eggs, cream, nutmeg, salt, and pepper. Stir in chives.

4. Pour egg mixture over the ingredients in the tart shell, gently pressing down on anything that floats to the top to keep it submerged.

5. Bake for 30 minutes until set. Serve warm.

Quiche

This pie is actually a form of quiche, made famous by the great Julia Child. It all started with Quiche Lorraine, an open-faced tart made with cheese, eggs, cream, onions, and ham. For high-fiber options, the fillings can include tomatoes, roasted peppers, and squashes. Accentuate it with various cheeses.

Apricot and Pistachio Couscous Chicken Roulades

Dried apricots and pistachios add flavor and fiber to the pasta stuffing for these chicken breasts. Couscous is so versatile you can mix it with anything you'd use with rice.

Serves 4
Serving Size 8 ounces

Calories: 474.60
Protein: 31.49 grams
Carbohydrates: 51.35 grams
Fiber: 3.11 grams
Fat: 16.61 grams

2 cups cooked couscous
¼ cup chopped dried apricots
¼ cup chopped pistachios
4 boneless, skinless chicken breast fillets, pounded thin
salt and pepper to taste
½ cup apricot preserves
¼ cup butter

1. Preheat oven to 350°F. Combine the couscous with the dried apricots and pistachios. Lay chicken breasts out on plastic wrap and sprinkle them with salt and pepper.

2. Lay a row of couscous mixture on each breast in the middle, then roll each breast into a roll.

3. Place the rolls seam-side down in a buttered baking dish.

4. Melt the apricot jam with the butter and pour it over the chicken rolls.

5. Bake chicken rolls uncovered for 45 minutes.

Couscous

A Moroccan specialty, couscous is used in salads, soups, stews, and appetizers and mixed with everything and anything available. Couscous can be sweetened with dried fruit, such as apricots. It's a wonderful dessert mixed with honey and fresh figs. Whatever your fiber allotment or goal for a given meal may be, add couscous and all sorts of fibrous vegetables and fruits will follow naturally.

Grilled Chicken with Mango Salsa

This salsa increases fiber and turns on taste buds for an otherwise simple chicken dish. The salsa makes an excellent accompaniment to cheese quesadillas or grilled shrimp. You can also up the fiber by serving the salsa with roasted peanuts on the side.

Serves 6
Serving Size ¼ cup

Calories: 462.86
Protein: 47.73 grams
Carbohydrates: 6.59 grams
Fiber: 0.85 grams
Fat: 26.39 grams

1 cup diced mango
½ cup diced red onion
1 jalapeño pepper
¼ bunch cilantro
1 tablespoon lime juice
3 teaspoons olive oil, divided
salt to taste
3 pounds chicken breasts

1. Combine the mango and red onion in a large bowl. Cut the jalapeño pepper in half, remove the seeds, and dice the flesh. Add to the bowl.

2. Chop the cilantro and add it to the bowl.

3. Add the lime juice, 1 tablespoon olive oil, and a pinch of salt. Stir well, taste, and add more salt if needed.

4. Prepare grill. Coat chicken breasts with 2 tablespoons olive oil and place on grill. Cook for 5 to 6 minutes per side or until chicken is cooked through. Serve with mango salsa.

Salsa Is Here to Stay!

It's food, music, and dancing! Starting with basic tomato salsa, the darling of the nacho tray, salsa has expanded to cover most fruit. The one requirement of salsa is that it be hot and spicy. Salsa can be fairly mild with just a bit of a bite or it can set your mouth on fire. Using various hot chili peppers adds more fiber than does hot sauce. If you use the seeds and interior veins of a chili, you increase the heat and fiber exponentially.

Chicken à la King

This classic recipe can also be made with turkey in the title role.

1. Combine the soup, milk, Worcestershire, mayonnaise, and pepper in a saucepan and bring to a boil.

2. Reduce heat and add the peas and pearl onions, mushrooms, and chicken. Simmer until the vegetables and chicken are heated through.

3. Serve over toast.

Serves 4

Calories: 335.40
Protein: 25.47 grams
Carbohydrates: 37.79 grams
Fiber: 6.99 grams
Fat: 9.78 grams

1 can condensed cream of chicken soup
¼ cup skim milk
½ teaspoon Worcestershire sauce
1 tablespoon mayonnaise
¼ teaspoon ground black pepper
2 cups frozen mix of peas and pearl onions, thawed
1 cup sliced mushrooms, stemmed
½ pound cooked, chopped chicken
4 slices whole-wheat bread, toasted

Yogurt "Gravy" Chicken Thighs

Za'atar is a mixture of sumac, sesame seeds, and herbs like oregano and hyssop. It's often used in Middle Eastern dishes.

Serves 4

Calories: 355.01
Protein: 32.20 grams
Carbohydrates: 45.60 grams
Fiber: 5.64 grams
Fat: 4.70 grams

16-ounce package hash browns
10-ounce package frozen vegetables
1 large sweet onion, sliced
4 (4-ounce) boneless, skinless chicken thighs
¼ teaspoon freshly ground black pepper
1 teaspoon garlic powder
1 tablespoon cornstarch
1 teaspoon dried parsley
2 cups plain nonfat yogurt
1 teaspoon za'atar or herb seasoning blend

1. Preheat oven to 350°F.

2. Place the hash browns, frozen vegetables, and onions in an oven- and microwave-safe casserole dish treated with nonstick spray. Cover with plastic wrap and microwave on high for 3 minutes. Turn the dish and microwave on high for an additional 2 to 3 minutes, until the vegetables are thawed and the onion is tender.

3. Remove and discard the plastic wrap. Season the chicken with the pepper and garlic powder. Arrange the thighs over the top of the vegetable mixture.

4. Stir the cornstarch and parsley into the yogurt. Pour the mixture over the chicken and vegetable mixture, spreading the yogurt so that it covers everything in an equal layer.

5. Bake for 45 minutes or until the yogurt is bubbling and thickened and the chicken thighs are done. Sprinkle the thighs with the za'atar. Serve immediately.

Sesame Tofu

Lots of crunchy sesame seeds are the coating for these chunks of chewy, crusty marvels. You can also add a cup of cooked chopped broccoli to get your greens. Sliced raw sugar snaps make a fine garnish.

Serves 4
Serving Size 1½ cups

Calories: 723.26
Protein: 30.13 grams
Carbohydrates: 75.74 grams
Fiber: 6.04 grams
Fat: 35.30 grams

1 pound fresh tofu, cubed
½ cup rice flour
pinch of five spice powder
1 teaspoon sesame oil
1 egg, beaten
¾ cup sesame seeds
½ cup peanut oil
½ cup teriyaki sauce
4 cups cooked rice or noodles
¼ cup sliced green onions

1. Drain the tofu cubes well on paper towels.

2. Mix the rice flour with the spice powder. Mix the sesame oil with the egg.

3. Dredge the tofu in the flour mixture, then dip in the egg mixture and toss in sesame seeds to coat. Lay the tofu in a single layer and let dry for 10 minutes.

4. Heat peanut oil in a skillet and pan fry the tofu until browned and crispy.

5. Drain the tofu on paper towels and then toss with teriyaki sauce. Serve over rice or noodles and scatter green onions on top.

Sea Bass Wrapped in Savoy Cabbage

Serves 4
Serving Size 6 ounces

Calories: 354.71
Protein: 25.39 grams
Carbohydrates: 6.93 grams
Fiber: 1.13 grams
Fat: 25.35 grams

4 large leaves Savoy cabbage
4 tablespoons unsalted
    butter, softened
1 tablespoon grated fresh
    ginger root
1 teaspoon grated orange
    zest
1 minced shallot
4 (1"-thick) sea bass fillets
salt and pepper to taste
½ cup coconut milk
¼ cup fresh lemon juice
3" piece lemongrass, thinly
    chopped
½ cup heavy cream
salt and pepper
1 tablespoon grated lemon
    zest

Serve this luscious fish over cooked brown rice that you've spiked with nuts, fresh ginger, fresh herbs, and a bit of minced green onion.

1. Preheat oven to 375°F.

2. Blanch the Savoy cabbage leaves in boiling water to soften and make them flexible, then plunge them into ice water to cool. Lay them out on paper towels to drain.

3. Combine the soft butter, grated ginger root, orange zest, and shallot to make a compound butter.

4. Divide the compound butter among the blanched cabbage leaves. Season the sea bass fillets with salt and pepper and place one on each cabbage leaf. Wrap the cabbage leaves around the fish fillets to make packages.

5. Place packages seam-side down in a baking dish. Pour the coconut milk and lemon juice over the packages. Top with lemongrass.

6. Cover and bake for 20 minutes. Remove the packages from the baking dish, place on a serving platter, and cover with foil. Strain the baking liquid into a saucepan and bring to a boil. Add the heavy cream and simmer to reduce into a slightly thickened sauce. Pour sauce over the packages on the platter. Sprinkle with lemon zest and serve hot.

Wrapping Food Before Cooking

Sea bass wrapped in Savoy cabbage produces the same moist results as wrapping it in pastry or a paper bag! However, the cabbage retains its nutritional and fiber value. The paper bag wrapping for food must be discarded and the puff pastry will get soggy and retain its fattening properties. Try wrapping chicken or duck breasts in cabbage and enjoy a healthy, super-succulent dinner.

Grilled Mahi-Mahi with Pineapple Salsa

This salsa is also good on pork tenderloin. The fruit and vegetables add fiber, texture, and piquancy to simple foods.

1. Combine the pineapple, red onion, green bell pepper, and red bell pepper in a large bowl.

2. Chop the cilantro and add it to the bowl.

3. Add the vinegar, hot sauce, and a pinch of salt. Stir well, taste, and add more salt if needed.

4. Prepare your grill. Coat the fish with olive oil and season with pepper. Place on hot grill. Let cook for 3 to 4 minutes per side or until fish is opaque. Top with pineapple salsa and serve.

Serves 8
Serving Size ¼ cup

Calories: 142.25
Protein: 21.30 grams
Carbohydrates: 3.87 grams
Fiber: 0.63 grams
Fat: 4.30 grams

1 cup diced pineapple
½ cup diced red onion
¼ cup minced green bell pepper
¼ cup minced red bell pepper
¼ bunch cilantro
1 tablespoon white wine vinegar
¼ teaspoon hot pepper sauce
salt to taste
2 pounds cod or other firm-fleshed white fish
2 tablespoons olive oil
pepper to taste

Halibut with Banana Salsa

This salsa is an excellent accompaniment to grilled scallops or firm-fleshed white fish. Try it with sautéed shrimp and brown rice to add some fiber and spice to otherwise bland fare.

Serves 6
Serving Size ¼ cup

Calories: 237.70
Protein: 31.86 grams
Carbohydrates: 8.19 grams
Fiber: 1.24 grams
Fat: 7.99 grams

1 cup diced bananas
¼ cup minced sweet onion
¼ cup minced green bell pepper
2 tablespoons lemon juice
2 tablespoons chopped cilantro
2 pounds halibut fillets
2 tablespoons olive oil

1. Combine the bananas, sweet onion, and green bell pepper in a large bowl.

2. Add the lemon juice and cilantro and toss to coat.

3. Prepare grill. Coat halibut with olive oil. Place fish on grill for 3–4 minutes per side or until fish is opaque.

Salsas and Salads

Transform a chicken or shrimp salad with pineapple or mango salsa. Spoon tomato salsa over ham salad. Make a fresh-flavored coleslaw with shredded Napa cabbage and absolutely any salsa for great taste and lots more fiber. Add even more protein and fiber by sprinkling toasted pepitas over the tops of these salads and the coleslaw.

Seafood in Thai-Curry Bean Sauce

*This recipe tastes as if it should have lots of sodium, but it doesn't.
The beans are a prime source of fiber.*

Serves 4

Calories: 234.58
Protein: 26.81 grams
Carbohydrates: 19.48 grams
Fiber: 6.53 grams
Fat: 4.18 grams

1. Bring the oil to temperature in a large, deep, nonstick sauté pan over medium heat. Add the curry powder, pepper, cumin, coriander, red pepper flakes, fennel seeds, cloves, and mace; sauté for 1 minute. Remove 1 teaspoon of the seasoned oil from the pan and set aside. Add the 1 tablespoon water and bring it to temperature, stirring to mix it with the seasoned oil remaining in the pan. Add the onion and sauté over moderately low heat until the onion is soft. Add the garlic and sauté for 1 minute, being careful not to burn the garlic.

2. Add the applesauce and wine and simmer the mixture until the wine is reduced by half. Add the chicken base and stir to dissolve it and mix it into the onion mixture. Add the ¼ cup water and bring to a boil. Add the lime juice granules, lemongrass, parsley, basil, shallots, and ⅓ cup of the beans. Reduce heat and simmer, stirring, for 1 minute.

3. Transfer the wine-bean mixture to a blender or food processor container; pulse to purée. Pour the wine-bean purée back into the saucepan and add the remaining beans. Simmer to bring the entire mixture to temperature, then keep warm.

4. Wash the shrimp and scallops under cold water. Blot dry between paper towels. Bring a nonstick skillet or sauté pan to temperature over moderately high heat. Add the seasoned oil. When the oil is hot (but not smoking), add the shrimp and sauté for 2 minutes on each side or until cooked through. Using a slotted spoon, transfer the shrimp to a plate and keep warm.

5. Add the scallops to the skillet and sauté for 1 minute on each side or until cooked through. Divide the bean sauce among 4 shallow bowls and arrange the shellfish on top.

*2 teaspoons sesame or
  canola oil*
1 teaspoon curry powder
*¼ teaspoon freshly ground
  black pepper*
⅛ teaspoon ground cumin
⅛ teaspoon ground coriander
pinch dried red pepper flakes
pinch ground fennel seeds
pinch ground cloves
pinch ground mace
1 tablespoon water
*1 small sweet onion, finely
  chopped*
2 cloves garlic, minced
*1 tablespoon no-salt-added,
  unsweetened applesauce*
¼ cup dry white wine
*¼ teaspoon low-sodium
  chicken bouillon*
¼ cup water
*⅛ teaspoon dried lime juice
  granules, crushed*
*⅛ teaspoon dried ground
  lemongrass*
*¼ packed cup fresh parsley
  leaves*
¼ packed cup fresh basil leaves
*1 tablespoon freeze-dried
  shallots*
*1⅓ cups canned no-salt-
  added cannellini beans,
  drained and rinsed*
*½ pound shelled and
  deveined shrimp*
½ pound scallops

Mixed Vegetable Tempura

Asparagus, carrot slices, and red bell pepper strips make this recipe delicious.
You could use any favorite vegetable that can hold up to steaming.

Serves 4
Serving Size 8 pieces

Calories: 524.48
Protein: 5.01 grams
Carbohydrates: 33.54 grams
Fiber: 4.70 grams
Fat: 42.60 grams

¾ cup beer
¾ cup flour
¾ teaspoon salt
2 cups vegetable oil
12 stalks asparagus
12 carrot sticks
8 red bell pepper strips

1. Whisk beer into flour until smooth, then stir in salt.

2. Heat oil to 375°F in a deep fryer or large pot.

3. Dip vegetables individually in batter, let excess drip off, and drop carefully into the hot oil. Cook in batches.

4. Cook about 3 minutes and remove from oil with a slotted spoon, chopsticks, or tongs.

5. Drain on paper towels and serve immediately.

Walnut and Mushroom Loaf

*This is a fantastic way to bring all the flavor and fiber
of nuts to your dinner table in a vegetarian-friendly way.*

Serves 4

Calories: 786.26
Protein: 26.49 grams
Carbohydrates: 57.98 grams
Fiber: 13.73 grams
Fat: 48.92 grams

5 teaspoons walnut or
    olive oil
1 large sweet onion, chopped
4 cups button mushrooms,
    sliced
1 cup ground walnuts
1 cup ground raw sunflower
    seeds
1 tablespoon lemon juice
1⅓ cups soymilk
1 cup whole-wheat bread
    crumbs
½ teaspoon dried parsley
⅛ teaspoon dried sage
1 teaspoon dried basil
½ cup oatmeal
1⅓ cups warm water
1 tablespoon yeast extract

1. Preheat oven to 350°F. Treat a baking dish with nonstick spray.

2. Bring a large nonstick sauté pan treated with nonstick spray to temperature over medium heat. Add 4 teaspoons of the oil, the onion, and mushrooms; sauté for 3 minutes. Add the walnuts and sunflower seeds; stir to mix, and sauté for 1 minute. Remove the pan from the heat and stir in the lemon juice, soymilk, bread crumbs, parsley, sage, and basil. Transfer to the prepared baking dish; bake for 45 minutes.

3. While the loaf bakes, prepare the gravy by putting the oatmeal, water, and the remaining 1 teaspoon oil in the bowl of a blender or food processor; pulse until liquefied. Pour the mixture into a small nonstick saucepan and heat over medium-low heat, stirring constantly until thickened. Stir in the yeast extract. Serve warm over the loaf.

Be Creative

You can substitute steamed vegetables like carrots and some cooked beans for some of the mushrooms in the Walnut and Mushroom Loaf. Likewise, experiment using your favorite seasoning blends instead of the recommended dried herbs.

Black Bean Chili

Serves 8

Calories: 304.06
Protein: 11.59 grams
Carbohydrates: 55.03 grams
Fiber: 9.11 grams
Fat: 4.85 grams

1½ cups dried black beans
2 tablespoons canola oil
2 large sweet onions, chopped
5 medium-size cloves garlic, minced
1 tablespoon ground cumin
1 tablespoon dried oregano
3 tablespoons salt-free chili powder
1 teaspoon freshly ground black pepper
1 teaspoon dried red pepper flakes
1 teaspoon dried lemon granules, crushed
3 jalapeño peppers, seeded and minced
2 (14½-ounce) cans no-salt-added diced tomatoes
1 cup chopped fresh pineapple
4 large carrots, peeled and sliced
1 cup uncooked long-grain brown rice
1 tablespoon apple cider or red wine vinegar
tamari sauce (optional)
no-salt-added peanut butter or other nut butter (optional)
fresh cilantro, for garnish

This vegetarian dish can easily be transformed into something to satisfy a meat-lover with the addition of ground turkey, beef, or pork.

1. Rinse the beans and cover them with water in a large, heavy pot. Bring to a full boil over medium-high heat, drain, and rinse again. Return the beans to the pot over medium-high heat and add 7 cups of water, or a combination of water and mushroom broth. Once the water comes to a boil, reduce heat and simmer for 1 hour.

2. While the beans cook, bring a large nonstick sauté pan to temperature over medium heat. Add the oil and onions; sauté for 4 minutes, stirring frequently. Lower the heat to medium-low. Add the garlic and sauté for 1 minute. Stir in the cumin, oregano, chili powder, pepper, red pepper flakes, lemon granules, and jalapeños; sauté for an additional 4 minutes, then add the tomatoes. Simmer for 10 minutes, stirring frequently.

3. Stir the sautéed mixture into the pot of beans. Add the pineapple, carrots, and rice. Simmer partially covered for another hour, or until the beans are soft and the rice is done. Stir in the vinegar. Have tamari sauce or Bragg Liquid Aminos, peanut or other nut butter, and freshly ground black pepper available at the table to flavor individual servings of the chili, if desired. Garnish with cilantro.

Chili Powders

Using a combination of chili powders such as ancho, chipotle, or specialty salt-free chili powder blends in the Black Bean Chili is an easy way to add layers of flavor. You can also substitute chunk pineapple canned in its own juice if fresh pineapple isn't available, or substitute 1 cup of fresh orange juice instead.

Chapter 11
One-Dish Casseroles

Broccoli Spinach Pie

This quiche-like casserole is made with a Whole-Wheat Pie Dough (page 282)
crust. You can also turn this into a deep-dish pie and put the dough on top.

Serves 6
Serving Size 1 slice

Calories: 527.61
Protein: 26.77 grams
Carbohydrates: 26.15 grams
Fiber: 3.77 grams
Fat: 35.90 grams

9" Whole-Wheat Pie Dough
round
1 cup cooked chopped
broccoli
½ cup cooked chopped
spinach leaves
½ cup crumbled feta cheese
3 eggs
1½ cups cream
⅟₁₆ teaspoon nutmeg
½ teaspoon salt
¼ teaspoon white pepper
2 tablespoons chopped
chives

1. Preheat oven to 375°F. Line a greased 1½-quart casserole dish with the pie dough. To keep the dough from puffing up, weigh it down by lining the dough with foil and covering the foil with dried beans. Bake for 20 minutes. Remove from the oven and discard the dried beans and foil. Return to the oven for 3 minutes.

2. Distribute the broccoli and spinach over the bottom of the crust. Sprinkle the feta cheese on top of the broccoli and spinach.

3. Combine the eggs, cream, nutmeg, salt, and pepper. Stir in the chives.

4. Pour the egg mixture over the ingredients in the tart shell.

5. Bake for 30 minutes or until the filling sets. Serve warm.

Squash Blossom Polenta

You can add additional edible flowers to this recipe for more color. Zucchini and lavender blossoms are wonderful in salads, battered and fried. Adding ½ cup fresh or frozen corn kernels will increase the texture and fiber.

Serves 4
Serving Size 1½ cups

Calories: 162.51
Protein: 2.62 grams
Carbohydrates: 23.73 grams
Fiber: 2.30 grams
Fat: 6.85 grams

4 cups water
1 teaspoon salt
1 cup coarse-ground yellow
    cornmeal
2 tablespoons butter
1 cup chopped zucchini
    squash blossoms

1. Put water and salt in a saucepan and bring to a boil. Reduce heat to medium low. Gradually add cornmeal and stir constantly until it has thickened, about 15 minutes.

2. Stir in butter, then add the chopped squash blossoms.

3. Serve immediately for soft polenta, or pour into a greased 9" × 13" baking dish and let cool. When cool, it can be cut into squares or triangles and grilled, sautéed, or baked.

Know Your Edible Flowers

Bean blossoms have a sweet, beanie flavor. Nasturtiums have a wonderfully peppery flavor similar to watercress. Violets, roses, and lavender lend a sweet flavor to salads or desserts. Bright yellow calendulas are an economic alternative to expensive saffron, though not quite as pungent. Other flowers may have a spicy or peppermint flavor.

Vegetable Pot Pie

Serves 6
Serving Size 2 cups

Calories: 480.55
Protein: 14.37 grams
Carbohydrates: 65.28 grams
Fiber: 8.99 grams
Fat: 19.13 grams

½ medium onion, diced
2 carrots, peeled and diced
2 celery stalks, diced
½ cup sliced leeks
2 tablespoons butter
¼ cup flour
3 cups chicken broth
1 potato, peeled and cubed
½ cup cut green beans
1 bay leaf
½ cup frozen peas
½ cup cream
salt and pepper to taste
¼ cup chopped chives
1 recipe Whole-Wheat
    Biscuits, unbaked
    (page 273)

1. Sauté onion, carrots, celery, and leeks in butter until tender. Dust with flour, stir, and cook a few minutes. Add chicken broth, potato, and green beans. Bring to a boil, add bay leaf, and simmer for 40 minutes until vegetables are cooked and liquid is thickened.

2. Stir in peas and cream and remove from heat. Remove bay leaf, season with salt and pepper, and stir in chopped chives. Pour filling into a 9" × 13" baking dish and place on a baking sheet with sides.

3. Preheat oven to 400°F.

4. Place the unbaked biscuits on top of the filling and bake for 45 minutes or until the biscuit top is baked.

5. Scoop out individual portions and serve hot.

Other Ways to Pot a Pie

You can make a country-style pie in an earthenware casserole. Try cornmeal batter on top, as opposed to whole-wheat pie crust. Biscuits are wonderful because they absorb some of the gravy or liquids in the pie as they bubble up, turning a pie into a cobbler. Try topping a pie with a nutty crust made with ground walnuts, butter, whole-wheat flour, and orange zest.

Acorn Squash, Cranberries, and Wild Rice

This is a quick and easy vegetarian meal made entirely in the microwave. The microwave takes the time factor out of cooking the squash, which can take 45–60 minutes in a conventional oven.

1. Pierce the squash all over with a fork. Place squash on a paper towel in the microwave oven. Cook on high for 5 minutes, turn over, and cook for 10 more minutes. Let stand 5 to 10 minutes.

2. Meanwhile, combine the cooked wild rice, balsamic vinegar, pecans, and dried cranberries. Set aside.

3. Cut the squash in half, remove the seeds, and place cut-side up in a casserole dish.

4. Spoon the wild rice mixture into the hollowed-out squash. Cover and cook on high in the microwave for several minutes to heat through.

5. Drizzle maple syrup on top before serving.

All-American

The combination of wild rice and cranberries is as American as a dish can be! Both of these ingredients were originally cultivated by Native Americans, who introduced them to the colonists. The sweet yet tart flavor of the cranberries pairs well with the nutty flavor of the rice and gives you all the fiber you need.

Serves 4
Serving Size ½ squash

Calories: 295.75
Protein: 4.74 grams
Carbohydrates: 48.93 grams
Fiber: 6.53 grams
Fat: 11.08 grams

2 acorn squash, whole
1 cup cooked wild rice
1 tablespoon balsamic vinegar
½ cup toasted pecans, chopped
½ cup dried cranberries
4 teaspoons maple syrup

Brown Rice Jambalaya

To make a truly authentic jambalaya, you should use ingredients indigenous to Louisiana, like filet gumbo, andouille sausage, crawfish, and tasso.

Serves 6
Serving Size 2½ cups

Calories: 583.29
Protein: 21.87 grams
Carbohydrates: 80.37 grams
Fiber: 5.46 grams
Fat: 18.87 grams

1 cup ham, cubed
½ cup vegetable oil
1 cup diced onion
1 cup diced celery
1 cup diced green bell pepper
5 cloves garlic, minced
½ teaspoon dried thyme
½ teaspoon ground black
    pepper
¼ teaspoon cayenne pepper
3 cups uncooked brown rice
4 cups chicken broth
2 bay leaves
¼ teaspoon salt
1 fully cooked andouille or
    kielbasa, sliced
½ cup diced tomatoes
½ pound shrimp, peeled and
    deveined

1. Brown the ham in the vegetable oil in a large pot. Remove it and set aside.

2. Add the onion, celery, green pepper, and garlic to the pot and sauté until tender.

3. Add the thyme, black pepper, cayenne pepper, and brown rice and cook for 5 minutes, stirring occasionally.

4. Add chicken broth, browned ham, bay leaves, salt, kielbasa, and tomatoes. Stir to combine, bring mixture to a simmer over medium heat, and cover the pot with a lid.

5. Simmer 40 minutes, add the shrimp on top, return the lid, and continue to cook 5–7 more minutes. Make sure the shrimp are pink. Remove the bay leaves and serve hot.

Mirepoix and the Louisiana Trinity

Mirepoix is the combination of onion, celery, and carrot in classic French cuisine, and it is the flavor base for sauces, soups, stews, and more. The combination of onion, celery, and green bell pepper is called the trinity in Bayou and Caribbean cuisine. It is used in the same manner as mirepoix. Cooks change the definition from house to house and village to village.

Broccoli Cheddar Rice

If you prefer a creamier texture, use American cheese instead of cheddar cheese. If you want extra fiber and flavor, add ½ cup roasted walnuts or pecans or top with sesame seeds.

1. Preheat oven to 350°F.

2. Heat olive oil in a saucepan and sauté the onion in it until tender.

3. Add rice and sauté for 3 to 5 minutes with the onion. Stir the broccoli into the rice mixture.

4. Pour the rice mixture into a 9" × 13" glass baking dish. Add chicken broth, salt, pepper, and cheese. Stir to incorporate. Cover with foil and bake for 45 minutes.

Serves 4
Serving Size 1½ cups

Calories: 437.21
Protein: 12.31 grams
Carbohydrates: 42.25 grams
Fiber: 2.72 grams
Fat: 24.07 grams

¼ cup olive oil
½ cup diced onion
1 cup long-grain white rice
2 cups chopped fresh broccoli
1¾ cups chicken broth
½ teaspoon salt
¼ teaspoon ground pepper
1 cup grated cheddar cheese

Baked Barley Casserole

Barley is a great food to eat when you want to feel full because it absorbs more liquid during cooking than other grains. That's why it's such a favorite in soups. It's also a highly digestible fiber.

1. Preheat oven to 350°F.

2. Sauté the barley in the olive oil until the barley starts to brown. Transfer the barley to a 3-quart casserole dish.

3. Sauté the onion in butter until it starts to brown and add to the casserole dish. Season with salt and pepper and add 3 cups beef broth.

4. Cover the casserole and bake for 60 minutes.

5. Add the remaining beef broth, cover, and bake until the liquid is absorbed, about 40 minutes. Add parsley for garnish.

Serves 4
Serving Size 2 cups

Calories: 394.05
Protein: 16.33 grams
Carbohydrates: 38.98 grams
Fiber: 9.04 grams
Fat: 20.81 grams

1 cup barley
3 tablespoons olive oil
1½ cups diced onion
2 tablespoons butter
½ teaspoon salt
¼ teaspoon pepper
6 cups beef broth
½ cup chopped Italian flat-leaf parsley for garnish

Black Beans, Plantains, and Rice

Ripe plantains are black on the outside. They look like big bananas and are featured in Caribbean and South American cuisine. They are not quite as sweet as bananas but just as loaded with fiber and nutrition.

Serves 4
Serving Size 2 cups

Calories: 698.75
Protein: 15.12 grams
Carbohydrates: 110.47 grams
Fiber: 12.73 grams
Fat: 23.85 grams

2 ripe plantains
¼ cup olive oil
3 tablespoons butter
2 minced cloves garlic
½ cup sliced sweet onion
1½ cups long-grain rice
2¾ cups chicken broth
1 teaspoon salt
2 cups cooked black beans, drained
2 tablespoons chopped cilantro
1 lemon

1. Peel the plantains and cut them into 1"-thick slices.

2. Heat the olive oil in a heavy skillet and brown the plantains on each side. Drain on paper towels and set aside.

3. Melt the butter in a large ovenproof pot and sauté the garlic, onions, and rice in it for 3 minutes. Add the chicken broth and salt and bring to a simmer.

4. Meanwhile, preheat the oven to 325°F.

5. Stir the simmering rice once. Cover and bake for 25 minutes. Uncover and add the black beans, plantains, and cilantro. Cover and return to the oven for 5 minutes. Remove from oven, squeeze the juice from the lemon over it, re-cover, and serve hot.

Going South!

Plantains, sweet potatoes, yams, mangoes, papayas, and wonderful spices will perk up tired recipes. Plantain chips add fiber and make a fine garnish for soups and stews. Break them into beef stew or sprinkle them over a pork roast. Shredded coconut is a delicious garnish for shrimp. Fresh pineapple will go a long way to perk up a chicken dish.

Corn Soufflé Pudding

*This recipe is perfect for holidays; it may be made a day
in advance, covered, refrigerated, and then baked the next day.
For extra spice, mince and stir in a jalapeño pepper.
Add some pepitas for garnish to sprinkle on at the last minute.*

1. Preheat oven to 400°F. Grease a 1½-quart casserole dish with 1 tablespoon of butter and set aside.

2. Melt the remaining butter in a saucepan, add the flour, and mix it with a whisk. Cook over medium heat for 30 seconds, add the milk, and stir with a whisk.

3. Cook while whisking for about 2 minutes over medium-high heat until the mixture thickens. Remove from heat, season with salt and pepper, and add the corn kernels.

4. Whisk in the eggs, cheese, and chives and scrape the batter into the prepared casserole dish.

5. Bake 40 minutes and serve immediately.

Serves 4
Serving Size 1½ cups

Calories: 612.23
Protein: 28.81 grams
Carbohydrates: 24.74 grams
Fiber: 1.30 grams
Fat: 44.98 grams

7 tablespoons butter
⅓ cup all-purpose flour
2 cups milk
½ teaspoon salt
¼ teaspoon pepper
1 cup frozen corn kernels
5 eggs, beaten
2 cups shredded Swiss cheese
2 tablespoons chopped
 chives

Cassoulet

This is a quick-cooking French meal in one dish. Other types of beans and cooked poultry may be used instead of the flageolets and confit.

Serves 4
Serving Size 1½ cups

Calories: 714.07
Protein: 46.93 grams
Carbohydrates: 58.63 grams
Fiber: 10.50 grams
Fat: 31.63 grams

1 tablespoon olive oil
½ cup diced onion
1 minced garlic clove
1 tablespoon tomato paste
1 teaspoon dried thyme
½ teaspoon salt
¼ teaspoon pepper
3 cups cooked flageolet
    beans
4 duck confit legs
1 cup sliced Polish sausage
1 cup coarse bread crumbs
1 tablespoon melted bacon
    fat

1. Preheat oven to 375°F. Rub half of the olive oil in a large casserole dish and set aside.

2. Sauté the onion and garlic in the remaining olive oil. Stir in the tomato paste, thyme, salt, and pepper.

3. Put the cooked beans in the prepared casserole dish and stir in the onion mixture. Arrange the duck confit legs and Polish sausage over the beans.

4. Toss the bread crumbs with the bacon fat and sprinkle them over the entire casserole.

5. Bake for 40 minutes or until crumbs are brown and casserole is heated well throughout.

Cassoulet Has Everything

This peasant dish was designed to feed a village. Made in a huge cauldron, hunters and farmers contributed what they had. There is no absolutely hard-and-fast recipe for cassoulet. Make it for a crowd of friends and/or family.

Zucchini Onion Casserole

*For added fiber and protein, sneak in a half-cup of
ground walnuts and mix them into the bread crumbs.
You may want to make your own Croutons (page 284) out of
whole-grain bread to boost the fiber content in this recipe.*

1. Preheat oven to 350°F.

2. In a 3-quart baking dish, layer half of each of the sweet onion, zucchini, and tomatoes. Season the vegetables with herbs, salt, and pepper.

3. Scatter half of the croutons over the seasoned vegetables and half of the cheese over the croutons.

4. Repeat the layering with the remaining vegetables, season with salt and pepper, and sprinkle the remaining croutons and cheese on top.

5. Cover with lid or aluminum foil and bake for 60 minutes. Serve hot.

Zucchini vs. Potatoes

Zucchinis are lower in calories and higher in fiber than potatoes. Try making scalloped zucchini, substituting it for potatoes, or mix zucchini with potatoes for added veggie-value. Yellow summer squash can also be used with zucchini and/or potatoes for added fiber. It has a sweet butter flavor that lets you use less butter and more squash!

**Serves 8
Serving Size 1½ cups**

Calories: 188.44
Protein: 9.34 grams
Carbohydrates: 12.96 grams
Fiber: 2.08 grams
Fat: 11.45 grams

*2½ cups thinly sliced sweet
 onion*
2½ cups sliced zucchini
*2 medium-large sliced ripe
 red tomatoes*
10 leaves fresh basil
1 tablespoon dried rosemary
salt and pepper to taste
2 cups seasoned croutons
*2 cups shredded cheddar
 cheese*

Bean Burrito Torte

This is a layered meal that has stripes of different ingredients so it resembles a layer cake or torte. The sauces and seasonings are available in most supermarkets or Latino markets. You can substitute Monterey Jack or pepper Jack cheese for cheddar for a different take on the classic.

Serves 6
Serving Size 1 wedge

Calories: 389.67
Protein: 13.62 grams
Carbohydrates: 45.21 grams
Fiber: 7.75 grams
Fat: 20.37 grams

1 cup refried beans
1 cup sour cream
1 tablespoon taco seasoning
9 (8") whole-wheat tortillas
½ cup enchilada sauce
1 cup shredded cheddar
    cheese
1 avocado, peeled, pitted,
    and sliced
¼ cup black olives
½ cup diced tomatoes
¼ cup chopped green onions
1 cup shredded iceberg
    lettuce

1. Preheat oven to 350°F. Oil a 9" cake pan.

2. Mix the refried beans, ½ cup of sour cream, and taco seasoning together.

3. Place 3 tortillas on the bottom of the cake pan. Spread half of the refried bean mixture over the tortillas. Spoon half of the enchilada sauce over the beans. Sprinkle half of the cheddar cheese over the enchilada sauce.

4. Place 3 tortillas on top of the cheese. Repeat the layering with the remaining bean mixture, enchilada sauce, and cheese.

5. Top with the last 3 tortillas, cover tightly with foil, and bake for 30 minutes. Remove from oven, remove the foil, cut into six wedges, and invert the pan onto a plate.

6. Remove the pan and garnish the top of the torte with the remaining sour cream, avocado, black olives, diced tomatoes, and green onions. Place the shredded lettuce around the torte on the plate and serve.

Southwest Flavors

You can do hundreds of variations on any southwestern recipe. By adding avocados to the Bean Burrito Torte, you add another dimension. A spritz of fresh lime served on the side acts like a sparkler. A layer of cooked corn also adds a dimension. A sprinkling of fresh cilantro, or parsley also adds fiber and savor. Just keep building!

Quinoa Pilaf

This grain is cooked the same way rice is cooked.
Feel free to add other ingredients such as sun dried tomatoes
and shredded zucchini for more texture and flavor.

Serves 4
Serving Size 1 cup

Calories: 280.41
Protein: 6.43 grams
Carbohydrates: 32.85 grams
Fiber: 3.61 grams
Fat: 14.22 grams

1. Preheat oven to 350°F.

2. Melt butter in a saucepan and sauté the onion, carrots, and celery in it until tender.

3. Add quinoa and sauté for 3–5 minutes with the vegetables.

4. Pour mixture into a baking dish, add chicken broth, salt, pepper, and bay leaf and stir to incorporate.

5. Cover and bake for 45 minutes. Remove bay leaf before serving.

¼ cup unsalted butter
½ cup diced onion
¼ cup diced carrots
¼ cup diced celery
1 cup quinoa
1½ cups chicken broth
½ teaspoon salt
¼ teaspoon white pepper
1 bay leaf

Quinoa

South American natives cultivated quinoa and had rituals to thank their creator for the miraculously sustaining food. This led the Spanish to prohibit the people from growing it in the seventeenth and eighteenth centuries. Terraced mountain slopes covered with cultivated quinoa were burned, and people starved. Enough seeds were secretly stored that quinoa, prized for its ability to grow on the chilly slopes of the Andes, is back.

Hoppin' John

This dish, a type of pilaf, consists of black-eyed peas and long-grain rice and is traditionally served on New Year's Eve in the southern United States. The peas are considered a good luck charm.

Serves 8
Serving Size 1½ cups

Calories: 302.01
Protein: 11.26 grams
Carbohydrates: 45.94 grams
Fiber: 4.95 grams
Fat: 8.23 grams

1¼ cups dried black-eyed
    peas
3 cups water
1½ cups diced onion
½ cup diced ham
½ teaspoon dried thyme
¼ teaspoon cayenne pepper
1 bay leaf
salt and pepper to taste
1 tablespoon butter
3 tablespoons bacon fat
1½ cups long-grain rice
2¾ cups chicken broth
1 teaspoon salt
2 tablespoons chopped
    parsley

1. Put the black-eyed peas in a large pot and cover them with water so it goes an inch above the peas. Bring to a boil and boil for 1 minute. Remove from heat and let sit for 90 minutes.

2. Drain and rinse the peas and return them to the pot along with the water, onion, ham, thyme, cayenne pepper, and bay leaf. Simmer uncovered for 25 minutes. Drain the liquid from the pot and remove the bay leaf. Season pea mixture with salt and pepper and set aside.

3. Melt the butter and bacon fat in a large ovenproof pot and sauté the rice in it for 1 minute. Add the chicken broth and teaspoon of salt and bring to a simmer.

4. Meanwhile, preheat the oven to 325°F.

5. Stir the simmering rice once, cover, and bake for 25 minutes. Uncover and add the pea mixture and parsley. Cover and return to the oven for 5 minutes. Remove from oven, fluff with a fork, and lightly toss to mix the ingredients together. Cover and let sit for 10 minutes, then serve.

Parsnip Curry

Related to carrots, parsnips are even more fibrous and have a stronger flavor.
They are a winter vegetable that contains a huge amount of vitamin A.

Serves 4
Serving Size 2½ cups

Calories: 660.24
Protein: 10.71 grams
Carbohydrates: 130.04 grams
Fiber: 15.07 grams
Fat: 11.59 grams

1. Put the oil in a large pot and turn the heat to medium. Add the garlic, ginger, red chili pepper, lemongrass, and onion and sauté for 10 minutes.

2. Stir in the tomato paste well, then add the coconut milk, chicken broth, and parsnips. Bring to a boil, then reduce and simmer for about 15 minutes, until the parsnips are tender.

3. Add the soy sauce, lime zest, lime juice, and cilantro. Stir and remove from heat. Pour the curry into a soup tureen or large serving bowl.

4. Put the steamed jasmine rice on a serving platter and serve it with the curry.

3 tablespoons vegetable oil
2 minced cloves garlic
1 tablespoon grated ginger root
1 teaspoon minced fresh red chili pepper
6" lemongrass stalk, thinly sliced
1 cup diced onion
⅓ cup tomato paste
1½ cups coconut milk
½ cup chicken broth
2 pounds parsnips, peeled and cubed
3 tablespoons light soy sauce
1 teaspoon grated lime zest
3 tablespoons fresh lime juice
2 tablespoons chopped cilantro
4 cups steamed jasmine rice

Winter Vegetables

Winter vegetables got their name because they could keep in a root cellar or cold pantry over the winter. They include parsnips, carrots, cabbages, Brussels sprouts, and onions. Apples keep well in a cool place, and they were dried for use as long as 300 years ago. Apple and pear cider hardened, giving the colonists a buzz all winter long. Before pasteurization, milk was suspect and people tended to use it for cheese and butter, so the juice of winter fruit slaked early American thirsts.

Chicken Salad Bake

This is a nice dish to take to a picnic, church supper, or pot luck dinner.
To stretch the dish and add more flavor, add a cup of cooked chopped broccoli
or a package of frozen artichoke hearts, thawed and thinly sliced.

Serves 6
Serving Size 2 cups

Calories: 994.46
Protein: 48.83 grams
Carbohydrates: 30.53 grams
Fiber: 5.63 grams
Fat: 74.30 grams

½ tablespoon soft butter
1 can concentrated cream of
    chicken soup
1 cup mayonnaise
1 cup sour cream
1 teaspoon seasoned salt
2 tablespoons lemon juice
4 cups diced cooked chicken
¼ cup sliced green onions
2 cups cooked brown rice
2 cups diced celery
¼ cup chopped black olives
1½–2 cups sliced almonds
2 cups shredded cheddar
    cheese

1. Preheat oven to 350°F.

2. Butter a 9" × 13" × 2" baking pan.

3. Mix the soup, mayonnaise, sour cream, seasoned salt, and lemon juice together.

4. Add the chicken, green onions, brown rice, celery, black olives, and ½ cup almonds to the soup mixture. Stir to combine. Scrape the mixture into the prepared baking pan.

5. Sprinkle the cheese and the remaining almonds over the top and bake 35–40 minutes. Serve hot.

Another Casserole

The variations on this recipe are nearly infinite. Substitute cream of mushroom or cream of celery soup for the cream of chicken soup. Use leftover diced cooked turkey rather than chicken. Use dried currants instead of black olives and crumbled blue cheese for the cheddar. All of the blues, such as Gorgonzola, Roquefort, and Danish Blue, are much stronger than cheddar or Jack cheese, so use less of them.

Quick Skillet Chicken Casserole

Lemon juice is often used to enhance the flavor.
It's also a good way to boost your daily fiber intake.

1. Add the milk, mayonnaise, water, chicken base, potato granules, onion powder, garlic powder, celery flakes, pepper, egg, Worcestershire sauce, and lemon juice to a blender or the bowl of a food processor; pulse until well mixed.

2. Pour the mixture into large, deep nonstick sauté pan; bring to a boil. Reduce heat and simmer, stirring until the mixture begins to thicken.

3. Add the frozen vegetables, mushrooms, and chicken; stir to combine. Cover and simmer for 5 minutes or until the mushrooms are cooked. Serve over the rice.

Serves 4

Calories: 307.71
Protein: 23.13 grams
Carbohydrates: 35.72 grams
Fiber: 5.03 grams
Fat: 8.06 grams

½ cup skim milk
2 tablespoons mayonnaise
1 cup water
½ teaspoon low-sodium chicken base
¼ cup unseasoned, no-fat-added instant mashed potato flakes
½ teaspoon onion powder
¼ teaspoon garlic powder
¼ teaspoon dried celery flakes
⅛ teaspoon freshly ground black pepper
1 large egg, beaten
1 teaspoon Worcestershire sauce
1 tablespoon lemon juice
10-ounce package frozen vegetables, thawed
1 cup sliced button mushrooms
½ pound cooked chicken, chopped
1⅓ cups cooked brown long-grain rice

Chicken and Green Bean Stovetop Casserole

Serves 4

Calories: 305.29
Protein: 22.85 grams
Carbohydrates: 35.59 grams
Fiber: 5.56 grams
Fat: 8.31 grams

1 can condensed cream of
   chicken soup
¼ cup skim milk
2 teaspoons Worcestershire
   sauce
1 teaspoon mayonnaise
½ teaspoon onion powder
¼ teaspoon garlic powder
¼ teaspoon ground black
   pepper
4-ounce can sliced water
   chestnuts, drained
2½ cups frozen green beans,
   thawed
1 cup sliced mushrooms,
   steamed
½ pound cooked, chopped
   chicken
1⅓ cups cooked brown long-
   grain rice

*This is a dressed-up variation of a popular Thanksgiving favorite.
It's meant to have a hint of the flavor of a green bean casserole,
but it can stand on its own as a meal.*

1. Combine the soup, milk, Worcestershire, mayonnaise, onion powder, garlic powder, and pepper in a saucepan and bring to a boil.

2. Reduce heat and add the water chestnuts, green beans, mushrooms, and chicken.

3. Simmer until vegetables and chicken are heated through.

4. Serve over rice.

Veggie Filler

Steamed mushrooms are a high-fiber, low-calorie way to add flavor to a dish and stretch the meat. If you don't like mushrooms, you can substitute an equal amount of other steamed vegetables like red and green peppers.

Chapter 12
Delicious Desserts

Carrot Cake

This cake can be served plain, sprinkled with powdered sugar, or frosted with cream cheese frosting. Coconut, carrots, nuts, and pineapple add a great amount of flavor to the fiber lode in this cake. It's very moist and will keep for a week in the refrigerator without drying out.

Serves 12
Serving Size 1 square

Calories: 466.40
Protein: 5.14 grams
Carbohydrates: 50.88 grams
Fiber: 2.05 grams
Fat: 28.65 grams

2 cups all-purpose flour
2 teaspoons baking powder
2 teaspoons baking soda
1 teaspoon salt
1¾ cups sugar
1¼ cups vegetable oil
4 eggs
3 cups shredded carrots
½ cup chopped walnuts
2 tablespoons shredded coconut
¾ cup crushed pineapple

1. Preheat oven to 300°F. Grease and flour a 9" × 13" × 2" rectangular pan. Set aside.

2. Combine the flour, baking powder, baking soda, and salt in a bowl and set aside.

3. Combine the sugar and oil in a mixing bowl. Add the eggs one at a time, beating after each addition. Add the flour mixture and mix well. Add the carrots, walnuts, coconut, and pineapple and mix well.

4. Scrape the batter into the prepared pan and bake for 45 minutes or until a toothpick inserted in the middle comes out clean.

5. Let cool to room temperature before cutting and serving.

Cream Cheese Frosting

To make frosting for the carrot cake, cream ½ cup softened cream cheese, ¼ cup softened butter, and 1 teaspoon vanilla using an electric mixer on low. Slowly add 1½ cups powdered sugar. When frosting is fluffy, spread on the cake. Garnish with orange or lemon zest for added tang.

Pineapple Upside-Down Cupcakes

Instead of a muffin tin, these cupcakes can be made in half-cup ramekins, custard cups, or ovenproof coffee cups. The fruit adds fiber and makes these very delicious.

1. Preheat oven to 350°F. Prepare the cups or tins with nonstick spray.

2. Melt unsalted butter and brown sugar in a saucepan over low heat until the mixture starts to foam and the sugar starts to caramelize. Remove from heat and pour into the muffin tin, dividing evenly among 10 cups.

3. Divide the pineapple and cherries among the muffin tin cups on top of the caramelized sugar mixture and set aside. Whip the egg whites to stiff peaks and set aside.

4. Cream the salted butter with the sugar with an electric mixer until fluffy. Beat in the egg yolks and vanilla. In a separate bowl combine the flour and baking powder. Add it to the butter-egg mixture in two parts, alternating with the milk. Fold the whipped egg whites into the cake batter and pour the batter over the fruit in the muffin tin.

5. Bake for 25 minutes. Remove the cupcakes from the oven, then invert the tin onto a cookie sheet with sides. Leave the muffin tin on top for 5 minutes, then remove it and let the cupcakes cool.

Serves 10
Serving Size 1 cupcake

Calories: 353.07
Protein: 4 grams
Carbohydrates: 50.65 grams
Fiber: 0.99 grams
Fat: 15.48 grams

¼ cup unsalted butter
¾ cup brown sugar
1 cup diced pineapple
¼ cup dried cherries
2 egg whites, room
    temperature
½ cup salted butter
1 cup sugar
2 egg yolks
1 teaspoon vanilla
1½ cups flour
2 teaspoons baking powder
½ cup milk

Blueberry Clafouti

Clafouti is a French custard pudding dessert that is traditionally made with unpitted cherries, but this recipe substitutes blueberries to make it easier to eat without worrying about the pits. Pears, peaches, apples, and prunes make a nice clafouti too.

Serves 6
Serving Size 1 slice

Calories: 253.15
Protein: 6.43 grams
Carbohydrates: 40.34 grams
Fiber: 2.98 grams
Fat: 7.52 grams

½ tablespoon soft butter
3 eggs
¼ cup cream
1 cup whole milk
¼ cup sugar
pinch of salt
1 tablespoon vanilla
⅔ cup flour
4 cups blueberries
¼ cup powdered sugar

1. Preheat oven to 350°F. Butter a 10" round baking dish.

2. Mix the eggs, cream, milk, sugar, salt, vanilla, and flour with an electric mixer on medium speed for about 5 minutes until frothy.

3. Pour ¼ of the batter into the prepared baking dish and bake for 5 minutes. Remove from the oven.

4. Sprinkle the blueberries evenly over the baked batter in the dish and then pour the rest of the batter over them.

5. Bake 35 minutes longer. Remove from the oven and let cool. Sprinkle powdered sugar over it and serve at room temperature.

French Country Desserts
French rustic tarts are a marvel of simplicity and ingenuity. A simple batter is transformed into a fruity delight. Fresh fruits straight from the orchard or garden are put to good use. Add nuts for extra fiber and spices to spike the flavors.

Fruitcake Bread Pudding

This fruitcake bread pudding can be served with warm caramel sauce, hard sauce, crème anglaise, or whipped cream. To cut the richness, you can add 2 cups of peeled and diced tart apple.

Serves 12

Calories: 516.86
Protein: 10.15 grams
Carbohydrates: 44.04 grams
Fiber: 1.45 grams
Fat: 34.12 grams

6 cups stale bread cubes
6 cups cubed fruitcake
5 egg yolks
7 eggs
2½ cups milk
3½ cups cream
1 cup sugar
1 teaspoon grated orange
   zest
1 teaspoon vanilla
½ cup melted butter

1. Preheat oven to 350°F. Generously butter a 9" × 13" baking dish.

2. Mix the bread cubes with the fruitcake and place them in the buttered dish. Set aside.

3. Mix the egg yolks, eggs, milk, cream, sugar, orange zest and vanilla together. Pour evenly over the fruitcake and bread cubes. Press down the bread cubes to submerge them in the custard and soak it up.

4. Drizzle the melted butter over the top.

5. Bake for 60 minutes until the custard is set. Serve warm.

Custard Sauce

These creamy sauces are very popular in Europe and in upscale American restaurants. They add no fiber, just a great, rich flavor. For a quick Crème Anglaise vanilla custard sauce, try this! Just let a good quality vanilla ice cream melt to pouring consistency and serve with bread pudding, chocolate cake, or fresh peach slices.

Fresh Fig and Raspberry Compote

Serve this fresh fruit compote chilled with a Hazelnut Stick (page 206) and a spoonful of vanilla yogurt for an elegant dessert. Figs are high in fiber and delicious, and raspberries are also an excellent source of fiber.

Serves 4
Serving Size 1 cup

Calories: 232.97
Protein: 1.32 grams
Carbohydrates: 61.55 grams
Fiber: 6.16 grams
Fat: 0.53 grams

½ cup honey
¼ cup water
12 ripe mission figs
1 cup ripe red raspberries
*1 tablespoon chopped fresh
    mint leaves*

1. Mix honey and water together in a glass bowl and microwave on high for 20 seconds. Remove, stir, and let chill in the refrigerator.

2. Cut the figs into quarters and add them to the chilled honey syrup.

3. Add the raspberries and mint to the chilled syrup and let sit for 15 minutes in the refrigerator.

4. To serve, scoop the figs and raspberries onto four dessert plates.

Fig Trouble

The Greek word for fig is syke, *and the word* sycophant *literally means "fig-eater." Ancient Athenians reputedly loved their figs and were proud to be called sycophants. The region of Attica (where Athens is located), famous for its cultivation of figs in the seventh century B.C., was forbidden by law to export its prized figs outside Greece. However, the Persian king, Xerxes, had a supply of them. The Athenian informants who alerted authorities to the illegal export of figs from Attica were derogatorily called sycophants, and that's where the modern definition of the term comes from.*

Blackberry Cobbler

This recipe can also be made from raspberries, blueberries, cherries, or a combination, which is sometimes called jumbleberry. The berry juice soaks into the biscuits, giving them enormous flavor. The whole wheat in the biscuits adds protein and fiber. The blackberries are also very fibrous.

1. Preheat oven to 350°F.

2. Prepare biscuit dough recipe, cut biscuit circles out, and set them aside.

3. Toss the blackberries, flour, and sugar together, then put the mixture into a 9" × 11" inch baking dish.

4. Bake the blackberries for 25 minutes, remove from oven, and place the unbaked biscuits on top of the hot berries.

5. Brush the biscuit tops with cream and return the cobbler to the oven to bake for another 25 minutes. Serve warm.

Serves 8
Serving Size 1½ cups

Calories: 441.3
Protein: 8.62 grams
Carbohydrates: 78.88 grams
Fiber: 11.09 grams
Fat: 12.13 grams

1 recipe Whole-Wheat Biscuits (page 273), unbaked
8 cups blackberries
¼ cup flour
¾ cup sugar
¼ cup cream

Raspberry-Rhubarb Crisp

This crisp can be baked ahead of time and reheated later or even served cold with cream poured over it. The berries and almonds will give you fiber. It's best to reheat the dessert so the crispy topping will be crisp!

Serves 8
Serving Size 1½ cups

Calories: 537.65
Protein: 7.68grams
Carbohydrates: 73.45 grams
Fiber: 6.63 grams
Fat: 25.54 grams

Crisp

6 cups chopped rhubarb
    stalks, red part only
¼ cup flour
1 cup sugar
2 cups raspberries

Topping

1 cup ground almonds
¼ cup rolled oats
1½ cups flour
½ cup brown sugar
¼ cup sugar
1 teaspoon cinnamon
½ teaspoon salt
¾ cup unsalted butter, cut in
    chunks

1. Preheat oven to 350°F.

2. Toss the rhubarb with ¼ cup flour and 1 cup sugar. Add the raspberries, toss gently, and then put the mixture into a 9" × 11" inch baking dish. Set aside.

3. In a bowl combine the almonds, oats, 1½ cups flour, brown sugar, sugar, cinnamon, and salt. Add the butter chunks and mix to a sandy consistency with an electric mixer. You can tell if the topping is ready if it clumps together when you squeeze it in the palm of your hand.

4. Cover the raspberry-rhubarb mixture evenly with the topping and bake for 60 minutes or until the juices start to bubble up and thicken.

5. Remove the crisp from the oven and cut around the sides to loosen. Cut into squares and serve warm with ice cream.

Poached Pears

These pears are used in the recipe for Pear Sorbet (page 173).
Pears are a wonderful late-summer and fall fruit. They are available for most
of the winter since they keep well under refrigeration. If the skin is left on,
they have loads of fiber and taste terrific.

Serves 4
Serving Size 2 pear halves

Calories: 197.30
Protein: 0.70 grams
Carbohydrates: 50.96 grams
Fiber: 4.17 grams
Fat: 0.67 grams

2 tablespoons lemon juice
4 ripe pears, peeled, halved,
    and cored
½ cup sugar
2 cups water
1 strip lemon peel
1 vanilla bean, split
    lengthwise

1. Rub the lemon juice on the pears.

2. In a saucepan, combine the sugar and water and heat over low to dissolve the sugar. Add the lemon peel and vanilla bean and simmer for 5 minutes.

3. Add the pear halves to the simmering liquid and place a piece of parchment paper over the surface of the liquid. Poke a few slits in the paper to let steam escape.

4. Simmer the pears until tender for 20–25 minutes. Poke them with a paring knife to test for tenderness.

5. Remove from heat and let pears cool in poaching liquid. Refrigerate in liquid until ready to serve.

Poached Fruit

Fruit can be poached in juice, wine, or water. The wonderful thing about poaching fruit is that it will keep for days if you refrigerate it; it'll keep for weeks if you freeze it. For fruits that tend to discolor—think apples and pears—use a bit of lemon juice in the poaching liquid to acidulate it and prevent browning.

Poached Quince

Quinces are too bitter to eat raw, but when they're cooked they attain a delightful flavor. They combine well with other fruit.

Serves 4
Serving Size ¾ cup

Calories: 125.58
Protein: 0.24 grams
Carbohydrates: 32.91 grams
Fiber: 1.06 grams
Fat: 0.05 grams

2 tablespoons lemon juice
2 quinces, peeled, cored, and sliced
½ cup sugar
2 cups water
1 strip lemon peel
1 vanilla bean, split lengthwise

1. Rub the lemon juice on the quinces.

2. In a saucepan, combine the sugar and water and heat over low to dissolve the sugar. Add the lemon peel and vanilla bean and simmer for 5 minutes.

3. Add the quince slices to the simmering liquid and place a piece of parchment paper over the surface of the liquid. Poke a few slits in the paper to let steam escape.

4. Simmer the quinces until tender, 20–25 minutes. Poke them with a paring knife to test for tenderness.

5. Remove from heat and let quinces cool in poaching liquid. Refrigerate in liquid until ready to serve.

The Allure of the Quince

Quinces were known by the ancient Greeks as "love apples." They grow on beautiful flowering trees, and the fruit looks a bit gnarled. They make excellent jams and jellies because they have a great deal of pectin, the stiffening agent in jams and jellies. Their distinctive flavor is very good in combination with other fruits in compotes.

Tea-Poached Prunes

*Save the leftover poaching liquid, reduce it until very thick,
and pour it over chocolate ice cream.*

1. In a saucepan, combine the sugar and water and heat over low to dissolve the sugar. Add the tea bags and simmer for 5 minutes.

2. Add the prunes to the simmering liquid and place a piece of parchment paper over the surface of the liquid. Poke a few slits in the paper to let steam escape.

3. Simmer the prunes for 15 minutes.

4. Remove from heat and let prunes cool in poaching liquid. Refrigerate in liquid until ready to serve.

Poached Quince, Pear, and Prune Compote

Poached fruits go well together. To get the fiber and flavor of three different fruits, make poached pears, poached quinces, and tea-poached prunes and arrange them on a serving platter. Drizzle a little poaching liquid over them and serve with biscotti. Add strawberries, raspberries, or blueberries to the poached fruits for even more excitement.

Serves 4
Serving Size ¾ cup

Calories: 289.81
Protein: 2.13 grams
Carbohydrates: 76.35 grams
Fiber: 6.29 grams
Fat: 0.51 grams

½ cup sugar
2 cups water
3 black currant tea bags
3 cups pitted prunes

Baked Apples

Serves 4
Serving Size 1 cup

Calories: 346.11
Protein: 1.49 grams
Carbohydrates: 50.90 grams
Fiber: 5.85 grams
Fat: 17.52 grams

4 apples, cored
⅓ cup brown sugar
¼ cup chopped pecans
1 teaspoon grated lemon zest
1 teaspoon ground cinnamon
¼ cup golden raisins
¼ cup butter, melted
⅔ cup apple juice

Baked apples make a wonderful breakfast or brunch treat. You can use almost any kind of apple for baking, but the tart Granny Smith is excellent for this recipe. These apples are good solo or accompanied with vanilla ice cream.

1. Preheat oven to 350°F.

2. Place the apples close together in a baking dish.

3. In a bowl, combine the brown sugar, pecans, lemon zest, cinnamon, and golden raisins. Sprinkle this mixture into the holes in the apples where the cores used to be. Drizzle the melted butter over the filling.

4. Pour juice into the baking dish around the bottom of the apples. Cover with foil and bake the apples for 30 minutes.

5. Uncover and baste the apples with the liquid at the bottom of the dish and return them to the oven for 10 minutes. Remove baked apples from the oven and serve warm with the basting liquid drizzled over them.

Cooked Fruit

Most fruit can be grilled, roasted, poached, and/or baked. Cooking fruit makes them more digestible for children and people with digestive or swallowing difficulties. Cooked fruits also make elegant desserts in the form of compotes, fruit parfaits, and pies. Ice cream, whipped cream, and custard sauces are excellent with cooked fruit. A spoonful of mascarpone cheese spooned over hot fruit is also delightful.

Oven-Roasted Pears

These pears are delicious served simply with a drizzle of crème fraîche and Walnut Biscotti (page 202), or with blue cheese and walnuts. The fiber in the pear will offset the sweetness of the wine with usable fiber.

1. Preheat oven to 450°F.

2. Place pears upright in a baking dish and pour the Marsala wine over them. Bake the pears for 20 minutes. Add water or more Marsala if the dish starts to get dry.

3. Baste the pears with the liquid in the dish and bake 20 minutes more.

4. Baste the pears again and bake longer until a knife inserted in a pear goes in easily.

5. Remove the pears from the oven and baste them several times as they cool. Serve at room temperature with a knife and fork.

Serves 4
Serving Size 1 pear

Calories: 217.41
Protein: 0.72 grams
Carbohydrates: 31.45 grams
Fiber: 3.34 grams
Fat: 0.56 grams

4 ripe Bosc pears
1½ cups Marsala wine

Stuffed Apricots

These warm apricots are good served with vanilla ice cream
or crème anglaise. You can boost the amount of fiber in this dessert
by adding toasted walnuts or pistachios as a garnish. Fresh blueberries are
also a pretty and fiber-rich counterpoint.

Serves 4
Serving Size 2 halves

Calories: 255.24
Protein: 3.28 grams
Carbohydrates: 24.42 grams
Fiber: 1.67 grams
Fat: 14.83 grams

4 ripe apricots
⅓ cup sugar
¼ cup soft butter
1 egg white
¼ cup ground almonds
⅛ cup bread crumbs
½ cup white wine

1. Preheat oven to 350°F. Butter a baking dish large enough to fit 8 apricot halves snugly in one layer.

2. Cut the apricots in half and remove the stones. Place apricot halves cut-side up in the prepared baking dish. Set aside.

3. In a bowl, cream the sugar and butter together until fluffy. Beat in the egg white, then stir in the almonds and bread crumbs.

4. Place a scoop of the almond filling on top of each apricot. Pour the white wine around the apricots on the bottom of the baking dish.

5. Bake apricots uncovered for 45 minutes, basting with the liquid at the bottom of the pan.

Rum-Raisin Rice Pudding

*This brown-rice pudding can be served warm with vanilla ice cream
or chilled with a bit of whipped cream. The brown rice is a fine source of fiber
and the raisins add to it as well. Don't worry about the alcohol in the rum;
it evaporates, leaving only flavor.*

1. Preheat the oven to 325°F.

2. Combine the raisins and rum and set aside.

3. Mix the milk and brown rice in a saucepan and bring to a boil, stirring occasionally. Cover, reduce heat to low, and simmer for 15 minutes. Remove from heat.

4. Stir in the raisins, rum, sugar, vanilla, orange zest, banana, and cream. Spoon the rice pudding into a baking dish, cover with foil, and place it in a larger roasting pan. Pour hot water around the sides of the pudding dish into the roasting pan to make a water bath and bake for 30 minutes. Take off the foil and bake another 15 minutes.

5. Remove from the oven and serve warm or let cool, cover, and chill in the refrigerator.

Fruit Puddings

Puddings come with many bases, including bread, tapioca, rice, and cornstarch. Most puddings include milk, cream, and lots of sugar. However, when you have too much coming from your orchard, garden, or bushes, you can use a lot more as it will cook down. Also, many puddings are extremely delicious and healthy, such as rice and tapioca.

Serves 6
Serving Size 1 cup

Calories: 390.73
Protein: 7.51 grams
Carbohydrates: 58.48 grams
Fiber: 2.39 grams
Fat: 10.36 grams

½ cup raisins
½ cup dark rum
3 cups milk
1 cup uncooked brown
　　basmati rice
½ cup sugar
1 teaspoon vanilla
1 tablespoon grated orange
　　zest
1 mashed banana
½ cup cream

Hasty Pudding

Serves 8
Serving Size 1½ cups

Calories: 680.77
Protein: 8.68 grams
Carbohydrates: 83.99 grams
Fiber: 4.03 grams
Fat: 36.05 grams

5 cups milk
½ cup cornmeal
1 teaspoon vanilla
½ cup molasses
1 teaspoon salt
1 cup sugar
1 cup unsalted butter, cubed
1 teaspoon ground dry ginger
1 teaspoon cinnamon
1 cup dried cherries
1 cup fresh corn kernels
1 cup raisins
1 cup cream

*Hasty pudding is a colonial American porridge that is made "hastily"
in contrast to the time-intensive, elaborate steamed puddings from England.
It also has loads of fiber and vitamins from the corn and dried fruit.*

1. Preheat oven to 350°F. Butter a 9" × 9" baking pan and set aside.

2. Scald 1 cup of milk in a saucepan, add cornmeal, and stir over medium heat until it thickens. Remove from heat.

3. Add all the remaining ingredients except the cream and 1 cup milk, to the cooked cornmeal. Stir to combine and pour the mixture into the prepared baking pan.

4. Pour the cream and 1 cup of milk over the top of the mixture to prevent a skin from forming during baking.

5. Bake uncovered for 30 minutes. Stir the cream and milk on top into the pudding and bake for 30 minutes more.

The Native American Influence

Native Americans introduced colonial settlers to corn, squash, beans, and peppers. Hasty pudding was a common dish when time and ingredients were scarce. Fortunately, all the ingredients can be found in modern supermarkets, and you won't have to do without the sweetness of cinnamon as you might have had to three centuries ago.

Cantaloupe Sorbet

This is delicious served with a glass of port. You can add crème fraîche or berries to this to enhance the color and flavor. Berries will give you extra fiber.

1. Combine sugar and water in a saucepan and heat just until sugar dissolves. Remove from heat and chill.

2. Combine chilled sugar syrup, cantaloupe purée, and lemon juice.

3. Freeze in an ice-cream freezer according to manufacturer's instructions. If you don't have one, you can freeze the mixture in a 9" × 13" pan until frozen. Break it into chunks, process in a food processor, and return to the freezer in the pan. Repeat the processing after the mixture has frozen again to make a smooth, scoopable sorbet.

Serves 12
Serving Size ½ cup

Calories: 51.58
Protein: 0.47 grams
Carbohydrates: 13.08 grams
Fiber: 0.43 grams
Fat: 0.14 grams

½ cup sugar
¼ cup water
3 cups cantaloupe purée
¼ cup lemon juice

Strawberry Sorbet

Try this with a slice of chocolate cake or add it to a glass of lemonade.

1. Combine sugar and water in a saucepan and heat just until sugar dissolves. Remove from heat and chill.

2. Combine chilled sugar syrup, strawberry purée, and lemon juice.

3. Freeze in an ice-cream freezer according to manufacturer's instructions.

Serves 12
Serving Size ½ cup

Calories: 50.92
Protein: 0.37 grams
Carbohydrates: 12.84 grams
Fiber: 1.35 grams
Fat: 0.21 grams

½ cup sugar
¼ cup water
3 cups strawberry purée
¼ cup lemon juice

Sorbet or Sherbet?

Sherbet (not sherbert, as it's often mispronounced) includes milk. It's like a watery ice cream. Sorbets, Italian ices, and granites are all related, giving you a great fruity chill-down on a hot day or after an evening meal. If they are puréed, they will have less fiber, but you can always serve them with berries, cut-up peaches, or whatever is in season.

Mango Sorbet

*This tastes like fresh mangoes with a velvet texture.
You can substitute lime juice for lemon for a different sparkle.
Mangoes are high in fiber and vitamin A. Throw a few blueberries
on top of each dish of sorbet for great color and added fiber.*

1. Combine sugar and water in a saucepan and heat just until sugar dissolves. Remove from heat and chill.

2. Combine chilled sugar syrup, mango purée, and lemon juice.

3. Freeze in an ice-cream freezer according to manufacturer's instructions.

Serves 12
Serving Size ½ cup

Calories: 60.33
Protein: 0.23 grams
Carbohydrates: 15.78 grams
Fiber: 0.76 gram
Fat: 0.11 grams

½ cup sugar
¼ cup water
3 cups mango purée
¼ cup lemon juice

Blueberry Sorbet

*This intensely flavored sorbet is really good served with a scoop
of vanilla ice cream. You can also scoop it into the center of a
small cantaloupe or drizzle it over a slice of honeydew.*

1. Combine sugar and water in a saucepan and heat just until sugar dissolves. Remove from heat and chill.

2. Combine chilled sugar syrup, blueberry purée, and lemon juice.

3. Freeze in an ice-cream freezer according to manufacturer's instructions.

Serves 12
Serving Size ½ cup

Calories: 53.82
Protein: 0.26 grams
Carbohydrates: 13.89 grams
Fiber: 1 gram
Fat: 0.14 grams

½ cup sugar
¼ cup water
3 cups blueberry purée
¼ cup lemon juice

Pear Sorbet

This is a great way to save leftover Poached Pears (page 163).

Serves 12
Serving Size ½ cup

Calories: 64.52
Protein: 0.23 grams
Carbohydrates: 16.79 grams
Fiber: 1.01 grams
Fat: 0.04 grams

½ cup sugar
¼ cup water
3 cups poached pear purée
¼ cup lemon juice

1. Combine sugar and water in a saucepan and heat just until sugar dissolves. Remove from heat and chill.

2. Combine chilled sugar syrup, pear purée, and lemon juice.

3. Freeze in an ice-cream freezer according to manufacturer's instructions.

Sorbet Ice Cubes

Before putting the purée in the ice-cream maker, spoon them into an ice-cube tray and freeze solid. You can add them to iced tea, lemonade, or fruit punch for a delicious extra flavor. Plus you will get vitamins, antioxidants, and fiber from the puréed fruit. At the very least, squeeze some fresh lemon into your ice-cube trays to give your water some flavor.

Hawaiian-Style Snow Cones

Serves 4
Serving Size 1 cone

Calories: 259.58
Protein: 3.24 grams
Carbohydrates: 48.05 grams
Fiber: 1.09 grams
Fat: 7.31 grams

4 tablespoons red bean paste
4 small scoops vanilla ice
  cream
4 cups shaved ice
½ cup flavored syrup for snow
  cones

The red bean paste in this recipe is the same as in the Red Bean Ice-Cream Shake (page 236). The red bean paste is the only fiber in this treat. If you sprinkle some chopped macadamia nuts on top as a garnish, you will stay with the Hawaiian theme but add protein and more fiber.

1. Place a tablespoon of sweet red bean paste in the bottom of four insulated paper cones or cups.

2. Top the sweet red bean paste with a scoop of vanilla ice cream in each cone or cup.

3. Put a cup of shaved ice on top of the vanilla ice cream in each cone or cup.

4. Drizzle 2 tablespoons of flavored syrup over each shaved ice mound. Serve immediately.

Flavored Syrup Recipe

To make your own flavored syrup for snow cones, follow this simple recipe. Bring 2 cups of sugar and 1¼ cups water to a boil in a saucepan; then remove from heat. Stir in one small packet of any flavor unsweetened drink mix, such as Kool-Aid, cover, and chill in the refrigerator. Pour into a plastic squeeze bottle for serving. You can also mix multiple flavors. Try combining mango and raspberry or lemon and lime.

Chapter 13
Popular Pies

Blueberry Pie

The addition of dried blueberries to fresh blueberries makes this pie even richer in fiber and flavor. If you can't find dried blueberries, use cut-up dried apples for the same high-fiber results.

1. Preheat oven to 350°F. Line pie pan with one circle of pie dough.

2. Mix blueberries with dried blueberries, sugar, lemon juice, lemon zest, and cornstarch and put them in the pie shell. Dot blueberries with butter pieces.

3. Cover the blueberries with the other pie-dough circle, crimp the edges to seal, and cut slits in the top. Sprinkle with sugar and bake for 50 minutes. Cool before slicing.

Serves 6
Serving Size 1 slice

Calories: 633.49
Protein: 4.12 grams
Carbohydrates: 104.88 grams
Fiber: 6.63 grams
Fat: 22.98 grams

2 rolled-out circles of Whole-Wheat Pie Dough (page 282)
4 cups blueberries
½ cup dried blueberries
1 cup sugar
¼ cup lemon juice
1 tablespoon grated lemon zest
4 tablespoons cornstarch
1 ounce butter, cut in pieces

Blackberry Pie

Canned berries are much too mushy to make a good pie, so be sure to make this when fresh blackberries are in season and reasonably priced. The seeds in the berries provide excellent fiber.

1. Preheat oven to 350°F. Line pie pan with one circle of pie dough.

2. Mix blackberries with sugar, orange juice, orange zest, and cornstarch and put them in the pie shell. Dot blackberries with butter pieces.

3. Cover the blackberries with the other pie-dough circle, crimp the edges to seal, and cut slits in the top. Sprinkle with sugar and bake for 50 minutes. Cool before slicing.

Serves 6
Serving Size 1 slice

Calories: 569.41
Protein: 3.61 grams
Carbohydrates: 88.58 grams
Fiber: 8.46 grams
Fat: 22.98 grams

2 rolled-out circles of Whole-Wheat Pie Dough (page 282)
5 cups blackberries
1 cup sugar
1 tablespoon orange juice
2 teaspoons grated orange zest
4 tablespoons cornstarch
2 tablespoons butter, cut in pieces

Strawberry Pie

Strawberries get even sweeter when cooked, but they lose none of their fiber. The aroma of a strawberry pie baking in the oven will have your kids eagerly anticipating something that's really healthful for dessert.

1. Preheat oven to 350°F. Line pie pan with one circle of pie dough.

2. Mix strawberries with sugar and cornstarch and put them in the pie shell. Dot strawberries with butter pieces.

3. Cover the strawberries with the other pie-dough circle, crimp the edges to seal, and cut slits in the top. Sprinkle with sugar and bake for 50 minutes. Cool before slicing.

Pies Around the World

The French make tarts and tortes, and the Germans fill strudel with fruit and bake them. Mexicans fry fruit-filled empanadas. Other versions are cobblers, deep-dish pies, crisps, and fruit-filled pastries, such as the Danish. You can spice up your pies with lemon and orange zest, cinnamon, or nutmeg. Always use whole-wheat pie crust dough.

Serves 6
Serving Size 1 slice

Calories: 543.10
Protein: 3.54 grams
Carbohydrates: 82.17 grams
Fiber: 5.11 grams
Fat: 22.99 grams

2 rolled-out circles of Whole-Wheat Pie Dough (page 282)
5 cups quartered strawberries
1 cup sugar
4 tablespoons cornstarch
1 ounce butter, cut in pieces

Rhubarb Pie

Serves 6
Serving Size 1 slice

Calories: 560.28
Protein: 4.12 grams
Carbohydrates: 85.20 grams
Fiber: 4.51 grams
Fat: 22.66 grams

2 rolled-out circles of Whole-
    Wheat Pie Dough (page
    282)
4 cups chopped rhubarb
½ cup dried sour cherries
1 cup sugar
¼ cup cornstarch
1 ounce butter, cut in pieces

The addition of dried cherries to rhubarb makes this pie even richer in fiber and flavor. The dried cherries have a special, natural sweetness of their own, which is a nice counterpoint to the naturally tart rhubarb.

1. Preheat oven to 350°F. Line pie pan with one circle of pie dough.

2. Mix rhubarb with dried cherries, sugar, and cornstarch and put the mixture in the pie shell. Dot the fruit with butter pieces.

3. Cover the filling with the other pie-dough circle, crimp the edges to seal, and cut slits in the top. Sprinkle with sugar and bake for 50 minutes. Cool before slicing.

Mixed Fruit Pies

Strawberry and rhubarb are a fabulous, classic combination. You can vary the berries, adding some blueberries to a strawberry or blackberry pie. You can add peaches to a raspberry pie, producing the classic combination called melba. Adding a cup of blueberries to a blackberry pie will thin out the seeds a bit. Experiment with fruits in season and enjoy your fiber!

Raspberry Pie

Tart and sweet, the seeds in raspberries add a lot of fiber to this pie, and the whole-grain pie dough adds vitamin B and fiber as well. The lemon juice and zest give it real sparkle.

1. Preheat oven to 350°F. Line pie pan with one circle of pie dough.

2. Mix raspberries with sugar, lemon juice, lemon zest, and cornstarch and put them in the pie shell. Dot raspberries with butter pieces.

3. Cover the raspberries with the other pie-dough circle, crimp the edges to seal, and cut slits in the top. Sprinkle with sugar and bake for 50 minutes. Cool before slicing.

Serves 6
Serving Size 1 slice

Calories: 556.43
Protein: 3.71 grams
Carbohydrates: 85.73 grams
Fiber: 9.14 grams
Fat: 23.07 grams

2 rolled-out circles of Whole-Wheat Pie Dough (page 282)
5 cups raspberries
1 cup sugar
¼ cup lemon juice
1 tablespoon grated lemon zest
4 tablespoons cornstarch
1 ounce butter, cut in pieces

Huckleberry Pie

It may be hard to find huckleberries, but if you can get them, make this pie. The best way to get huckleberries is to make friends with a grower or go to green markets. Huckleberries are loaded with fiber and vitamins.

1. Preheat oven to 350°F. Line pie pan with one circle of pie dough.

2. Mix huckleberries with sugar, lemon juice, and cornstarch and put them in the pie shell. Dot huckleberries with butter pieces.

3. Cover the huckleberries with the other pie-dough circle, crimp the edges to seal, and cut slits in the top. Sprinkle with sugar and bake for 50 minutes.

4. Cool before slicing to prevent running.

Serves 6
Serving Size 1 slice

Calories: 573.41
Protein: 3.57 grams
Carbohydrates: 90.79 grams
Fiber: 5.35 grams
Fat: 22.96 grams

2 rolled-out circles of Whole-Wheat Pie Dough (page 282)
5 cups huckleberries
1 cup sugar
¼ cup lemon juice
4 tablespoons cornstarch
1 ounce butter, cut in pieces

Cherry Pie

The addition of dried cherries to fresh cherries makes this pie even richer in fiber and flavor. When cherries are in season, buy yourself a cherry pitter and mix the varieties of cherries in your pie—Queen Anne, sour red, and black Bing—for excitement.

Serves 6
Serving Size 1 slice

Calories: 557.53
Protein: 4.42 grams
Carbohydrates: 84.55 grams
Fiber: 4.69 grams
Fat: 22.81 grams

2 rolled-out circles of Whole-Wheat Pie Dough (page 282)
4 cups pitted cherries
½ cup dried cherries
¾ cup sugar
3 tablespoons cornstarch
1 ounce butter, cut in pieces

1. Preheat oven to 350°F. Line pie pan with one circle of pie dough.

2. Mix cherries with dried cherries, sugar, and cornstarch and put them in the pie shell. Dot cherries with butter pieces.

3. Cover the cherries with the other pie-dough circle, crimp the edges to seal, and cut slits in the top. Sprinkle with sugar and bake for 50 minutes. Cool before slicing.

Freeze Your Pies!

When berries and fruits are in season, make a lot of pies but do not bake them. Wrap them well in cling wrap and freeze them. You'll have pies even when your favorite fruits are not in season. Just remove them from the freezer and bake them whenever you're ready.

Apple Pie

Apple butter adds an extra dimension to this homey pie.
Garnish your apple pie with cheddar cheese, and throw some toasted
walnut pieces in with the apples for extra fiber.

1. Preheat oven to 350°F.

2. Line pie pan with one of the pie-dough circles. Cut slits in the other pie-dough circle and set aside.

3. Mix apples in a bowl with cornstarch, sugar, and spice.

4. Pile the apples into the dough-lined pie pan, then dot them with the apple butter. Cover apples with the pie-dough circle with slits to form the top crust. Crimp edges together to seal the crust.

5. Brush the crust with water and sprinkle with sugar. Bake for 60 minutes.

Apple Pie Spice

To make your own apple pie spice, simply mix 2 teaspoons ground cinnamon, ½ teaspoon ground allspice, and ½ teaspoon nutmeg. Store the spice mixture in an airtight jar. It's best to grind your own spices fresh. Many stores now sell fresh spices in bulk. You can vary the spicing with ground ginger and cloves for a different flavor.

Serves 6
Serving Size 1 slice

Calories: 489.33
Protein: 2.91 grams
Carbohydrates: 77.78 grams
Fiber: 4.53 grams
Fat: 18.96 grams

2 rolled-out circles of Whole-Wheat Pie Dough (page 282)
5 cups peeled, sliced apples
4 tablespoons cornstarch
½ cup sugar
1 tablespoon apple pie spice
4 tablespoons apple butter
2 tablespoons sugar, for sprinkling on top crust

Pecan Pie

Buttery, nutty, and fibrous, this luscious pie is a delicious treat for any occasion.

Serves 6
Serving Size 1 slice

Calories: 821.38
Protein: 8.09 grams
Carbohydrates: 92.20 grams
Fiber: 4.96 grams
Fat: 50 grams

2 cups pecans
1 prebaked Whole-Wheat Pie Dough crust (page 282)
½ cup brown sugar
½ cup sugar
1 cup corn syrup
6 tablespoons melted brown butter
3 eggs
1 teaspoon vanilla
½ teaspoon salt

1. Preheat oven to 350°F.

2. Spread out nuts evenly in the pie crust.

3. Whisk together sugars, corn syrup, brown butter, eggs, vanilla, and salt to make filling.

4. Pour filling in crust over the pecans.

5. Bake for 50 minutes, let cool before cutting.

Beurre Noisette

To make brown butter, which is called beurre noisette *in French cuisine, melt unsalted butter and let the solids turn a nutty brown, like hazelnuts. Be careful not to let it burn though! Add a small piece of vanilla bean for added flavor. This lends itself to many desserts and can also be used to flavor vegetables, such as squash, pumpkins, and green string beans.*

Squash Pumpkin Pie

The combination of kabocha squash and butternut is a real favorite. However, you can also substitute cooked buttercup squash, turban squash, or acorn squash for lots of fiber.

Serves 6
Serving Size 1 slice

Calories: 437.45
Protein: 5.36 grams
Carbohydrates: 51.04 grams
Fiber: 3.03 grams
Fat: 24.19 grams

1. Preheat oven to 400°F.

2. In a bowl, combine all the ingredients except the pie dough with a whisk.

3. Line a pie pan with the pie dough, flute the edges, and pour filling into it.

4. Bake 15 minutes. Turn the oven down to 350°F and bake another 45 minutes. Cover crust edge with foil if it starts to get too dark during baking.

5. Cool completely before cutting.

1 cup cooked pumpkin purée
1 cup cooked butternut
*   squash purée*
1 cup brown sugar
1 tablespoon flour
½ teaspoon salt
1 tablespoon pumpkin pie
*   spice*
¼ teaspoon ground coriander
1⅓ cups cream
2 eggs
1 teaspoon vanilla
1 rolled-out circle of Whole-
*   Wheat Pie Dough (page*
*   282)*

Pumpkin Pie Spice

Although you can buy prepared pumpkin pie spice mixes, you can adapt it to your own tastes by making it yourself. Mix 1½ teaspoons ground cinnamon, ½ teaspoon freshly grated nutmeg, ½ teaspoon ground ginger, ¼ teaspoon allspice, ¼ teaspoon ground cloves. If you are going to use the spices immediately, mince some fresh ginger into the mixture and omit the dried ginger.

Green Tomato–Raisin Pie

Serves 6
Serving Size 1 slice

Calories: 511.72
Protein: 4.58 grams
Carbohydrates: 78.56 grams
Fiber: 4.07 grams
Fat: 20.88 grams

2 rolled-out circles of Whole-Wheat Pie Dough (page 282)
2 tablespoons cornstarch
¾ cup sugar
1 teaspoon cinnamon
4 cups large green tomatoes, chopped
½ cup golden raisins
2 tablespoons lemon juice
1 teaspoon grated lemon zest
1 tablespoon cold salted butter

This recipe is a good way to use up end-of-the-season tomatoes that haven't ripened. It's really a delicious way to get lots of fiber from the tomatoes and raisins, and the whole-wheat crust will give you another good reason to eat healthful food.

1. Preheat oven to 425°F.

2. Line pie pan with one of the pie-dough circles. Cut slits in the other pie-dough circle and set both aside in the refrigerator.

3. Mix cornstarch, sugar, and cinnamon together in a bowl.

4. Toss the chopped tomatoes, golden raisins, lemon juice, and lemon zest with the sugar mixture.

5. Put the tomato filling into the dough-lined pie pan and put the butter on top of it. Cover the filling with the pie-dough circle with slits to form the top crust. Crimp the edges together to seal the crust.

6. Bake for 20 minutes, reduce the temperature to 325°F, and bake 40 minutes longer. Cool completely and serve at room temperature or warmed.

Mincemeat Pie

This recipe is a meatless variety of mincemeat.
The Sherry Hard Sauce under the recipe for Mincemeat Loaf (page 265)
is a good accompaniment for this pie too.

Serves 8
Serving Size 1 slice

Calories: 652.63
Protein: 5.88 grams
Carbohydrates: 91.77 grams
Fiber: 7.02 grams
Fat: 29.94 grams

1. Preheat oven to 400°F.

2. Line pie pan with one of the pie-dough circles. Cut slits in the other pie-dough circle and set both aside in the refrigerator.

3. Mix remaining ingredients in a large saucepan and bring to a boil.

4. Stir, turn heat to low, and simmer for 25 minutes, stirring often. Set the mixture aside to cool to room temperature.

5. Pour the cooled filling into the dough-lined pie pan, cover the filling with the pie-dough circle with slits to form the top crust. Crimp the edges together to seal the crust. Bake for 30 minutes, reduce heat to 350°F, and bake 30 more minutes. Cool completely, then warm slightly before serving.

Mincemeat

In the old days, cooks used to put real meat in mincemeat, and some people still do it today. Ground pork is a favorite, but beef, veal, or turkey are also popular. When meat is added, mincemeat pie ceases to be a dessert, but it is an excellent lunch or late supper on a cold night. Try cutting the sugar to a tablespoon and adding ½ pound meat.

2 rolled-out circles of Whole-Wheat Pie Dough (page 282)
5 cups Granny Smith apples, peeled, cored, and chopped
¼ cup brandy
1 cup sugar
1 teaspoon cinnamon
1 teaspoon nutmeg
¼ teaspoon ground cloves
1 tablespoon grated lemon zest
1 tablespoon grated orange zest
2 tablespoons lemon juice
2 tablespoons orange juice
¼ cup apple cider
1 cup raisins
½ cup currants
1 cup chopped pecans
4 tablespoons salted butter

Fresh Peach Pie

Serves 6
Serving Size 1 slice

Calories: 526.78
Protein: 3.71 grams
Carbohydrates: 79.02 grams
Fiber: 4.87 grams
Fat: 22.63 grams

2 rolled-out circles of Whole-Wheat Pie Dough (page 282)
5 cups peaches, peeled, pitted, and sliced
¾ cup sugar
3 tablespoons cornstarch
2 tablespoons butter, cut in pieces

Nectarines or plums can be made into pies in the same way as this recipe. Adding some toasted pecans or walnuts enhances the flavor and gives the pie a bit of crunch.

1. Preheat oven to 350°F. Line pie pan with one circle of pie dough.

2. Mix peach slices with sugar and cornstarch and put them in the pie shell. Dot peaches with butter pieces.

3. Cover the peaches with the other pie-dough circle, crimp the edges to seal, and cut slits in the top. Sprinkle with sugar and bake for 50 minutes. Cool before slicing.

Apple Tart Tatin

Serves 6
Serving Size 1 slice

Calories: 414.06
Protein: 3.29 grams
Carbohydrates: 49.42 grams
Fiber: 3.04 grams
Fat: 23.79 grams

4 tablespoons butter
½ cup brown sugar
6 apples, peeled, cored, and quartered
1 sheet frozen puff pastry, thawed in the refrigerator

A slice of this upside-down tart needs nothing more than a dollop of crème fraîche to accompany it. The apples provide the only fiber.

1. Preheat oven to 375°F.

2. Sauté the butter and brown sugar in a cast-iron skillet until the foam subsides and it caramelizes. Remove from heat.

3. Place the apple quarters on the bottom of the pan, lining them up around the edge and ending in the center.

4. Cut the corners off the puff pastry to make a rough round and place it on the apples. Cut a small slit in the center to let steam escape.

5. Bake the skillet in the oven for 45 minutes. Remove, invert onto a plate, and carefully lift, leaving the tart on the plate. Cut into wedges and serve hot.

Shaker Lemon Pie

This pie filling is made from whole lemons sliced paper thin, and it needs to be started the day before baking. It's tart enough to require some hard sauce or whipped cream on top. Eating the whole lemon gives you a shot of ascorbic acid and plenty of excellent fiber.

1. Grate the zest from the lemons into a glass bowl and set aside. Slice the lemons as thinly as possible, remove any seeds, and put the slices in the bowl. Add the sugar and salt and toss to distribute. Cover and let stand at room temperature overnight. Stir the lemons in the morning and let them continue to macerate for up to 24 hours.

2. Preheat oven to 425°F. Line pie pan with one of the pie-dough circles. Cut slits in the other pie-dough circle and set aside.

3. Beat the eggs with a whisk until foamy. Add the butter and flour and whisk to incorporate. Stir the lemons into the egg mixture, juice and all.

4. Pour the mixture into the dough-lined pie pan; spread out evenly. Cover the filling with the pie-dough circle with slits to form the top crust. Crimp the edges together to seal the crust.

5. Bake for 30 minutes, reduce heat to 350°F, and bake 25–30 more minutes. Cool completely and serve at room temperature.

Serves 6
Serving Size 1 slice

Calories: 709.35
Protein: 7.03 grams
Carbohydrates: 106.41 grams
Fiber: 2.65 grams
Fat: 29.37 grams

2 large lemons
2 cups sugar
¼ teaspoon salt
2 rolled-out circles of Whole-Wheat Pie Dough (page 282)
4 eggs
¼ cup unsalted butter, melted
3 tablespoons flour

Polenta Pear Tart

*Tender Poached Pears (page 163) are nestled between 2 layers of
Sweet Cornmeal Tart Dough (page 283) in this recipe. Using polenta
as your pie crust gives an added dimension of fiber to the recipe.*

Calories: 345.03
Protein: 8.05 grams
Carbohydrates: 68.21 grams
Fiber: 4.08 grams
Fat: 4.28 grams

*2 rolled-out circles of Sweet
    Cornmeal Tart Dough
    (page 283)*
¼ cup ground almonds
2 tablespoons sugar
6–8 poached pear halves
1 egg, beaten
2 tablespoons coarse sugar

1. Preheat oven to 375°F.

2. Line a 9" fluted tart pan with a removable bottom with one of the dough circles.

3. Sprinkle the dough in the tart pan with the ground almonds and sugar. Arrange the pear halves on the almond-sugar mixture, cut-sides down and points facing in.

4. Place the second dough circle on top of the pears and press down around the rim to cut off extra dough, if any. Brush with egg and sprinkle with coarse sugar.

5. Bake 40 minutes, let cool to room temperature, slice, and serve.

Polenta Is Versatile

Puddings, pie crust, muffins, and other lovely creations from polenta are healthful and so good for you. Polenta was commonly used by peasants in the past, but you can benefit from its nutrients today. Avoid white-flour pie crusts, cornstarch puddings, and muffins made with white flour.

Chapter 14
Cookies

Sunflower Seed Shortbread

These delicate cookies are simple to make and you enjoy the nutty, crunchy fiber content of whole-wheat flour and sunflower seeds. They are wonderful as an after school snack or at tea time to give your friends a fiber boost!

Serves 12
Serving Size 1 wedge

Calories: 163.22
Protein: 2.82 grams
Carbohydrates: 15.27 grams
Fiber: 1.18 grams
Fat: 10.47 grams

½ cup butter, softened
¼ cup sugar
½ teaspoon vanilla
1 cup all-purpose flour
¼ cup whole-wheat flour
½ teaspoon salt
1 egg white
½ cup toasted sunflower
   seeds, shelled

1. Preheat oven to 325° F.

2. Combine butter and sugar in a bowl and mix with a wooden spoon or electric mixer until slightly fluffy but not whipped.

3. Add vanilla and mix well.

4. Add flours and salt and mix to form a smooth dough.

5. Press dough into a 9" pie plate, and brush the dough with the egg white. Sprinkle the sunflower seeds on top of the dough, press in, and bake for 20 minutes. Remove from oven and cut into 12 wedges immediately. Let cool.

Oatmeal Raisin Cookies

You may substitute shortening for half of the butter in this recipe as long as it is the kind with no trans fat in it. Everyone loves this classic cookie, rich in fiber and nutrition.

1. Preheat oven to 350°F.

2. Cream the butter, brown sugar, and sugar with an electric mixer until fluffy.

3. Add eggs, water, and vanilla and combine well, scraping the sides of the bowl frequently.

4. Mix the oats, flour, salt, and baking soda together in a bowl. Add it to the butter mixture, stirring well to combine into a smooth dough. Stir in the raisins.

5. Drop dough in mounds onto a cookie sheet. Press down with a wet palm to flatten them slightly. Bake cookies 12 minutes. Cool on a rack.

Oatmeal

Sneak oatmeal into brownies, bars, and other rich cookies to scrub the fat, cholesterol, and trans fat out of your arteries and intestines. Cook up some Irish oatmeal for breakfast and then add it to other foods, including cookies.

Serves 24
Serving Size 2 cookies

Calories: 327.58
Protein: 5.46 grams
Carbohydrates: 53.10 grams
Fiber: 3.15 grams
Fat: 11.41 grams

1½ cups butter, softened
1½ cups brown sugar
1 cup sugar
2 eggs
½ cup water
2 teaspoons vanilla
6 cups rolled oats, quick-cook
2 cups flour
2 teaspoons salt
1 teaspoon baking soda
3 cups raisins

Whole-Wheat Peanut Butter Cookies

Try these cookies with pieces of banana pressed into each one before baking for a different treat that adds more fiber to the recipe. The kids will love this variation, and it will sustain them from after school until dinner.

Serves 18
Serving Size 2 cookies

Calories: 283.24
Protein: 6.09 grams
Carbohydrates: 32.31 grams
Fiber: 2.03 grams
Fat: 15.45 grams

6 ounces soft butter
1 cup peanut butter
1 cup brown sugar
½ cup sugar
2 eggs
2 teaspoons vanilla
1½ cups all-purpose flour
1 cup whole-wheat flour
¼ teaspoon salt
1¼ teaspoons baking powder
½ teaspoon baking soda
½ cup sugar in a bowl

1. Preheat oven to 350°F.

2. Cream together the butter, peanut butter, brown sugar, and sugar with an electric mixer until fluffy.

3. Add eggs and vanilla and combine well. Scrape the sides of the bowl.

4. Mix the flours, salt, baking powder, and baking soda together in a bowl. Add it to the butter mixture, stirring well to combine into a smooth dough.

5. Form dough into 1" balls and place them on a cookie sheet. Dip a dinner fork into the bowl of sugar and press a crosshatch mark into each cookie. Dip fork frequently into the sugar to prevent sticking. Bake cookies 10 minutes. Cool on a rack.

Sesame Seed Cookies

These delicate cookies are a type of lace cookie, full of delicious and fiber-rich sesame seeds. The seeds add a touch of protein. These cookies are also elegant enough for dessert, topped with ice cream.

1. Stir the honey, butter, powdered sugar, and water together in a saucepan. Turn the heat to medium and bring to a boil. Boil for 1 minute and remove from heat.

2. Stir in the sesame seeds, salt, and flour. Let cool to room temperature.

3. Preheat oven to 350°F. Line baking sheets with parchment paper or silicone mats.

4. Roll the cookie dough into balls, and place them 4" apart from each other on the prepared baking sheets.

5. Bake for 8 minutes, then let cool on racks. Peel off the cooled cookies and store in an airtight container.

Learning about Seeds

Seeds are delicious, high in both fiber and in protein. However, people with diverticulitis or diverticulosis cannot eat them. They get caught in the little intestinal pockets that these diseases produce. There they go bad and cause pain, gas, and attendant swelling. Children and people without these diseases will benefit from a good daily dose of seeds in the diet. Eating nuts and seeds while you're healthy will help prevent intestinal problems.

Serves 15
Serving Size 2 cookies

Calories: 65.37
Protein: 1.45 grams
Carbohydrates: 6.99 grams
Fiber: 0.46 grams
Fat: 3.90 grams

4½ teaspoons honey
1½ tablespoons butter
½ cup powdered sugar
1 tablespoon water
½ cup sesame seeds
pinch of salt
2 tablespoons flour

Dandy Candy

*Many versions of this no-bake cookie recipe have been around
for a long time. This is what grade school kids named and "manufactured" for
years for their fund-raising projects. It's still a great, healthy project
for your kids to make for school sales.*

Serves 18
Serving Size 2 pieces

Calories: 201.59
Protein: 3.53 grams
Carbohydrates: 30.42 grams
Fiber: 1.62 grams
Fat: 8.25 grams

2 cups sugar
2 tablespoons cocoa powder
½ cup milk
6 tablespoons butter
½ cup peanut butter
2 cups rolled oats
½ teaspoon vanilla

1. Mix the sugar and cocoa powder together in a saucepan.

2. Add the milk and butter and bring to a boil. Cook for 2 minutes and remove from heat.

3. Stir in the peanut butter, oats, and vanilla.

4. Lay out waxed paper. Drop teaspoons of the mixture onto it and let them cool.

Unbaked Sweets

There are many kinds of fudge-type candies that do not require baking. The more seeds, nuts, and dried fruit you can add to them, the better. Big bowls and wooden spoons will facilitate the process. Start with the Dandy Candy recipe and then invent your own variations.

Pecan Pie Bars

Honey or corn syrup may be substituted for the brown rice syrup in these chewy, nutty bars. They are a quick fiber fix when you don't have time to make a pecan pie.

Serves 24
Serving Size 1 bar

Calories: 236.28
Protein: 2.26 grams
Carbohydrates: 20.08 grams
Fiber: 1.70 grams
Fat: 17.34 grams

1¼ cups butter, divided
1 cup all-purpose flour
1 cup whole-wheat flour
½ teaspoon salt
1½ cups brown sugar, divided
⅓ cup brown rice syrup
2 tablespoons cream
2 cups chopped pecans

1. Preheat oven to 350°F. Line a 13" × 9" × 2" baking pan with nonstick foil.

2. Cut ¾ cup of the butter into small pieces and put them in a food processor with the flours, salt, and ½ cup brown sugar. Pulse until sandy in texture.

3. Press the mixture into the bottom of the prepared pan and bake for 20 minutes.

4. Meanwhile, melt the remaining ½ cup butter in a saucepan, add the remaining 1 cup brown sugar, brown rice syrup, and cream. Simmer for 1 minute. Stir, remove from heat, add the pecans, and stir to combine.

5. Pour the filling onto the crust and spread to make it even. Return to the oven to bake for 20 minutes. Cool completely before cutting.

Apricot–Chocolate Chip Squares

Serves 18
Serving Size 2 squares

Calories: 411.91
Protein: 7.15 grams
Carbohydrates: 47.11 grams
Fiber: 3 grams
Fat: 22.66 grams

1 cup unsalted butter,
   softened
¾ cup brown sugar
¾ cup sugar
2 eggs
1 teaspoon vanilla
2¼ cups all-purpose flour
½ teaspoon salt
1 teaspoon baking soda
1 cup chocolate chips
1 cup chopped dried apricots
2 cups granola
1 cup chopped cashews

*These cookies are easy and have the added crunch of granola and cashews.
Pack these instead of trail mix when you go camping or to the park. These are
so loaded with vitamins, protein, and fiber that you will go for miles.*

1. Preheat oven to 375°F.

2. Cream the butter, brown sugar, and sugar with an electric mixer until fluffy.

3. Add eggs and vanilla and combine well. Scrape the sides of the bowl.

4. Mix the flour, salt, and baking soda together in a bowl. Add it to the butter mixture, stirring well to combine into a smooth dough. Stir in chocolate chips, dried apricots, granola, and cashews.

5. Press dough into a foil-lined 15½" × 10½" × 1" baking pan and bake for 20 minutes. Cool on a rack and cut into squares.

Popcorn Cookies

Air-popped popcorn is best for this recipe, but any unbuttered popcorn will work. Omit the salt if you use prepopped salted popcorn.

Serves 18
Serving Size 2 cookies

Calories: 50.56
Protein: 0.86 grams
Carbohydrates: 8.56 grams
Fiber: 0.17 grams
Fat: 1.58 grams

2–3 cups plain popcorn
1 tablespoon butter, melted
2 egg whites, room
   temperature
⅔ cup sugar
1 teaspoon vanilla
½ teaspoon salt
36 blanched, skinless
   almonds, toasted

1. Preheat oven to 325°F. Line baking sheets with parchment paper or silicone mats.

2. Mince the popcorn in a food processor by pulsing several times. Measure 1½ cups for the recipe. (Discard any extra.) Toss the popcorn with the melted butter.

3. Whip the egg whites until frothy. Add the sugar gradually, continuing to whip the egg whites to stiff peaks.

4. Fold the egg whites and popcorn together. Stir in the vanilla and salt.

5. Drop teaspoons of the popcorn mixture onto the prepared baking sheets and top each one with an almond. Bake for 7 minutes. Let cool and store in an airtight container.

Blanching and Toasting Almonds

To blanch and skin whole almonds, boil them for 1 minute. Drain and cool for a few minutes. Slip the skins off by pinching the almonds between your thumb and forefinger. The skins will slip right off and the almonds will pop out. To toast almonds, place them on a cookie sheet in a 350°F oven for 12 to 15 minutes.

Cornmeal Cookies

Serves 9
Serving Size 2 cookies

Calories: 248.83
Protein: 2.87 grams
Carbohydrates: 35.55 grams
Fiber: 1.17 grams
Fat: 11.11 grams

½ cup soft butter
¾ cup sugar
1 egg
1 cup all-purpose flour
½ cup cornmeal
½ teaspoon baking soda
½ teaspoon salt
¼ cup dried currants
1 teaspoon grated orange
    zest

A pretty variation of these cookies is to add a tablespoon of chopped candied violets and leave out the currants. However, the cornmeal and currants are a tasty source of fiber.

1. Preheat oven to 350°F. Line baking sheets with parchment paper or silicone mats.

2. Combine the butter, sugar, and egg with an electric mixer until smooth.

3. Add the flour, cornmeal, baking soda, and salt. Mix to combine.

4. Stir in the currants and orange zest. Put tablespoons of the dough onto the prepared baking sheets, 1" apart from each other.

5. Bake 10–12 minutes. Cool on a rack.

Cornmeal in Your Cookies!

Coarsely ground cornmeal crisps up nicely when baked. Cornmeal is satisfying and loaded with fiber that takes time to digest. It leaves you feeling full for a good long time and releases energy slowly without any peaks or valleys. Experiment with white or yellow cornmeal, adding it to brownies and other super-rich treats for a healthful note.

Caramel Corn–Chocolate Truffles

If you have leftovers, store them in an airtight container in a cool place, but not the refrigerator. Caramel corn may get less crunchy since it absorbs moisture quickly.

Serves 18
Serving Size 2 truffles

Calories: 99.34
Protein: 1.01 grams
Carbohydrates: 9.64 grams
Fiber: 0.56 grams
Fat: 6.75 grams

2–3 cups caramel corn
⅔ cup cream
1 cup chocolate chips

1. Mince the caramel corn in a food processor by pulsing several times. Set aside in an airtight container.

2. Bring the cream to a boil in a saucepan and immediately remove from heat.

3. Add the chocolate chips, cover, and let sit for 3 minutes. Stir the chocolate and cream together until smooth. Refrigerate for 45 to 60 minutes.

4. Scoop heaping teaspoons of the chocolate mixture onto foil-lined cookie sheets and refrigerate until firm.

5. Roll the firm truffle balls in the minced caramel corn and serve within a few hours.

Almond Macaroons

To dress these up you may dip the bottoms of the cooled macaroons in chocolate. Try substituting candied ginger for the candied orange peel. However, including the coconut, applesauce, and orange peel adds yummy fiber.

Serves 12
Serving Size 2 macaroons

Calories: 156.17
Protein: 3.18 grams
Carbohydrates: 15.88 grams
Fiber: 2.62 grams
Fat: 9.31 grams

2 egg whites
¼ cup sugar
¼ cup applesauce
1¼ cups shredded coconut
¼ cup chopped candied
    orange peel
¾ cup ground almonds
2 tablespoons flour

1. Preheat oven to 350°F. Line baking sheet pan with parchment paper.

2. Whip the egg whites with the sugar until frothy. Stir in the remaining ingredients.

3. Form mixture into walnut-size balls and place them on the prepared cookie sheet.

4. Bake for 20 minutes.

5. Cool, then peel cookies off the parchment paper.

Macadamia Mandelbrot

Mandelbrot is like biscotti, twice-baked cookies that are perfect with tea, coffee, and after-dinner drinks. The whole-wheat flour and the nuts add to the fiber, and the nuts provide a delectable flavor.

1. Preheat oven to 350°F. Grease a baking sheet pan.

2. Cream the butter and sugar with an electric mixer. Add egg and vanilla and beat to incorporate.

3. In a separate bowl combine the baking powder, salt, and flours. Add this dry mixture to the egg-butter mixture and combine to make a smooth dough. Stir in macadamia nuts.

4. Scrape dough out onto the prepared baking sheet pan and form it into a domed log using wet fingers. Bake for 30 minutes, remove from oven and cool for 5 minutes. Turn the oven down to 275°F.

5. Cut the log into ¾"-wide slices and place the slices back on the baking sheet, cut-sides facing up. Bake 15 minutes, turn cookies over, and bake 10 minutes more. Cool on a rack.

Serves 6
Serving Size 2 Mandelbrot

Calories: 265.65
Protein: 4.31 grams
Carbohydrates: 25.58 grams
Fiber: 2.39 grams
Fat: 17.19 grams

2 ounces unsalted butter, softened
¼ cup sugar
1 egg
½ teaspoon vanilla
1 teaspoon baking powder
pinch of salt
½ cup all-purpose flour
½ cup whole-wheat flour
½ cup toasted macadamia nuts

Walnut Biscotti

This is a delicious basic cookie that's not too sweet. It goes well with Poached Quince, Pear, and Prune Compote (page 165). You can intensify the almond flavor in this recipe by adding a spoonful of almond extract.

1. Preheat oven to 350°F. Grease a baking sheet pan or line it with parchment.

2. Whip the egg and sugar together with an electric mixer until light yellow in color and very fluffy.

3. In a separate bowl combine the baking powder, salt, and flours. Add dry mixture to the egg mixture and combine to make a smooth dough. Stir in walnuts.

4. Scrape dough out onto the prepared baking sheet pan and form it into a broad, flat log using wet fingers. Bake for 30 minutes, remove from oven, and cool for 5 minutes. Turn the oven down to 275°F.

5. Cut the log into ½"-wide slices and place the slices back on the baking sheet, cut-sides facing up. Bake 15 minutes, turn cookies over, and bake 10 minutes more. Cool on a rack.

Biscotti

Biscotti *means "twice baked" in Italian. It starts out like a sweet bread and then, cut into slices and rebaked, turns into a delicious cookie with endless variations. Various dried fruits, different kinds of nuts, and other flavorings spike biscotti. You can throw in seeds to add to the crunch and fiber.*

Cranberry Pistachio Biscotti

This is a festive cookie to have around holiday time, studded with red and green. Serve it with eggnog. You will be serving rich and delicious fiber in the nuts and cranberries.

1. Preheat oven to 350°F. Grease a baking sheet pan.

2. Cream the butter and sugar with an electric mixer. Add egg and vanilla and beat to incorporate.

3. In a separate bowl combine the nutmeg, baking powder, salt, and flour. Add this dry mixture to the egg-butter mixture and combine to make a smooth dough. Stir in pistachios and cranberries.

4. Scrape dough out onto the prepared baking sheet pan and form it into a broad, flat log using wet fingers. Bake for 30 minutes, remove from oven, and cool for 5 minutes. Turn the oven down to 275°F.

5. Cut the log into ½"-wide slices and place the slices back on the baking sheet, cut-sides facing up. Bake 15 minutes, turn cookies over, and bake 10 minutes more. Cool on a rack.

Serves 10
Serving Size 2 biscotti

Calories: 152.89
Protein: 3.33 grams
Carbohydrates: 17.87 grams
Fiber: 1.75 grams
Fat: 7.92 grams

2 ounces unsalted butter, softened
¼ cup sugar
1 egg
½ teaspoon vanilla
¼ teaspoon grated nutmeg
1 teaspoon baking powder
pinch of salt
½ cup all-purpose flour
½ cup whole-wheat flour
½ cup shelled pistachios
¼ cup dried cranberries, chopped

Mom's Golden Squares

*Any loving mother can rouse the family by making these late at night.
The aroma of the cookies will wake a heavy sleeper who will
want a cookie and a late-night glass of milk*

Serves 12;
Serving Size 2 squares

Calories: 275.16
Protein: 5.13 grams
Carbohydrates: 38.21 grams
Fiber: 1.37 grams
Fat: 12.28 grams

½ tablespoon soft butter
*2 cups graham cracker
    crumbs*
1 cup chocolate chips
½ cup chopped walnuts
*1 can sweetened condensed
    milk*

1. Preheat oven to 350°F.

2. Butter an 8"-square baking pan, line it with waxed paper, and grease the waxed paper. Set aside.

3. Combine the graham cracker crumbs, chocolate chips, and walnuts in a mixing bowl. Add the sweetened condensed milk and mix to combine.

4. Scrape the mixture into the prepared pan and bake for 40 minutes until the top is golden brown.

5. Remove from the oven and invert the pan onto a foil-lined flat surface. Remove the waxed paper and let mixture cool before cutting into squares.

When You Can't Go Wrong
It's hard to make a nondelicious cookie or bar when you use chocolate chips and nuts. Stick with whole-wheat flour whenever possible or cut white flour with a grain flour. All sorts of nuts work for the fiber balance. Try mixing various sorts of toasted nuts, such as sweet hazelnuts with more tart walnuts. Mix almonds with pecans for a new crunch.

Pecan Lace Cookies

Pecan lace cookies are thin and crisp and are the perfect accompaniment to Pear Sorbet (page 175). They can also be crumbled to go over the sorbet. Whatever you do, the pecans have lots of fiber.

Serves 15
Serving Size 2 cookies

Calories: 62.52
Protein: 0.48 grams
Carbohydrates: 6.81 grams
Fiber: 0.41 grams
Fat: 4.02 grams

4½ teaspoons dark corn syrup
1½ tablespoons butter
½ cup powdered sugar
1 tablespoon water
½ cup finely chopped pecans
pinch of salt
2 tablespoons flour

1. Stir the corn syrup, butter, powdered sugar, and water together in a saucepan. Turn the heat to medium and bring to a boil. Boil for 1 minute and remove from heat.

2. Stir in the pecans, salt, and flour. Let cool to room temperature.

3. Preheat oven to 350°F. Line baking sheets with parchment paper or silicone mats.

4. Roll the cookie dough into balls and place them 4" apart from each other on the prepared baking sheets.

5. Bake for 8 minutes, then let cool on racks. Peel off the cooled cookies and store in an airtight container.

Tuiles

Tuiles are lace cookies that have been molded into a curved shape while they are still warm. The name is French for "tiles" and refers to curved terra cotta roof tiles. To mold them, put a piece of parchment paper over the cookies right after they come out of the oven and roll the two parchment papers with the cookies sandwiched between them up on a rolling pin. Let cool completely, then carefully unroll the tuiles.

Hazelnut Sticks

*This dough can be rolled into a log instead of a rectangle
for round cookies. Hazelnuts have a sweet flavor
and also contain a great deal of protein and fiber.*

Serves 12
Serving Size 2 sticks

Calories: 178.20
Protein: 3.02 grams
Carbohydrates: 17.92 grams
Fiber: 1.21 grams
Fat: 11.09 grams

5 tablespoons soft butter
½ cup sugar
1 egg
1 cup toasted hazelnuts
1 cup all-purpose flour

1. Cream the butter and sugar with an electric mixer until smooth.

2. Add the egg, beat it in, and scrape down the sides of the bowl.

3. Add the hazelnuts and mix. Add the flour and mix to combine.

4. Wrap the dough in plastic wrap, press it down into a ½"-thick, 3"-wide rectangle and refrigerate for 4 hours.

5. Preheat oven to 350°F. Line baking sheets with parchment paper or silicone mats. Remove the dough from the freezer, unwrap, and slice into ½"-thick sticks. Bake 10 minutes, turn the cookies over, and bake 5–10 minutes longer, depending on how dark you want them to be. Cool on a rack.

Chapter 15
Homemade Crackers

Sesame Seed Wafers

The rectangular candies made with sesame seeds are the inspiration for these savory wafers. However, the wafers are far less fattening and much more fiber-full and healthful!

Serves 4

Calories: 143.28
Protein: 3.04 grams
Carbohydrates: 12.66 grams
Fiber: 0.83 grams
Fat: 9.10 grams

½ cup all-purpose flour
2 tablespoons sesame seeds
2 tablespoons cold butter, cut
   in small pieces
1 tablespoon sour cream
1½ teaspoons lemon juice
1 tablespoon kosher salt

1. Mix the flour, sesame seeds, and butter in a food processor until the mixture is the texture of cornmeal.

2. Add the sour cream and lemon juice and mix until the dough comes together.

3. Roll the dough into a ball, wrap in plastic, flatten it into a disc, and chill for 15 minutes.

4. Preheat the oven to 400°F and line a baking sheet pan with parchment paper or silicone mat.

5. Roll the chilled dough out thin and cut out 2" rounds with a cookie cutter or wineglass. Put the crackers on the prepared baking sheet pan and sprinkle them with kosher salt. Bake 12 minutes, let cool, and serve.

Crackers vs. Cookies

Crackers are a much healthier option than cookies. To begin with, they tend not to contain sugar. The difference between crackers and cookies is the same as between snacks and treats. Treats are defined as special occasion goodies, not everyday food. Snacks are defined as part of a healthful diet, small meals to keep you going in between full meals. Snacks are particularly important for growing children, dieters, diabetics, and hypoglycemics. Everyone needs to keep a level of energy going to be healthy and feel well.

Toffee Crackers

This recipe transforms saltine crackers into an unbelievably delicious sweet treat. The hazelnuts and Grape-Nuts do mitigate the sugar and butter.

1. Preheat oven to 350°F. Line a sheet pan with sides with nonstick aluminum foil. Lay the crackers out on the foil in rows of 4" × 5".

2. Combine the brown sugar and butter in a 2-quart saucepan. Bring to a boil, turn to medium-low, and simmer for 5 minutes, stirring occasionally with a wooden spoon.

3. Pour the hot sugar and butter mixture over the crackers. Spread to cover evenly with a heat-resistant silicone spatula. Bake for 10 minutes. Remove from the oven and let rest about 5 minutes.

4. Sprinkle the chocolate chips and cereal evenly over the toffee crackers. Let rest 10 minutes.

5. Smooth the chocolate and cereal out evenly over the top of the toffee crackers with a spatula. Sprinkle the hazelnuts over the chocolate mixture, and let the toffee crackers cool completely. Break into pieces and store in an airtight container.

Yields 10 servings
Serving Size 2 crackers

Calories: 698.56
Protein: 8.35grams
Carbohydrates: 68.62 grams
Fiber: 4.69 grams
Fat: 47.04 grams

20 whole-wheat saltine crackers
1 cup brown sugar
1 cup butter
4 cups chocolate chips
1 cup Grape-Nuts cereal
1 cup hazelnuts, chopped

Poppy Seed Crackers

*This recipe is a nice addition to a salad or cheese and fruit plate.
Make homemade crackers to serve with cheese, salad, or soup.*

Serves 4

Calories: 131.10
Protein: 2.66 grams
Carbohydrates: 12.06 grams
Fiber: 0.75 grams
Fat: 7.87 grams

½ cup all-purpose flour
2 tablespoons poppy seeds
2 tablespoons cold butter, cut
    in small pieces
1 tablespoon sour cream
1½ teaspoons lemon juice
1 tablespoon kosher salt

1. Mix the flour, poppy seeds, and butter in a food processor until the mixture is the texture of cornmeal.

2. Add the sour cream and lemon juice and mix until the dough comes together.

3. Roll the dough into a ball, wrap in plastic, flatten it into a disc, and chill for 15 minutes.

4. Preheat the oven to 400°F and line a baking sheet pan with parchment paper or silicone mat.

5. Roll the chilled dough out thin and cut out 2" rounds with a cookie cutter or wineglass. Put the crackers on the prepared baking sheet pan and sprinkle them with kosher salt. Bake 12 minutes, let cool and serve.

Poppy Seeds

You can find poppy seed paste in Danish pastries, turnovers, and other desserts. They are also a favorite on rolls and breads. These crackers, loaded with poppy seeds, are piquant while adding a healthful dose of fiber to the diet. By making your own crackers, you can avoid a great deal of the sugar and sodium that commercially manufactured crackers contain.

Seeded Saltine Crackers

This is one of the easiest ways to "make" your own crackers, starting with premade crackers. You can make these crackers more dietetic by substituting canola oil for butter. You will get fiber from the whole wheat and seed. Seeds also add a protein kick.

1. Preheat oven to 475°F.

2. Lay the saltines out in one layer in a roasting pan with sides. Pour the ice water over them and let them soak for 3 minutes. Remove the crackers with a slotted metal spatula to drain on paper towels for 5 minutes. Pour the water out and dry the roasting pan.

3. Pour half of the melted butter over the bottom of the roasting pan, then carefully pick up the crackers and place them on the butter. Pour the rest of the melted butter over the crackers.

4. Sprinkle the crackers with the seeds.

5. Bake 18 minutes. Serve warm.

Serves 6

Calories: 291.36
Protein: 6.05 grams
Carbohydrates: 11.24 grams
Fiber: 2.30 grams
Fat: 25.80 grams

24 whole-wheat saltines
2 quarts ice water
½ cup unsalted butter, melted
¼ cup poppy seeds
½ cup sesame seeds

Toffee Graham Crackers

This recipe has graham crackers in it as an ingredient, and the result is sweet and crunchy. Use commercial graham crackers, not homemade for this.

Serves 6
Serving Size 2 pieces

Calories: 412.90
Protein: 2.78 grams
Carbohydrates: 35.23 grams
Fiber: 2.23 grams
Fat: 30.80 grams

10 graham crackers, broken
    in half
1 cup brown sugar
½ cup butter
1 cup finely chopped pecans

1. Preheat oven to 350°F. Line a sheet pan with sides with nonstick aluminum foil. Lay the graham crackers out on the foil in rows, touching each other.

2. Combine the brown sugar and butter in a 2-quart saucepan. Bring to a boil, turn to medium-low, and simmer for 5 minutes, stirring occasionally with a wooden spoon.

3. Pour the butter-sugar mixture evenly over the crackers. Sprinkle the pecans evenly over the top and bake for 10 minutes.

4. Let the crackers cool completely. Break into pieces and store in an airtight container.

Making New Ones
Taking a package of old-fashioned graham crackers and turning them into toffee grahams is a highly creative way to make something good into something better. The pecans add crunch, protein, and fiber to the grahams, which are also high in fiber. The Toffee Grahams are a version of brittle and very delicious, but fattening.

Cornmeal Crackers

*Use the coarsest ground cornmeal available for the maximum fiber.
The thinner the crackers are rolled, the crunchier they will be.*

1. Mix the flour, cornmeal, lemon zest, pepper, and butter in a food processor until the mixture is the texture of cornmeal.

2. Add the sour cream and lemon juice and mix until the dough comes together.

3. Roll the dough into a ball, wrap in plastic, flatten it into a disc, and chill for 15 minutes.

4. Preheat the oven to 400°F and line a baking sheet pan with parchment paper or silicone mat.

5. Roll the chilled dough out thin and cut out 2" rounds with a cookie cutter or wineglass. Put the crackers on the prepared baking sheet pan and sprinkle them with kosher salt. Bake 12 minutes, let cool, and serve.

Serves 4

Calories: 111.68
Protein: 1.57 grams
Carbohydrates: 11.49 grams
Fiber: 0.80 grams
Fat: 6.65 grams

¼ cup all-purpose flour
¼ cup cornmeal
1 teaspoon grated lemon zest
½ teaspoon black pepper
2 tablespoons cold butter, cut in small pieces
1 tablespoon sour cream
1½ teaspoons lemon juice
1 tablespoon kosher salt

Graham Crackers

These homemade graham crackers are good with cheese or made into s'mores. Using all-purpose flour adds little nutritional value to the crackers, but upping the quantity of whole-wheat flour adds grain and fiber.

Serves 12

Calories: 239.92
Protein: 4.19 grams
Carbohydrates: 38.85 grams
Fiber: 2.80 grams
Fat: 8.39 grams

½ cup unsalted butter, soft
¾ cup brown sugar
⅓ cup honey
1 teaspoon vanilla
1 cup all-purpose flour
2 cups whole-wheat flour
1 teaspoon baking powder
½ teaspoon baking soda
1 teaspoon cinnamon
¼ teaspoon salt
½ cup whole milk

1. Preheat oven to 350°F. Line baking sheets with parchment paper or silicone mats. Set aside.

2. Cream the butter, brown sugar, honey, and vanilla together until smooth and slightly fluffy.

3. Mix the flours, baking powder, baking soda, cinnamon, and salt together in a separate bowl.

4. Alternately add the flour mixture and the milk to the butter mixture to form a dough. Roll out and cut into squares. Place the squares on the prepared baking sheets and poke them all over with a fork.

5. Bake 15 minutes, then cool on a rack.

Keeping Crackers

Place crackers in airtight tins or jars. When packing crackers in school lunches, be sure to put them on top. Giving your children a nourishing soup for lunch and some healthful crackers will keep them going until they get out of school and are ready for a snack.

Pita Crisps

Serve these fresh chips with Hummus (page 68) or White Bean Dip (page 69), or use them instead of crackers for soup. You can also melt soft cheese on them and top with raisins for a satisfying, high-fiber snack.

Serves 8

Calories: 82.50
Protein: 2.73 grams
Carbohydrates: 16.71 grams
Fiber: 0.66 grams
Fat: 0.36 grams

4 rounds pita bread

1. Preheat the oven to 350°F. Separate the pita rounds in half, making two rounds out of each. Cut the eight halves into wedges and place them on a baking sheet.

2. Bake the pita wedges for 10 minutes until crisp. Let cool.

Whole-Wheat Pita Breads

Whatever you do, use whole-wheat pitas to make sure the fiber intake is as high as it can be. Aside from hummus, you can put cheese, fruit, dried fruit, and different veggies in the pockets. Try a mixture of chopped olives sprinkled over cream cheese on a pita cracker. Roquefort cheese spread on top, melted slightly, and then decorated with strips of roasted red pepper make a divine cocktail snack.

Date Parmesan Crackers

Serves 16
Serving Size 2 crackers

Calories: 139.77
Protein: 2.28 grams
Carbohydrates: 15.72 grams
Fiber: 1.55 grams
Fat: 8.23 grams

¼ cup unsalted butter, soft
1 tablespoon grated
    Parmesan cheese
½ cup shredded cheddar
    cheese
⅓ teaspoon salt
pinch ground cayenne
    pepper
½ cup all-purpose flour
16 whole pitted dates
¼ cup slivered almonds
¼ cup salted butter, melted

The date and almond stuffing add fiber while the cheese give you some protein. This makes a nice addition to a picnic buffet.

1. Preheat oven to 350°F. Line baking sheet pan with parchment paper or silicone mat.

2. Cream the unsalted butter, Parmesan and cheddar cheeses, salt, and cayenne pepper together with an electric mixer. Add the flour and combine to form a dough.

3. Roll the dough into a 1" diameter log and refrigerate.

4. Cut dates in half lengthwise, and stuff each date half with a slivered almond.

5. Remove dough from refrigerator and cut into ¼"-thick slices. Put the slices on the prepared baking sheet ½" apart. Press an almond-stuffed date onto each slice, almond-side up, and brush each cracker with melted butter.

6. Bake 10 minutes. Serve warm or at room temperature.

Pecan–Blue Cheese Crackers

You can use Danish Blue, Gorgonzola, or Roquefort cheese to vary this recipe.
The cheese and egg provide protein, and the pecans are loaded with fiber.

Serves 12
Serving Size 2 crackers

Calories: 143.55
Protein: 3.11 grams
Carbohydrates: 5.46 grams
Fiber: 1.05 grams
Fat: 12.68 grams

¼ cup unsalted butter, soft
½ cup blue cheese (¼ pound),
  soft
1 egg, separated
½ cup all-purpose flour
½ cup chopped toasted
  pecans
24 pecan halves

1. Cream the butter and blue cheese together with an electric mixer until smooth. Add the egg yolk and mix. Add the flour and pecans and mix to form a dough.

2. Roll the dough into a 1" diameter log and refrigerate 30 minutes.

3. Preheat oven to 375°F. Line baking sheet pan with parchment paper or silicone mat.

4. Cut the dough log into ¼"-thick slices. Put the slices on prepared baking sheet ½" apart. Press a pecan half onto each slice and brush each cracker with egg white.

5. Bake 12 minutes and cool on a rack.

Cheese, Not on, but in the Cracker

Combining cheese with cracker dough adds enormous flavor and makes the fiber go down more easily. The flavors of seeds, dates, raisins, and other dried fruits make excellent combinations when blended into cracker dough. You can also add savory herbs to cheese dough. Try some rosemary, oregano, or dried basil, kneaded right into the mixture.

Mustard Seed–Cheddar Crackers

*The fiber here comes from the seeds and whole-wheat flour.
When serving them to company, place a slice of tart apple on
top of each cracker to add fiber and brighten the flavor.*

1. Mix the cheddar cheese, Swiss cheese, and butter together in a food processor until smooth. Add the remaining ingredients and process until the mixture comes together.

2. Roll the dough into a 1" diameter log and refrigerate 2 hours.

3. Preheat oven to 350°F. Line baking sheet pan with parchment paper or silicone mat.

4. Cut the dough log into ¼"-thick slices. Put the slices on prepared baking sheet 1" apart.

5. Bake 15 minutes, then cool.

Whole-Wheat Bacon Crackers

*The flavor from the bacon and bacon fat in this recipe is the real thing,
but you may substitute imitation bacon bits and vegetable shortening
(without trans fats) for a vegetarian version. Whole-wheat flour and wheat
germ are important nutrients, adding flavor and fiber.*

1. Mix the flours, wheat germ, bacon, and bacon fat in a food processor until the mixture is the texture of cornmeal.

2. Add the sour cream and Dijon mustard and mix until the dough comes together.

3. Roll the dough into a ball, wrap in plastic, flatten it into a disc and chill for 15 minutes.

4. Preheat the oven to 400°F and line a baking sheet pan with parchment paper or silicone mat.

5. Roll the chilled dough out thin and cut out 2" rounds with a cookie cutter or wineglass. Put the crackers on the prepared baking sheet pan and sprinkle them with celery seeds. Bake 12 minutes, let cool, and serve.

Wheat Germ

You can sneak wheat germ into cookies, crackers, muffins, pancakes, and even omelets. Aside from being high in dietary fiber, it's high in protein, magnesium, phosphorus, and selenium. All of these nutrients are not typically consumed in high levels in the American diet. Whenever you can put really good nutrition back into your family's diet, do it.

Serves 4

Calories: 131.22
Protein: 2.70 grams
Carbohydrates: 12.21 grams
Fiber: 1.43 grams
Fat: 8.09 grams

¼ cup all-purpose flour
¼ cup whole-wheat flour
2 teaspoons wheat germ
1 tablespoon minced cooked bacon
2 tablespoons cold bacon fat
1 tablespoon sour cream
1½ teaspoons Dijon mustard
1 tablespoon celery seeds

Millet Cracker Bread

Millet is an excellent source of fiber, as are mustard and sesame seeds.
They are all delicious.

Serves 4

Calories: 270.82
Protein: 6.56 grams
Carbohydrates: 41.90 grams
Fat: 2.39 grams
Fat: 4.94 grams

½ package yeast
3 tablespoons warm water
¼ teaspoon sugar
1¼ cups flour, plus more for
   kneading
2 tablespoons olive oil,
   divided
¼ cup cool water
pinch of kosher salt
pinch of curry powder
2 tablespoons millet
1 tablespoon mustard seeds
2 tablespoons black sesame
   seeds

1. Combine yeast with the warm water, sugar, and ¼ cup flour. Let sit 10 minutes. Add 1 tablespoon olive oil, cool water, kosher salt, and ½ cup flour and combine with a wooden spoon. Add remaining flour and pinch of curry powder and mix to form dough.

2. Knead dough on a floured board for 5 minutes, adding flour as needed to prevent sticking.

3. Cover and set dough in an oiled bowl. Set aside in a warm place and let dough rise for 60 minutes. Punch down dough, cover, and let rise for 60 minutes.

4. Preheat oven to 400°F. Roll out the dough into one large, thin rectangle on a lightly floured surface. Place the rectangle on an oiled baking sheet. Stretch it out as thin as it will stay (it will shrink a little).

5. Brush 1 tablespoon olive oil over the dough and sprinkle the millet, mustard seeds, and black sesame seeds over it. Bake for 20 minutes, until crisp. Cool completely.

Oat Crackers

These crackers make a great snack to keep in the car. Oats are both satisfying and great artery cleansers.

1. Mix the flour, oats, wheat germ, and butter in a food processor until the mixture is the texture of cornmeal.

2. Add the sour cream and lemon juice and mix until the dough comes together.

3. Roll the dough into a ball, wrap in plastic, flatten into a disc, and chill for 15 minutes.

4. Preheat the oven to 400°F and line a baking sheet pan with parchment paper or silicone mat.

5. Roll the chilled dough out thin and cut out 2" rounds with a cookie cutter or wineglass. Put the crackers on the prepared baking sheet pan and sprinkle them with kosher salt. Bake 12 minutes, let cool, and serve.

Playing with Your Food

Try chestnut flour mixed with all-purpose flour for a whole different experience. Experiment with rice and rice flour too. Find ways to make every snack a real treat as well as something that's good for you. Healthful eating does not have to be boring when you play with your food.

Serves 4

Calories: 106.06
Protein: 1.92 grams
Carbohydrates: 9.49 grams
Fiber: 0.84 grams
Fat: 6.73 grams

¼ cup all-purpose flour
¼ cup rolled oats, minced in food processor
2 teaspoons wheat germ
2 tablespoons cold butter, cut in small pieces
1 tablespoon sour cream
1½ teaspoons lemon juice
1 tablespoon kosher salt

Herb and Cheddar Savory Shortbread

It's like a cookie, but it's not too sweet, and it will take the place of a scone for breakfast. You can top off an elegant dinner by serving this with cheese and fruit.

Serves 12

Calories: 473.50
Protein: 6.89 grams
Carbohydrates: 38.74 grams
Fiber: 0.23 grams
Fat: 32.78 grams

1 pound unsalted butter, soft
¼ cup sugar
4 cups flour
¼ cup wheat germ
¼ teaspoon salt
1 teaspoon thyme
¼ teaspoon onion powder
½ cup grated cheddar cheese

1. Preheat oven to 350°F.

2. Combine butter and sugar in a bowl and mix with a wooden spoon or electric mixer.

3. Toss the flour with the wheat germ, salt, thyme, onion powder, and cheddar cheese.

4. Add flour mixture to the butter mixture and mix to form a smooth dough.

5. Press dough into a 9" tart pan with a removable bottom, prick all over with a fork, and bake for 40 minutes. Remove from oven and let cool. Remove the side of the pan and cut the savory shortbread into 12 wedges.

Chapter 16
Special Snacks

Caramel Cashew Popcorn

This is a snack that needs to be protected from humidity after it is baked, so store it in an airtight container.

Serves 8;
Serving Size 2 cups

Calories: 482.35
Protein: 7.29 grams
Carbohydrates: 56.35 grams
Fiber: 3.65 grams
Fat: 27.85 grams

½ cup butter
1 cup brown sugar
½ teaspoon salt
¼ cup corn syrup
16 cups popped corn
½ teaspoon baking soda
2 cups honey roasted
    cashews

1. Preheat oven to 200°F.

2. Put the butter, brown sugar, salt, and corn syrup in a saucepan and heat over medium-high heat. When the mixture boils, set the timer for 5 minutes.

3. Meanwhile, put the popped corn in a roasting pan.

4. Remove the boiled mixture from heat and stir in the baking soda. It will foam up a bit. Pour the mixture over the popped corn and toss to coat evenly.

5. Bake for 15 minutes, stir; bake another 15 minutes, stir; bake another 15 minutes, stir and add the cashews; bake 15 minutes longer. Spread the caramel corn on baking sheets in one layer and let cool.

High Fiber and Sugar
The fiber in these recipes will mitigate the sugar. However, refined sugar, white sugar, honey, maple syrup, and corn syrup should be limited for growing children and adults who want to watch their weight. The higher the fiber content in a sugary snack, the slower it will be digested.

Popcorn Snack Mix

This party mix with popcorn is perfect for movie night at home.
Just serve it in a big bowl with individual plastic cups for each person.

1. Preheat oven to 250°F.

2. Combine popcorn, cereals, peanuts, cashews, and pretzels in a large roasting pan.

3. Combine melted butter, Worcestershire sauce, garlic powder, onion powder, and seasoning salt in a small bowl. Drizzle the butter mixture over the popcorn mixture and toss to distribute.

4. Bake in the oven for 15 minutes, stir; repeat four more times.

5. Remove from oven. Spread mix out on baking sheets and let cool. Toss the chocolate-covered raisins in and mix to distribute evenly. Store in an airtight container.

Serves 12
Serving Size 1 cup

Calories: 432.53
Protein: 10.20 grams
Carbohydrates: 53.67 grams
Fiber: 5.60 grams
Fat: 22.55 grams

4 cups popped popcorn
2 cups toasted oat rings
    cereal
3 cups wheat cereal squares
1 cup peanuts
1 cup cashews
1 cup mini pretzel twists
6 tablespoons butter, melted
2 tablespoons Worcestershire
    sauce
1 teaspoon garlic powder
½ teaspoon onion powder
1 teaspoon seasoning salt
1 cup chocolate-covered
    raisins

Pink Popcorn

This is a lovely pale-pink glazed popcorn treat that is crunchy and sweet.

Serves 8
Serving Size 1 cup

Calories: 161.48
Protein: 1.15 grams
Carbohydrates: 26.86 grams
Fiber: 1.21 grams
Fat: 6.09 grams

¼ cup butter
3 tablespoons corn syrup
½ cup sugar
1 small box strawberry kiwi
　　gelatin
8 cups popped popcorn

1. Preheat oven to 300°F. Line a baking sheet pan with foil.

2. Melt the butter with the corn syrup in a 6-quart pot over medium heat. Add the sugar and gelatin. Stir and bring the mixture to a boil.

3. Reduce heat to low and simmer for 5 minutes, stirring occasionally.

4. Remove the mixture from the heat and immediately pour in the popcorn. Toss the popcorn to coat and then spread it out on the foil.

5. Bake the coated popcorn for 10 minutes. Cool and break up into smaller pieces. Store in an airtight container.

Cotton Candy Colors

If you make several different batches of this popcorn using different shades (and flavors) of pink, blue, and purple gelatin you can combine them to make a beautiful bowl of variegated popcorn that is as colorful as cotton candy but with way more fiber.

Peanut Bananas

Try this recipe with almond or cashew butter for variation;
honey may be substituted for the brown rice syrup.

1. Peel the bananas and cut them into quarters crosswise.

2. Stand the banana pieces cut-sides up on a platter. (Cut the pointed tips off the end pieces so they can stand up.)

3. Mix the peanut butter with the brown rice syrup in a glass bowl and microwave on high for 15 to 20 seconds. Stir together well.

4. Spoon the peanut butter mixture onto the banana pieces.

5. Sprinkle granola over the peanut butter and serve.

Nature's Flatware

You may serve these banana snacks with bamboo skewers or tooth-picks, but fingers are just fine. However, it's important to do so with clean hands. Bananas are loaded with fiber and potassium; they really fill you up. They are especially wonderful for the lonely traveler, sitting in the airport, waiting for a plane that's late.

Serves 4
Serving Size 3 pieces

Calories: 615.29
Protein: 19.54 grams
Carbohydrates: 68.44 grams
Fiber: 7.49 grams
Fat: 33.50 grams

3 bananas
1 cup crunchy peanut butter
¼ cup brown rice syrup
1 cup granola

Trail Mix

Serves 8
Serving Size 1 cup

Calories: 647.58
Protein: 12.60 grams
Carbohydrates: 73.28 grams
Fiber: 8.89 grams
Fat: 35.54 grams

2 cups dried cherries
2 cups roasted pecans
1 cup M&Ms
2 cups granola
1 cup shelled sunflower seeds
1 cup Pretzel Goldfish

Pack individual servings of these to take in the car when running errands so you have something to snack on if you don't have time to stop for a meal.

1. Combine everything in a large bowl.

2. Divide into individual portions and store in resealable plastic bags or serve in individual paper cups.

Sweets and Fiber

The more fiber you add to a sweet snack, the easier it is to pass it out of the body. Add nuts for high fiber and protein. Walnuts, almonds, and pecans are readily available. Add some seeds—especially sesame seeds—for more fiber. Flavorful seeds, such as poppy seeds, anise, caraway, and celery seeds, are more an addition to flavor than raw fiber. Add them anyway because every little bit counts.

Almond-Stuffed Dates

Combining almonds and dates is a delicious way to create candylike sweets that are fiber-rich. If you roast or toast the almonds, they will be crunchier and more satisfying.

1. Place the powdered sugar in a bowl.

2. Cut a slit on one side of each date and remove the pit. Replace it with an almond.

3. Roll the dates in the powdered sugar.

Dates and Nuts

Dates are special. They are loaded with dietary fiber and they're sweet to the point of being gooey. However, people like them more because they are delicious than because they are good for you. If you love sweets, mix them with almonds to scrub out your colon and eat almond-filled high-fiber dates rather than candy.

Serves 6

Calories: 194.33
Protein: 2.78 grams
Carbohydrates: 34.48 grams
Fiber: 2.70 grams
Fat: 6.06 grams

1 cup powdered sugar
12 Medjool dates
½ cup whole almonds

Apple Cheddar Rye Rounds

*You may toast the bread before cutting out circles for a crisper finished texture.
Your fiber here comes from the caraway seeds, the rye flour, and the apples.
Cheddar cheese and apples—especially tart apples—are a classic
combination. If you leave the skin on, this snack is even higher in fiber.*

Serves 4

Calories: 236.45
Protein: 9.23 grams
Carbohydrates: 33.89 grams
Fiber: 4.06 grams
Fat: 7.18 grams

*8 slices rye bread with
caraway seeds
1 tablespoon Dijon mustard
½ cup diced apples, skin on
½ cup shredded cheddar
cheese*

1. Preheat broiler.

2. Cut 2 circles out of each slice of bread with a small cookie cutter or champagne glass. Discard the crusts.

3. Mix the Dijon mustard, apples, and cheddar cheese together in a bowl.

4. Spread the apple mixture onto each round evenly and place on a foil-lined baking sheet. Broil for 3 to 5 minutes, until cheese melts. Let cool a bit before eating.

Caramel Nut Apple Wedges

*Another way to serve this is to arrange the undipped apple wedges on a
platter and let diners dip their own apples into the caramel and hazelnuts.
This becomes a fondue. However, the caramel may be superhot,
so be careful. Nuts and apples give you some fiber.*

Serves 6

Calories: 596.46
Protein: 10.28 grams
Carbohydrates: 81.33 grams
Fiber: 7.16 grams
Fat: 29.78 grams

*1 pound of caramels,
unwrapped
¼ cup evaporated milk
2 cups chopped hazelnuts
2 red apples
1 Golden Delicious apple
2 Granny Smith apples*

1. Melt the caramels and evaporated milk over low heat.

2. Toast the hazelnuts in the oven for 12 minutes at 350°F.

3. Cut the apples into quarters, cut out the cores, and cut the quarters into slices for dipping.

4. Dip the apple wedges into the caramel and then in the hazelnuts. Place the wedges on waxed paper.

5. Refrigerate for 15 minutes or until caramel is set.

Celery–Peanut Butter Boats

*Great for a picnic or potluck, these are a good way
to get children to eat raw vegetables.*

Serves 4

Calories: 217.56
Protein: 8.67 grams
Carbohydrates: 9.41 grams
Fiber: 3.47 grams
Fat: 17.96 grams

*4 ribs of celery, washed or
    wiped clean*
½ cup crunchy peanut butter
*2 tablespoons toasted
    sesame seeds*

1. Fill celery ribs with peanut butter and smooth out the top.

2. Cut the celery on the diagonal in to 1" slices.

3. Sprinkle the sesame seeds over the bites and serve.

Snacking with Celery

Crisp and spicy, celery is perfect with savory or slightly sweet fillings. Celery adds fiber to anything you pile into it, and its crunch is important in snacks. Fill it with light cream cheese and seeds or chopped toasted nuts. In a pinch, dip it in salad dressing. Celery will give your colon exactly what it needs. Fortunately, it's low in calories and tastes wonderful.

Energy Balls

*These yummy bites are great to have on hand for quick energy,
especially for kids. There's good protein in the peanut butter and milk.
The peanut butter, oats, raisins, and corn flakes give this snack high fiber.*

Serves 12

Calories: 190.92
Protein: 6.35 grams
Carbohydrates: 31.23 grams
Fiber: 2.19 grams
Fat: 5.76 grams

½ cup honey
½ cup peanut butter
1 cup nonfat dry milk
1 cup uncooked quick-cook
    rolled oats
½ cup raisins
2 cups crushed corn flakes
    cereal

1. Mix the honey and peanut butter together.

2. Add the dry milk, oats, and raisins. Mix together well.

3. Roll the mixture into 2 dozen balls.

4. Roll the balls in the crushed cereal.

5. Cover and refrigerate.

Oat Cakes

*These are like a bowl of oatmeal to go. They're a great alternative
to purchased energy bars. You get protein from the egg
and yogurt and lots of fiber from the oatmeal and apricots.*

1. Preheat oven to 325°F.

2. Pulse the oats in a food processor 10 times, then add the flour and baking soda and pulse to mix.

3. In a bowl, whisk the egg white until frothy, then add the yogurt, sugar, honey, and vanilla. Add the oat mixture and dried apricots to the yogurt mixture. Mix with a wooden spoon.

4. Roll the mixture into 8 balls and flatten them into thick, cylindrical patties.

5. Bake them on a parchment-lined baking sheet for 15–20 minutes. Let cool and refrigerate unless eating right away.

Serves 8

Calories: 377.55
Protein: 9.22 grams
Carbohydrates: 80.72 grams
Fiber: 4.59 grams
Fat: 2.56 grams

3 cups rolled oats
2 cups flour
¼ teaspoon baking powder
1 egg white
⅓ cup plain yogurt
½ cup sugar
½ cup honey
½ teaspoon vanilla extract
*½ cup dried apricots,
    chopped*

Pretzel Gorp

Serves 8
Serving Size ½ cup

Calories: 210.70
Protein: 6.50 grams
Carbohydrates: 27.44 grams
Fiber: 3.23 grams
Fat: 9.75 grams

2 cups small pretzel twists
1 cup raisins
1 cup roasted peanuts

*Adding pretzels to Good Old Raisins and Peanuts (GORP)
gives another dimension to this classic snack.
Here you get some extra crunch along with your fiber and protein.*

Combine everything in a large bowl and serve.

Banana Malted Soymilk Shake

Serves 2
Serving Size 8 ounces

Calories: 329.57
Protein: 9.46 grams
Carbohydrates: 67.38 grams
Fiber: 4.93 grams
Fat: 4.13 grams

2 bananas
2 tablespoons malt powder
1 cup vanilla frozen yogurt
½ cup soymilk
1 teaspoon honey

*Malted milk and bananas are good. The bananas are the
prime source of fiber in this lovely smoothie. If you like chocolate,
make this using chocolate frozen yogurt instead of vanilla.*

Place all ingredients in a blender and blend until smooth.

Date Milkshake

This is a smooth and creamy milkshake with lots of fiber and natural date sugar. It makes a great breakfast smoothie with loads of fiber and protein as well as flavor.

Serves 2
Serving Size 12 ounces

Calories: 643.95
Protein: 19.60 grams
Carbohydrates: 131.64 grams
Fiber: 8.74 grams
Fat: 8.36 grams

1 cup chopped dates
1 cup milk
1 banana, peeled
1 cup plain yogurt
¼ cup orange juice
1 pint vanilla frozen yogurt

1. To soften the dates, soak them in the milk for 30 minutes.

2. Purée the dates and milk in a blender, then add the banana and blend.

3. Add the yogurt, orange juice, and frozen yogurt and blend until smooth.

Yogurt Is a Carrier for Fibers

Many great fibers are very dry. These include dried fruits, seeds, and nuts. However, when these nourishing dry ingredients are mixed with some yogurt, they slip right down the hatch without any problems. Lots of little children have trouble swallowing too-dry foods. Add some yogurt to their high-fiber snacks and they will be very happily nourished.

Red Bean Ice-Cream Shake

Serves 2
Serving Size 16 ounces

Calories: 634.89
Protein: 23.24 grams
Carbohydrates: 80.52 grams
Fiber: 17.07 grams
Fat: 26.19 grams

1 pint vanilla ice cream
1½ cups red bean paste
1 cup milk

Red bean paste is a sweetened purée found in Asian groceries.
You can make your own by puréeing a can of red beans and adding honey
to taste. Substitute red bean ice cream for the paste if available.
Red bean paste is an excellent source of both protein and fiber.
There is some protein in the ice cream and milk.

Combine everything in a blender and blend until smooth.

Make Your Own

To make your own sweet red beans, which can be puréed in a food processor to make red bean paste, soak 1 cup dried adzuki beans in water overnight. Drain and put the beans in a saucepan with 4 cups water and simmer for 1½ hours. Stir in ½ cup sugar and cook for 10 more minutes, stirring often. Squash the beans with a wooden spoon in the saucepan and stir to thicken. Remove from heat and purée in a food processor for a smoother paste. Chill in the refrigerator before using.

Chapter 17
Yeast Breads

Whole-Wheat Pita Bread

The famous Middle Eastern flatbread is made with whole-wheat flour in this recipe. Pita is one of the most useful breads for snacks, lunches, and suppers. The whole wheat gives this recipe fiber and protein as well as B-vitamins.

Serves 6
Serving Size 1 pita

Calories: 131.72
Protein: 4.43 grams
Carbohydrates: 27.01 grams
Fiber: 2.51 grams
Fat: 0.89 grams

½ packet yeast
¾ cup warm water
1½ teaspoons olive oil
½ teaspoon salt
1 cup all-purpose flour
¾ cup whole-wheat flour

1. Combine yeast with the warm water and stir. Add olive oil and salt and mix. Combine all-purpose and whole-wheat flours in another bowl. Add 1¼ cups flour mixture to yeast mixture and combine with a wooden spoon. Add another ¼ cup flour mixture and mix with hands to form dough.

2. Knead dough on a floured board for 10 minutes, adding the remaining flour mixture as needed to prevent sticking. (Use more all-purpose flour if necessary.)

3. Cover and let dough rise in an oiled bowl for 90 minutes in a warm place. Punch down dough and divide it into 6 pieces. Roll them into balls, cover, and let rest 5 minutes.

4. Roll the balls into 6" flat rounds on a floured board. Cover and let rest again for 15 minutes.

5. Preheat the oven to 500°F and place 2 pitas on a baking sheet. Bake for 5 to 10 minutes. Repeat for the next batch. Bake them in the oven for 3 to 5 minutes (the preheated pan will make the baking time less). Repeat with the remaining 2 rounds.

Whole-Wheat Bread

This is a basic loaf of bread that can be used for sandwiches or toast or used to make stuffing and croutons. The fiber is in the wheat flour. Throw in 2 ounces of wheat germ to give it more fiber and nutrition.

1. Combine yeast, ½ teaspoon sugar, and ⅓ cup water in a bowl. Let sit for 5 minutes.

2. In a mixing bowl combine remaining water, butter, remaining sugar, salt, and baking powder. Mix in the all-purpose flour, followed by the yeast mixture with an electric mixer. Add the whole-wheat flour and knead with dough hook for 10 minutes.

3. Turn dough into an oiled bowl. Cover and set in a warm place. Let rise for 1 to 2 hours until doubled in bulk.

4. Punch down dough, then shape into a cylinder and place in an oiled loaf pan. Cover and let rise in a warm place for 90 minutes until doubled in size.

5. Preheat oven to 350°F. Uncover and bake for 40 minutes.

Whole-Wheat to Whole-Grain Bread

You can add all kinds of grains to your whole-wheat bread. Mix in some ground corn, millet, wheat bran flakes, ground soy or soy flour, and malt. You can sweeten the bread with honey, maple syrup, or red bean paste. The flavors expand geometrically, and the grainy texture makes fabulous toast, French toast, and sandwiches. Giving your body what it needs is not that hard; it simply takes a little time and thought.

Serves 8
Serving Size 1 slice

Calories: 247.39
Protein: 6.80 grams
Carbohydrates: 44.94 grams
Fiber: 4.12 grams
Fat: 5.11 grams

1 packet yeast
3 tablespoons sugar
1⅓ cups warm water
3 tablespoons soft butter
1 teaspoon salt
¼ teaspoon baking powder
1¾ cups all-purpose flour
1¾ cups whole-wheat flour

Multigrain Bread

*Whole-wheat flour, rolled oats, sunflower seeds, and millet
are the grains in this hearty loaf. The fiber comes from whole wheat,
millet, oats, and sunflower seeds. They all add some protein too.*

Serves 8
Serving Size 1 slice

Calories: 281.71
Protein: 8.20 grams
Carbohydrates: 45.74 grams
Fiber: 4.70 grams
Fat: 7.96 grams

1 packet yeast
3 tablespoons sugar
1⅓ cups warm water
3 tablespoons soft butter
1 teaspoon salt
¼ teaspoon baking powder
1½ cups all-purpose flour
1½ cups whole-wheat flour
½ cup rolled oats
¼ cup sunflower seeds
2 tablespoons uncooked
    millet

1. Combine yeast, ½ teaspoon sugar, and ⅓ cup water in a bowl. Let sit for 5 minutes.

2. In a mixing bowl combine remaining water, butter, remaining sugar, salt, and baking powder. Mix in the all-purpose flour, followed by the yeast mixture, with an electric mixer. Add the whole-wheat flour, rolled oats, sunflower seeds, and millet. Knead with a dough hook for 10 minutes.

3. Turn dough into an oiled bowl and let sit in a warm place. Cover and let rise for 1 to 2 hours until doubled in bulk.

4. Punch down dough, then shape it into a cylinder, and place it in an oiled loaf pan. Cover and let rise in a warm place for 90 minutes until doubled in size.

5. Preheat oven to 350°F, uncover bread, and bake for 40 minutes.

Friendship Bread

This bread is a fun project that takes a couple weeks to complete, but the result is well worth the wait. This recipe is an adaptation of the one my daughter's friend gave her. It's got plenty of flavor and some fiber.

1. For the starter, dissolve the yeast in the warm water in a nonmetal bowl. Stir in the all-purpose flour, sugar, and milk with a wooden spoon. Cover loosely and let sit at room temperature, stirring once a day for 3 days.
2. On the fourth day, stir in 1 cup each of flour, sugar, and milk. Stir once a day for the next 4 days.
3. On the eighth day, stir in 1 cup each of flour, sugar, and milk. Place 1 cup of the mixture into a 1-gallon plastic zipper bag and leave it out at room temperature. Divide the remaining starter in two and give to two friends.
4. Squish the bag once a day for the next 4 days, letting air out as needed. Keep the starter at room temperature.
5. On the thirteenth day, add 1 cup each of flour, sugar, and milk. Squish the bag and leave at room temperature. Squish the bag once a day for the next 3 days, letting air out as needed.
6. On the sixteenth day, empty the bag into a large nonmetal bowl and add 1½ cups each of flour, milk, and sugar. Mix well, then take 4 cups of the mixture out of the bowl. Divide the 4 cups into four 1-gallon plastic zipper freezer bags. Seal out the air. Date the bags and give two of them away to friends with a copy of the recipe. Use one bag to complete the recipe. Save one bag as the starter for the next batch. (Freeze it until you want to make the next batch; leave at room temperature for step 4 to make more starters.)
7. Preheat oven to 325°F. Butter two 9" × 5" loaf pans and set aside. Add the eggs, oil, applesauce, milk, 1 cup sugar, 2 teaspoons cinnamon, baking powder, baking soda, salt, whole-wheat flour, all-purpose flour, and pudding mix to the remaining starter in the bowl. Mix well and pour the batter into the prepared loaf pans.
8. Combine 1 teaspoon cinnamon with ¼ cup sugar and sprinkle it on top of the batter. Bake for 60 minutes. Cool on a rack.

Serves 16
Serving Size 1 slice

Calories: 279.46
Protein: 3.47 grams
Carbohydrates: 49.94 grams
Fiber: 1.35 grams
Fat: 8.00 grams

Starter:
¼ ounce package yeast
¼ cup warm water
1 cup all-purpose flour
1 cup sugar
1 cup whole milk

Days 4, 8, and 13:
1 cup all-purpose flour
1 cup sugar
1 cup whole milk

Day 16:
1½ cups all-purpose flour
1½ cups sugar
1½ cups whole milk

Final Day:
1 tablespoon soft butter
3 eggs, beaten
½ cup vegetable oil
½ cup applesauce
½ cup milk
1¼ cups sugar, divided
3 teaspoons cinnamon, divided
½ teaspoon baking powder
½ teaspoon baking soda
½ teaspoon salt
1 cup whole-wheat flour
1 cup all-purpose flour
1 large box instant vanilla pudding mix

Individual Stollens

Stollen is a German holiday bread studded with dried fruits and nuts. This version is baked in muffin tins instead of the traditional loaf shape. It uses the same batter as the Friendship Bread (page 241), so you can make one loaf of that and make this recipe with the other half of the batter. It's deliciously loaded with fiber in the nuts and fruit.

1. Soak the currants and raisins in the rum for 2 hours.

2. Preheat oven to 325°F. Line 12 muffin tin cups with fluted paper liners.

3. Mix the almond extract, nutmeg, and rum-soaked dried fruit into the prepared Friendship Bread batter. Stir in the almonds and candied lemon peel.

4. Fill the muffin tin cups ¾ full with the batter.

5. Bake for 15 minutes. Let cool and dust with powdered sugar to serve.

Holiday Breads

These yummy gifts are easily made in advance and frozen with a quick warm-up at the last minute. You can use any and all of your favorite nuts. Dried fruits and candied fruits are excellent. Some regional specialties add saffron to the bread to give it a beautiful golden color.

Serves 12
Serving Size 1

Calories: 233.52
Protein: 3.945 grams
Carbohydrates: 38.64 grams
Fiber: 5.49 grams
Fat: 8.17 grams

½ cup dried currants
½ cup golden raisins
½ cup dark rum
½ teaspoon almond extract
¼ teaspoon nutmeg
1 cup Friendship Bread (page 241, step 6)
¾ cup chopped almonds
¼ cup chopped candied lemon peel
¼ cup powdered sugar

Raisin Foccacia

*This is the bread to use when making the Walnut Tarragon
Chicken Salad sandwich (page 56). You can use fresh or dried rosemary.
The bread garners its fiber from raisins.*

Serves 8

Calories: 535.94
Protein: 12.96 grams
Carbohydrates: 102.61 grams
Fiber: 4.83 grams
Fat: 8.05 grams

*2 packets yeast
1 teaspoon honey
2½ cups warm water
4 cups flour
3 tablespoons olive oil
1 tablespoon salt
1 cup raisins
½ cup chopped scallions
additional olive oil for pan
    and top of dough*

1. Combine yeast, honey, and warm water in a mixing bowl and let it sit for 5 minutes.

2. Add 2 cups flour, olive oil, and salt. Mix for 2 minutes, then let sit for 10 minutes.

3. Add remaining 2 cups flour, raisins, and green onions. Mix with dough hook for 5 minutes. Let dough rise covered in an oiled bowl for 60 minutes in a warm place.

4. Punch down dough, then stretch and press it out onto a well-oiled 11" × 18" sheet pan. Cover and let rise in a warm place for 60 minutes.

5. Preheat oven to 400°F. Uncover dough and drizzle with olive oil. Poke holes all over the dough with your fingertips and bake for 25 minutes. Cool on a rack.

Foccacia

Richly redolent with olive oil and herbs, this foccacia also tastes great with nuts. A typically Italian version of foccacia has toasted pine nuts and several dried Mediterranean herbs. It's excellent as a dinner bread, a sandwich bread, or spread with fruit preserves for breakfast. Leftovers can be made into bread salad or pudding.

Shallot-Walnut Herb Bread

This flavorful loaf is perfect with a cheese plate, fruit, and paté. Set it out with the cheese and fruit for a light lunch. The excellent fiber comes from whole-wheat flour, shallot, and walnuts. The fresh sage and thyme add color and flavor but not a great deal of fiber.

Serves 8
Serving Size 1 slice

Calories: 306.64
Protein: 8.78 grams
Carbohydrates: 46.98 grams
Fiber: 4.58grams
Fat: 10.36 grams

1 packet yeast
3 tablespoons maple syrup
1⅓ cups warm water
3 tablespoons walnut oil
1 teaspoon salt
¼ teaspoon baking powder
1¾ cups all-purpose flour
1¾ cups whole-wheat flour
1 shallot, minced
½ cup chopped walnuts
1 tablespoon minced fresh sage
1 tablespoon minced fresh thyme

1. Combine yeast, ½ teaspoon maple syrup, and ⅓ cup water in a bowl. Let sit for 5 minutes.

2. In a mixing bowl combine remaining water, walnut oil, remaining maple syrup, salt, and baking powder. Mix in the all-purpose flour, then the yeast mixture with an electric mixer. Add the whole-wheat flour, shallot, walnuts, and herbs. Knead with a dough hook for 10 minutes.

3. Turn dough into an oiled bowl. Cover and let rise for 1 to 2 hours until doubled in bulk in a warm place.

4. Punch down dough, then shape into a cylinder and place in an oiled loaf pan. Cover and let rise in a warm place for 90 minutes until doubled in size.

5. Preheat oven to 350°F. Uncover bread and bake for 40 minutes.

Olive Bread

Serve this bread dressed with olive oil and softened cheese for a cocktail snack. The fiber comes in deliciously with the olives and whole-wheat flour.

1. Combine yeast, ½ teaspoon honey, and ⅓ cup water in a bowl. Let sit for 5 minutes.

2. In a mixing bowl combine remaining water, olive oil, remaining honey, salt, and baking powder. Mix in the all-purpose flour, then the yeast mixture with an electric mixer. Add the whole-wheat flour, olives, and thyme. Knead with a dough hook for 10 minutes.

3. Turn dough into an oiled bowl. Cover and let rise in a warm place for 1 to 2 hours until doubled in bulk.

4. Punch down dough, then shape into a cylinder and place in an oiled loaf pan. Cover and let rise in a warm place for 90 minutes until doubled in size.

5. Preheat oven to 350°F. Uncover bread and bake for 40 minutes.

Mediterranean Breads

Olive oil, olives, nuts, dried fruits, herbs, and nuts make Mediterranean breads more than just bread. Adding corn, barley, brown rice flour, and other goodies adds to the nutritional value and fiber in these breads. You can take any recipe and adapt it with your favorite flavors and ingredients. Try adding chestnut flour for a very Italian experience.

Serves 8
Serving Size 1 slice

Calories: 284.32
Protein: 6.95 grams
Carbohydrates: 47.73 grams
Fiber: 4.29 grams
Fat: 8.09 grams

1 packet yeast
3 tablespoons honey
1⅓ cups warm water
3 tablespoons olive oil
1 teaspoon salt
¼ teaspoon baking powder
1¾ cups all-purpose flour
1¾ cups whole-wheat flour
1 cup pitted Niçoise olives
2 tablespoons minced fresh thyme

Pecan Bread

*Chicken, tuna, or egg salad sandwiches made with this
bread are great for a brown bag lunch or picnic. You can also slice it
thinly for tea sandwiches filled with cream cheese and cucumber.
Whole wheat and pecans add plenty of fiber.*

Serves 8
Serving Size 1 slice

Calories: 401.57
Protein: 8.85 grams
Carbohydrates: 48.03 grams
Fiber: 6.27 grams
Fat: 21.17 grams

1 packet yeast
3 tablespoons sugar
1⅓ cups warm water
3 tablespoons soft butter
1 teaspoon salt
¼ teaspoon baking powder
1¾ cups all-purpose flour
1¾ cups whole-wheat flour
1½ cups chopped pecans

1. Combine yeast, ½ teaspoon sugar, and ⅓ cup water in a bowl. Let sit for 5 minutes.

2. In a mixing bowl combine remaining water, butter, remaining sugar, salt, and baking powder. Mix in the all-purpose flour and then the yeast mixture with an electric mixer. Add the whole-wheat flour and pecans. Knead with a dough hook for 10 minutes.

3. Turn dough into an oiled bowl, cover, and let rise in a warm place for 1–2 hours until doubled in bulk.

4. Punch down dough, then shape into a cylinder and place in an oiled loaf pan. Cover and let rise in a warm place for 90 minutes until doubled in size.

5. Preheat oven to 350°F. Uncover bread and bake for 40 minutes.

Cinnamon-Swirl Raisin Bread

*Toast this bread for breakfast for a healthy start to a long workday
or spread blue cheese and drizzle honey on toast points with Poached Pears
(page 163). The whole-wheat flour gives you both protein and fiber,
and the raisins add flavor and fiber.*

Serves 8
Serving Size 1 slice

Calories: 301.04
Protein: 7.26 grams
Carbohydrates: 59.16 grams
Fiber: 5.36 grams
Fat: 5.21 grams

1 packet yeast
3 tablespoons sugar
1⅓ cups warm water
3 tablespoons soft butter
1 teaspoon salt
¼ teaspoon baking powder
1¾ cups all-purpose flour
1¾ cups whole-wheat flour
1 cup raisins
3 tablespoons cinnamon

1. Combine yeast, ½ teaspoon sugar, and ⅓ cup water in a bowl. Let sit for 5 minutes.

2. In a mixing bowl combine remaining water, butter, remaining sugar, salt, and baking powder. Mix in the all-purpose flour and then the yeast mixture with an electric mixer. Add the whole-wheat flour and raisins. Knead with dough hook for 10 minutes.

3. Turn dough into an oiled bowl, cover and let rise in a warm place for 1–2 hours until doubled in bulk.

4. Punch down dough, then roll into a rectangle. Sprinkle the cinnamon over the dough, roll it into a cylinder, and place in an oiled loaf pan. Cover and let rise in a warm place for 90 minutes until doubled in size.

5. Preheat oven to 350°F. Uncover bread and bake for 40 minutes.

Multigrain Dinner Rolls

Serves 12
Serving Size 1 roll

Calories: 249.23
Protein: 7.91 grams
Carbohydrates: 35.23 grams
Fiber: 3.44 grams
Fat: 9.01 grams

1 packet yeast
3 tablespoons warm water
1 cup warm milk
2½ ounces melted butter
1 teaspoon salt
1 egg, beaten
3 tablespoons sugar
2 cups all-purpose flour
1¾ cups whole-wheat flour
¼ cup rolled oats
1 egg, beaten
½ cup sunflower seeds

Whole-wheat flour, rolled oats, and sunflower seeds make up the multiple grains in these fiber-rich dinner rolls. They are also delicious with butter, herbed olive oil, or cream cheese.

1. Combine yeast and water and let sit for 5 minutes to proof.

2. Add milk, butter, salt, egg, and sugar to the yeast mixture. Mix well.

3. Stir in the all-purpose flour with a wooden spoon or the paddle attachment to an electric stand mixer. Gradually add whole-wheat flour and rolled oats. Knead with a dough hook for 10 minutes. Put dough in an oiled bowl, cover and let rise in a warm place for 90 minutes.

4. Punch down dough, divide into 12 pieces, and roll each piece in a ball. Place dough balls on a greased baking sheet. Cover and let rise until doubled, about 60 minutes.

5. Preheat oven to 350°F. Uncover rolls, brush with egg, and sprinkle with sunflower seeds. Bake for 15 minutes.

Popcorn Bread

*This is a fun and light bread. Loaded with corn fiber, it's excellent
with apple butter. Be sure to pick out any unpopped corn kernels before
mincing the popcorn in the food processor.*

1. Mix the water, milk, sugar, and yeast in a mixing bowl. Let sit for 10 minutes.

2. Meanwhile, mince the popcorn in a food processor by pulsing until it reaches the consistency of cornmeal. Add it with the salt to the yeast mixture. Stir and add the egg and 2 tablespoons melted butter, beating with an electric mixer.

3. Stir in the flour and then knead with a dough hook or by hand on a floured surface for 10 minutes. Oil a large bowl, place the dough in the bowl, and turn to coat. Cover the bowl and let the dough rise in a warm place for 30 minutes.

4. Punch the dough down and let rise another 30 minutes. Shape the dough into a loaf and place in a 9" × 13" loaf pan that has been brushed with 1 tablespoon butter. Cover and let rise 60 minutes.

5. Preheat oven to 350°F. Uncover the loaf and bake it for 35–40 minutes. Brush with 1 tablespoon butter and let cool.

Serves 8
Serving Size 1 slice

Calories: 235.23
Protein: 5.23 grams
Carbohydrates: 37.94 grams
Fiber: 1.35 grams
Fat: 6.85 grams

⅓ cup boiling water
⅓ cup cold milk
¼ cup sugar
½ package dry yeast
1½ cups popcorn
⅓ teaspoon salt
1 egg, beaten
4 tablespoons melted butter, divided
2½ cups all-purpose flour

Whole-Wheat Hamburger Buns

*These buns are a good way to add more fiber to a cheeseburger
or veggie burger. They also make good sandwich rolls for mixed deli meats.
The ginger adds a lot of flavor.*

Serves 6
Serving Size 1

Calories: 308.71
Protein: 9.66 grams
Carbohydrates: 53.78 grams
Fiber: 5.51 grams
Fat: 6.82 grams

1 packet yeast
3 tablespoons sugar
pinch of dried ginger
1⅓ cups warm water
3 tablespoons soft butter
1 teaspoon salt
¼ teaspoon baking powder
1¾ cups all-purpose flour
1¾ cups whole-wheat flour
1 egg, beaten

1. Combine yeast, ½ teaspoon sugar, ginger, and ⅓ cup water in a bowl. Let sit for 5 minutes.

2. In a mixing bowl combine remaining water, butter, remaining sugar, salt, and baking powder. Mix in the all-purpose flour and then the yeast mixture with an electric mixer. Add whole-wheat flour. Knead with a dough hook for 10 minutes.

3. Turn dough into an oiled bowl. Cover and let rise in a warm place for 1 to 2 hours until doubled in bulk.

4. Punch down dough, then divide into 6 pieces, and shape into buns. Cover and let rise in a warm place for 1½ hours until doubled in size.

5. Preheat oven to 350°F. Uncover buns, gently brush with egg, and bake for 20 minutes.

Yeast Breads

Yeast has its own special flavor and aroma. It will stand up to fruits, nuts, and olives better than baking powder quick breads. It's also much more fun to knead, push, pull, and work with as it develops. If you've never kneaded a good yeast dough, try it sometime—it's good for developing a sense of peace and well-being.

Apple Bread

Moist and full of apples, this bread is a great snack with a piece of cheddar cheese. You give your family fiber with great flavor coming from the whole-wheat flour and apples.

1. Combine yeast, ½ teaspoon sugar, and ⅓ cup water in a bowl. Let sit for 5 minutes.

2. In a mixing bowl combine remaining water, butter, remaining sugar, salt, and baking powder. Mix in the all-purpose flour and then the yeast mixture with an electric mixer. Add the whole-wheat flour. Knead with a dough hook for 10 minutes.

3. Turn dough into an oiled bowl. Cover and let rise in a warm place for 1 to 2 hours until doubled in bulk.

4. Punch down dough, then roll it into a rectangle. Scatter the apples over the dough and sprinkle them with the cinnamon sugar. Roll into a cylinder and place in an oiled loaf pan. Cover and let it rise in a warm place for 90 minutes until doubled in size.

5. Preheat oven to 350°F. Uncover bread and bake for 50 minutes.

Serves 8
Serving Size 1 slice

Calories: 255.22
Protein: 6.82 grams
Carbohydrates: 46.98 grams
Fiber: 4.39 grams
Fat: 5.16 grams

1 packet yeast
3 tablespoons sugar
1⅓ cups warm water
3 tablespoons soft butter
1 teaspoon salt
¼ teaspoon baking powder
1¾ cups all-purpose flour
1¾ cups whole-wheat flour
1 cup peeled, chopped apples
1 tablespoon cinnamon
    mixed with 1 tablespoon
    sugar

Onion Rye Flatbread

Onions and caraway seeds are only part of the fiber equation in this flatbread. The additional sesame and poppy seeds add to the crunch and fiber. This flatbread is so much healthier than store-bought crackers, and it lends itself to every meat and cheese you enjoy.

Serves 4
Serving Size ¼ flatbread

Calories: 228.66
Protein: 5.33 grams
Carbohydrates: 34.14 grams
Fiber: 2.63 grams
Fat: 7.64 grams

½ package yeast
3 tablespoons warm water
¼ teaspoon sugar
1¼ cups flour, plus more for kneading
2 tablespoons olive oil
¼ cup cool water
¾ teaspoon salt
¼ cup rye flour
½ onion, peeled
1 teaspoon caraway seeds
1 teaspoon sesame seeds
1 teaspoon poppy seeds
pinch of kosher salt
pinch of ground black pepper

1. Combine yeast with the warm water, sugar, and ¼ cup flour. Let sit 10 minutes. Add 1 tablespoon olive oil, cool water, salt, rye flour, and ½ cup flour and combine with a wooden spoon. Add remaining flour and mix to form dough.

2. Knead dough on a floured board for 5 minutes, adding flour as needed to prevent sticking.

3. Cover the dough in an oiled bowl. Let dough rise for 60 minutes in a warm place. Punch down dough and roll it into a tight ball. Cover and let rise for 60 minutes.

4. Meanwhile, dice the onion and mix it with the remaining olive oil, caraway seeds, sesame seeds, poppy seeds, salt, and pepper.

5. Preheat oven to 450°F. Roll the dough into a thin 14" round on a lightly floured surface. Place the dough onto a cornmeal-dusted baking sheet. Poke holes with a fork in the dough.

6. Spread the onion mixture over the dough round and bake for 15 minutes, until crisp. Cut into irregular triangles to serve.

Quick Breads

Strawberry Banana Oatmeal Bread

*This recipe makes a moist pink loaf that has healthful oatmeal,
strawberries, and bananas for fiber and grain.*

1. Preheat oven to 350°F.

2. Spray a 5" × 9" loaf pan with nonstick oil.

3. Combine flour, sugar, baking powder, salt, and oats in a mixing bowl.

4. Add oil, eggs, strawberries, and bananas, and stir together just until combined.

5. Scrape batter into the prepared loaf pan and bake for 60 minutes or until a wooden skewer inserted in the middle comes out clean. Cool on a rack.

Serves 8
Serving Size 1 slice

Calories: 307.14
Protein: 4.75 grams
Carbohydrates: 48.36 grams
Fiber: 2.64 grams
Fat: 11.21 grams

1½ cups all-purpose flour
⅔ cup sugar
2 teaspoons baking powder
½ teaspoon salt
¾ cup quick-cooking oats
⅓ cup canola oil
2 eggs, beaten
½ cup mashed strawberries
½ cup mashed bananas

Grape-Nuts Bread

*Instead of cereal you may substitute chopped nuts,
such as pecans or hazelnuts, for a nutty loaf. The nuts accomplish
the same thing the cereal does: they add fiber to the bread.*

1. Preheat oven to 350°F.

2. Combine the flour, sugar, baking powder, salt, and baking soda in a large mixing bowl.

3. Combine the oil, milk, and egg in another bowl.

4. Add the milk mixture to the flour mixture and stir just to combine. Fold in the cereal and scrape the batter into an oiled 9" × 5" × 3" loaf pan.

5. Bake for 60 minutes, cool on a rack, and wrap when cool.

Serves 8
Serving Size 1 slice

Calories: 361.53
Protein: 6.92 grams
Carbohydrates: 66.40 grams
Fiber: 2.57 grams
Fat: 8.37 grams

2 cups all-purpose flour
1 cup sugar
1½ teaspoons baking powder
1 teaspoon salt
½ teaspoon baking soda
¼ cup canola oil
¾ cup milk
1 egg, beaten
1½ cups Grape-Nuts cereal

Cranberry Orange Tea Bread

*This bread can be baked, cooled, sliced, wrapped, and frozen to serve later.
The cranberries give it a fine amount of fiber, and the orange adds to the flavor.*

1. Preheat oven to 350°F.

2. Combine the flour, sugar, baking powder, salt, and baking soda in a large mixing bowl.

3. Combine the oil, orange juice, egg, and orange zest in another bowl.

4. Add the juice mixture to the flour mixture and stir just to combine. Fold in the cranberries and scrape the batter into an oiled 9" × 5" × 3" loaf pan.

5. Bake for 60 minutes, cool on a rack, and wrap when cool.

Quick Breads

Quick breads are leavened with baking power and/or baking soda rather than yeast. They don't have to sit and rise. You can bake them as soon as the dough is made. You can use all kinds of different grains, nuts, fruits, and vegetables in quick breads. Try substituting various kinds of flour for whole wheat, and your family will be surprised each time you make bread.

Serves 8
Serving Size 1 slice

Calories: 291.92
Protein: 3.91 grams
Carbohydrates: 53.64 grams
Fiber: 1.63 grams
Fat: 7.20 grams

2 cups all-purpose flour
1 cup sugar
1½ teaspoons baking powder
1 teaspoon salt
½ teaspoon baking soda
¼ cup canola oil
¾ cup orange juice
1 egg, beaten
*2 tablespoons grated orange
    zest*
1 cup cranberries, chopped

Blueberry Graham Coffeecake

Serves 12
Serving Size 1 piece

Calories: 457.79
Protein: 5.02 grams
Carbohydrates: 64.97 grams
Fiber: 1.80 grams
Fat: 20.71 grams

½ cup brown sugar
2 teaspoons cinnamon
2⅓ cups all-purpose flour
1 cup butter
1½–2 cups sugar
3 eggs
1 cup graham cracker crumbs
2 teaspoons baking powder
1 teaspoon baking soda
½ teaspoon salt
1 cup sour cream
2 cups blueberries

Graham flour is a slightly coarser grind than whole-wheat flour because it has the bran and germ layers of the wheat kernel's endosperm mixed in, which makes a coarse, brown flour with a nutty and slightly sweet flavor.

1. Preheat oven to 350°F; then butter a Bundt pan.

2. Make filling by combining the brown sugar, cinnamon, ⅓ cup all-purpose flour, and ¼ cup butter with fingertips until crumbly. Set aside.

3. For batter, cream together ¾ cup butter and sugar until fluffy. Add eggs, one at a time, and beat them in to form a smooth batter.

4. In a separate bowl, whisk together 2 cups flour, 1 cup graham cracker crumbs, baking powder, baking soda, and salt. Add flour mixture alternately with sour cream to the butter-egg mixture until fully incorporated. Fold in the blueberries, then layer half the batter in the Bundt pan, sprinkle it with the filling mixture, and layer the rest of the batter on top.

5. Bake for 50 minutes, or until a toothpick inserted in the middle comes out clean.

Graham Crumbs

Use graham crumbs whenever you can. Adding the wheat in this coarse form compensates for the butter and sour cream in many cake and cookie recipes. If you don't have graham crumbs handy, add wheat germ for fiber and vitamins. The sweet flavor of graham also allows you to cut back on the sugar in any cake or cookie recipe. Adding berries is also important to the fiber quotient.

Dried Fig–Anise Bread

Other dried figs to consider for this bread are the Calimyrna and Smyrna. All dried figs are chewy, sweet, and high in fiber. Incorporate figs in your cooking and baking whenever you can find them in the market.

Serves 8
Serving Size 1 slice

Calories: 347.70
Protein: 4.48 grams
Carbohydrates: 68.02 grams
Fiber: 3.79 grams
Fat: 7.45 grams

2 cups all-purpose flour
1 cup sugar
1½ teaspoons baking powder
1 teaspoon salt
½ teaspoon baking soda
¼ cup canola oil
¾ cup apple juice
1 egg, beaten
1 cup chopped dried black mission figs
½ teaspoon anise seed

1. Preheat oven to 350°F.

2. Mix together the flour, sugar, baking powder, salt, and baking soda in a large mixing bowl.

3. Combine the oil, apple juice, egg, figs, and anise seed in another bowl.

4. Add the juice mixture to the flour mixture and stir just to combine. Scrape the batter into an oiled 9" × 5" × 3" loaf pan.

5. Bake for 60 minutes, cool on a rack, and wrap when cool.

What's in a Name?
The Calimyrna fig is California's version of the Smyrna fig, which is indigenous to the town of the same name in Turkey. It is golden in its dried form. Mission figs, which are purple on the outside when fresh, are black when dried.

Date Nut Bread

*This is another excellent snacking bread for breakfast
or with cheese. If you can stand to wait, wrap it and
let it sit for a day before slicing to let the bread settle.*

Serves 8
Serving Size 1 slice

Calories: 396.31
Protein: 4.95 grams
Carbohydrates: 68.91 grams
Fiber: 3.27 grams
Fat: 12.62 grams

2 cups all-purpose flour
1 cup sugar
1½ teaspoons baking powder
1 teaspoon salt
½ teaspoon baking soda
¼ cup canola oil
¾ cup orange juice
1 egg, beaten
1 cup chopped dates
½ cup chopped pecans

1. Preheat oven to 350°F.

2. Mix together the flour, sugar, baking powder, salt, and baking soda in a large mixing bowl.

3. Combine the oil, orange juice, and egg in another bowl.

4. Add the juice mixture to the flour mixture and stir just to combine. Fold in the dates and pecans and scrape the batter into an oiled 9" × 5" × 3" loaf pan.

5. Bake for 60 minutes, cool on a rack, and wrap when cool.

Cornbread

The corn and cornmeal make this a high-fiber bread, and adding a diced red bell pepper to the batter will add color and vitamin C.

Serves 12
Serving Size 1 piece

Calories: 351.92
Protein: 4.80 grams
Carbohydrates: 26.42 grams
Fiber: 1.45 grams
Fat: 23.77 grams

1. Preheat oven to 350°F. Grease a 9" × 11" brownie pan, then dust it with cornmeal.

2. Combine cornmeal, flour, sugar, salt, and baking powder in a bowl.

3. In another bowl, mix together egg yolks, cream, half-and-half, and corn kernels.

4. Mix the dry ingredients with the wet ingredients and let sit for 20 minutes. Stir again after 20 minutes.

5. In a separate bowl, whip egg whites to soft peaks. Fold whipped egg whites into batter, then fold in melted butter. Pour batter into prepared pan and bake 20–25 minutes.

1¼ cups cornmeal
¾ cup cake flour
¾ cup sugar
1 tablespoon salt
2¼ teaspoons baking powder
3 egg yolks
1 cup cream
1¼ cups half-and-half
1 cup corn kernels
3 egg whites
⅞ cup melted butter

Grits-Cornmeal-Polenta-Corn Flour

Cornmeal is ground in coarse, medium coarse, and fine grades. The finest is flour or starch. The next finest is your usual grainy stuff that is about the consistency of coarse salt. You use this for polenta, cornbread, and corn cake. The coarsest cornmeal is used for grits and polenta. Cornmeal is available in lovely canary yellow, white, and purple. The purple cornmeal is a bit harder to find. They all taste exactly the same and have the same nutritional value.

Pumpkin Cranberry Bread

Serves 8
Serving Size 1 slice

Calories: 274.28
Protein: 3.83 grams
Carbohydrates: 48.17 grams
Fiber: 1.66 grams
Fat: 7.86 grams

1½ cups all-purpose flour
1 cup sugar
1 teaspoon baking powder
1 teaspoon salt
½ teaspoon baking soda
¼ teaspoon cinnamon
¼ teaspoon nutmeg
¼ teaspoon ginger
¼ cup canola oil
¾ cup pumpkin purée
1 egg, beaten
1 cup cranberries, chopped
½ cup shelled pumpkin seeds
   (pepitas)

Pepitas can be found in Hispanic groceries and in many supermarkets.
If you can't find pepitas, substitute walnuts to add protein and fiber.
The pumpkin purée also has a high level of vitamin A.

1. Preheat oven to 350°F.

2. Combine the flour, sugar, baking powder, salt, baking soda, and spices in a large mixing bowl.

3. Combine the oil, pumpkin purée, and egg in another bowl.

4. Add the pumpkin mixture to the flour mixture and stir just to combine. Fold in the cranberries and scrape the batter into an oiled 9" × 5" × 3" loaf pan.

5. Sprinkle the pumpkin seeds on top of the batter and bake for 60 minutes. Cool on a rack and wrap when cool.

Zucchini Bread

This interesting zucchini bread has crunchy pecans and chewy raisins for added flavor and fiber. When you add nuts to any recipe, you also add protein.

1. Preheat oven to 350°F. Oil 2 loaf pans and set aside.

2. Combine the flour, salt, baking soda, baking powder, and cinnamon in a bowl.

3. Mix the eggs, oil, and sugar in another bowl.

4. Add the zucchini and dry ingredients alternately until fully incorporated into a smooth batter. Fold in the pecans and raisins and scrape the batter into the loaf pans.

5. Bake for 60 minutes, cool on a rack, and wrap when cool.

Zucchini and Carrot Bread

Adding vegetables to bread started during World War II when flour was rationed. Resourceful cooks substituted vegetables for flour. Today, we do this to add fiber and flavor to quick breads. Zucchini is a wonderful bread to make when you have a garden that is overproducing zucchini! Make extra loaves and freeze them for a nice treat in December.

Serves 16
Serving Size 1 slice

Calories: 388.19
Protein: 4.10 grams
Carbohydrates: 52.14 grams
Fiber: 2.08 grams
Fat: 19.28 grams

3 cups all-purpose flour
1 teaspoon salt
1 teaspoon baking soda
¼ teaspoon baking powder
1 tablespoon cinnamon
3 eggs, beaten
1 cup canola oil
2 cups sugar
2 cups grated zucchini
1 cup chopped pecans
1 cup raisins

Scallion Spoon Bread

This quick bread has a texture that is like a cross between Cornbread (page 259) and Corn Soufflé Pudding (page 145). The fiber content is very high, and there's protein in the eggs and cheese.

Serves 6
Serving Size 1 cup

Calories: 212.19
Protein: 11.47 grams
Carbohydrates: 18.76 grams
Fiber: 1.48 grams
Fat: 10.19 grams

1 teaspoon corn oil
1 tablespoon butter
2 cups milk
½ cup corn kernels
⅔ cup cornmeal
salt
cayenne pepper
1 cup chopped scallions
1 cup shredded cheddar cheese
4 eggs

1. Preheat oven to 375°F. Oil a 2-quart casserole dish and set aside.

2. Melt butter in a saucepan over low heat. Add the milk, corn kernels, cornmeal, salt, and cayenne pepper and bring to a boil. Lower the heat and simmer for 5 minutes, stirring often.

3. Take off the heat, stir in the scallions and cheese, and let sit for 15 minutes.

4. Meanwhile, separate the eggs and whip the whites to soft peaks. Whisk the egg yolks into the cornmeal mixture, then fold the whipped egg whites in.

5. Scrape the batter into the prepared casserole dish and bake for 30 minutes. Serve warm with a large spoon.

Cracked Wheat Bread

This is an adaptation of a recipe that dates back to 1913, according to an old community cookbook. When traveling, always pick up a regional cookbook as a souvenir; they are often full of gems, loaded with nutrition and fiber.

1. Preheat oven to 325°F.

2. Mix together the flours, brown sugar, baking powder, salt, and baking soda in a large mixing bowl.

3. Combine the oil, buttermilk, and egg in another bowl.

4. Add the buttermilk mixture to the flour mixture and stir just to combine. Scrape the batter into an oiled 9" × 5" × 3" loaf pan.

5. Bake for 45 minutes, cool on a rack, and wrap when cool.

Weekend Breads

Breads naturally have lots of usable soluble fiber, but cracked wheat bread also has insoluble fiber and vitamin B. You can make nutritious spreads for breads by mixing nuts and dried cranberries into whipped cream cheese. Flavored butters also melt nicely into hot breads; try adding a tablespoon of concentrated orange juice to a couple of ounces of softened butter.

Serves 8
Serving Size 1 slice

Calories: 202.36
Protein: 5.45 grams
Carbohydrates: 37.34 grams
Fiber: 2.96 grams
Fat: 4.22 grams

1½ cups whole-wheat flour
½ cup all-purpose flour
½ cup brown sugar
½ teaspoon baking powder
½ teaspoon salt
½ teaspoon baking soda
2 tablespoons canola oil
1 cup buttermilk
1 egg, beaten

Pineapple Cheddar Bread

Serves 8
Serving Size 1 slice

Calories: 329.80
Protein: 7.89 grams
Carbohydrates: 48.08 grams
Fiber: 1.60 grams
Fat: 12.11 grams

2 cups all-purpose flour
¾ cup sugar
1½ teaspoons baking powder
1 teaspoon salt
½ teaspoon baking soda
2 tablespoons canola oil
1 cup crushed pineapple
2 eggs, beaten
¾ cup shredded cheddar
    cheese
½ cup chopped walnuts

This bread is made with sharp white cheddar cheese, but any kind of cheddar or Monterey Jack cheese can be used. This is an excellent bread to have with tea—it's sweet from the pineapple and full of fiber to hold guests over in case dinner is late.

1. Preheat oven to 350°F.

2. Combine the flour, sugar, baking powder, salt, and baking soda in a large mixing bowl.

3. Combine the oil, pineapple, and eggs in another bowl.

4. Add the pineapple mixture to the flour mixture and stir just to combine. Fold in the cheese and nuts and scrape the batter into an oiled 9" × 5" × 3" loaf pan.

5. Bake for 60 minutes, cool on a rack, and slice when cool.

Mincemeat Loaf

*This bread is made with meatless mincemeat, which consists
of raisins and spices. Serve slices with sherry hard sauce for a special occasion.
It's also got more fiber than most special festive breads
because it contains whole-wheat flour.*

Serves 8
Serving Size 1 slice

Calories: 242.03
Protein: 5.90 grams
Carbohydrates: 41.24 grams
Fiber: 2.51 grams
Fat: 6.52 grams

1. Preheat oven to 400°F.

2. Combine the flours, sugar, baking powder, salt, and nutmeg in a large mixing bowl.

3. Combine the butter, buttermilk, eggs, and mincemeat in another bowl.

4. Add the mincemeat mixture to the flour mixture and stir just to combine. Scrape the batter into an oiled 9" × 5" × 3" loaf pan.

5. Bake for 50–60 minutes, cool on a rack, and slice when cool.

1 cup all-purpose flour
¾ cup whole-wheat flour
¼ cup sugar
1 tablespoon baking powder
¼ teaspoon salt
¼ teaspoon nutmeg
2 tablespoons butter, melted
1 cup buttermilk
2 eggs, beaten
1 cup mincemeat

Sherry Hard Sauce

Hard sauce is used on all sorts of heavy bread puddings. It's traditional, delicious, and very fattening. It adds no fiber at all. However, if you decide to go for it, use ½ teaspoon per serving. To make it, combine ½ cup soft unsalted butter with ½ cup powdered sugar and 2 teaspoons sherry with an electric mixer until fluffy and light. Refrigerate until ready to serve.

Peanut Bread

Serves 8
Serving Size 1 slice

Calories: 546.22
Protein: 15.75 grams
Carbohydrates: 61.09 grams
Fiber: 3.72 grams
Fat: 28.78 grams

2 cups all-purpose flour
1 cup brown sugar
1½ teaspoons baking powder
1¼ teaspoons salt
½ teaspoon baking soda
¼ cup peanut oil
¾ cup smooth peanut butter
2 eggs, beaten
1¼ cups milk
1 cup roasted peanuts

This bread is best when made with "homemade" peanut butter like the kind you can grind yourself at a health food store. The crunch and nutritional value of peanuts also ups the fiber of this bread.

1. Preheat oven to 350°F.

2. Combine the flour, brown sugar, baking powder, salt, and baking soda in a large mixing bowl.

3. Combine the oil, peanut butter, eggs, and milk in another bowl.

4. Add the peanut butter mixture to the flour mixture and stir well to combine. Fold in the peanuts and scrape the batter into an oiled 9" × 5" × 3" loaf pan.

5. Bake for 40 minutes, turn the heat down to 325°F, cover with foil, and bake 30 minutes longer. Cool on a rack before slicing.

Parsnip Bread

To cook parsnips for this bread, peel and boil them in water for about 15 minutes, until tender. You will have a nice, sweet, and savory bread with high fiber from the parsnips and whole wheat.

1. Preheat oven to 350°F.

2. Combine the whole-wheat flour, brown sugar, salt, and baking soda in a mixing bowl.

3. Combine the butter, yogurt, eggs, parsnips, and carrots in another bowl.

4. Add the flour mixture to the parsnip mixture and stir to combine. Fold in the chives and scrape the batter into an oiled 9" × 5" × 3" loaf pan.

5. Bake for 60 minutes, cool on a rack, and wrap when cool.

Carrots vs. Sugar

Carrots came to be used in breads and muffins during World War II when sugar was rationed. Carrots are naturally extremely sweet, so you can cut back on the sugar in your recipes and still have a very sweet bread, muffin, or cake. Carrots also add an enormous amount of fiber to any baked product. What used to be considered a stop-gap measure is now considered good nutrition.

Serves 16
Serving Size 1 slice

Calories: 228.86
Protein: 4.15 grams
Carbohydrates: 40.97 grams
Fiber: 3.64 grams
Fat: 6.49 grams

3 cups whole-wheat flour
1½ cups brown sugar
½ teaspoon salt
1 teaspoon baking soda
½ cup butter, melted
½ cup plain yogurt
2 eggs, beaten
2 cups cooked mashed
    parsnips
½ cup grated carrots
2 tablespoons chopped
    chives

Raisin Bran Muffins

A breakfast of a glass of orange juice (with pulp!) and a bran muffin is a delicious way to start your day with fiber. The raisins add sweetness and fiber, and you can substitute whole-wheat flour for all-purpose flour to add even more fiber.

Serves 36

Calories: 113.72
Protein: 2.10 grams
Carbohydrates: 21.33 grams
Fiber: 2.66 grams
Fat: 3.42 grams

1 cup boiling water
2½ cups All-Bran cereal
2½ cups all-purpose flour
2½ teaspoons baking soda
1 teaspoon salt
½ cup vegetable oil
1 cup sugar
2 eggs, beaten
2 cups buttermilk
1½ cups raisins
1 cup bran flakes

1. Preheat oven to 400°F. Grease a muffin tin or line it with fluted paper cups. Pour the boiling water over 1 cup All-Bran, and let sit for 10 minutes.

2. Mix the flour, baking soda, and salt in a mixing bowl and set aside.

3. Mix the oil into the bran and water mixture, then add the remaining bran, sugar, eggs, and buttermilk.

4. Add the flour mixture to the bran mixture and mix to combine. Stir in the raisins and bran flakes and fill the muffin cups ¾ full with the batter.

5. Bake muffins for 20 minutes.

Quick Breads vs. Muffins

Most quick-bread recipes can be used for muffins. You will get a dozen standard muffins or 24 mini-muffins. Always prepare your muffin tins with nonstick spray, even those that are supposedly nonstick. Muffins bake in about 15–20 minutes and make nice equal portions. Never overfill the muffin cups or they will rise and lap over the pan.

Prune–Sour Cream Muffins

Whether you call them prunes or dried plums, the deep purple bits of fruit studding these muffins are one of the best sources of fiber. Use prunes in lots of breads and muffins as a dietary staple that will keep your arteries clean.

Serves 12

Calories: 149.17
Protein: 1.66 grams
Carbohydrates: 14.89 grams
Fiber: 1.11 grams
Fat: 9.85 grams

2 cups all-purpose flour
⅔ cup sugar
1 tablespoon baking powder
½ teaspoon salt
2 eggs
1 cup sour cream
⅜ cup butter, melted
1 teaspoon grated orange zest
1 cup pitted prunes, chopped
¼ cup sugar

1. Preheat oven to 400°F. Grease a muffin tin or line it with fluted paper cups.

2. Whisk together flour, sugar, baking powder, and salt in a large bowl.

3. Whisk together eggs, sour cream, butter, and orange zest in another bowl.

4. Stir the wet ingredients into the dry ingredients, fold in prunes with a spatula, and fill muffin cups ¾ full with the batter.

5. Sprinkle tops with sugar and bake 15 minutes.

Poppy Seed–Lemon Muffins

Make these breakfast muffins into a dessert with sliced strawberries.
Poppy seeds are a high-fiber and high-protein seed, and the wheat germ
adds even more vitamins and fiber to this recipe.

Serves 12

Calories: 219.41
Protein: 5.20 grams
Carbohydrates: 31.49 grams
Fiber: 1.60 grams
Fat: 8.34 grams

2 cups all-purpose flour
⅔ cup sugar
1 tablespoon baking powder
½ teaspoon salt
¼ cup wheat germ
½ cup poppy seeds
2 eggs
¾ cup milk
⅜ cup butter, melted
¼ cup lemon juice
¼ cup grated lemon zest

1. Preheat oven to 400°F. Grease a muffin tin or line it with fluted paper cups.

2. Whisk together flour, sugar, baking powder, salt, wheat germ, and poppy seeds in a large bowl.

3. Whisk together eggs, milk, and butter in another bowl.

4. Stir the wet ingredients into the dry ingredients, stir in the lemon juice and lemon zest, and fill muffin cups ¾ full with the batter.

5. Bake 15 minutes.

Seeds

Seeds are great fillers, adding protein and fiber to your diet. Sesame seeds are a staple of Asian cooking, and sesame oil, flavored with the toasted seeds, is delicious. You can add celery seeds to most savory dishes. Poppy seeds are very important to Russian and Eastern European cooking and add a delicious, high-fiber crunch to breads, cakes, and cookies.

Chapter 19
Doughs, Batters, and Pastry

Baking Mix

Serves 12
Serving Size 1 cup

Calories: 648.01
Protein: 14.50 grams
Carbohydrates: 78.47 grams
Fiber: 5.36 grams
Fat: 31.94 grams

6 cups all-purpose flour
3 cups whole-wheat flour
⅓ cup baking powder
1 tablespoon salt
2 tablespoons sugar
½ cup nonfat dry milk
2 cups cold unsalted butter

*This is nice to have on hand for making quick biscuits,
shortcakes, or cobblers. You may substitute non-trans-fat shortening
for the butter. It's like making your own standard mix with the addition
of healthful, high-fiber whole-wheat flour.*

1. Combine flours, baking powder, salt, sugar, and nonfat dry milk in a mixing bowl.

2. Cut butter into small pieces and add to dry ingredients. Mix butter into dry ingredients with a pastry cutter, your fingers, or an electric mixer until mixture reaches the texture of cornmeal.

3. Store in the freezer or refrigerator in an airtight container.

Baking Mix

Be sure to keep your baking mix in the refrigerator. If you are going to leave it unrefrigerated, leave the butter out until you are going to use it. To make biscuits or shortcakes, mix 3 cups baking mix with ⅔ cup whole milk, heavy cream, or buttermilk. Knead 10 times on a floured surface, roll to ¾" thickness, cut into rounds, and bake 12–15 minutes at 400°F.

Whole-Wheat Biscuits

You can make breakfast sandwiches from these hearty biscuits for a boost in fiber to start your day.

1. Preheat oven to 400°F.

2. Combine flours, baking powder, salt, and sugar in a mixing bowl.

3. Cut butter into small pieces and add to dry ingredients. Mix butter into dry ingredients with a pastry cutter or your fingers. Add buttermilk and mix with a wooden spoon to form the dough.

4. Roll dough on a floured board to 1" thickness. Cut circles with a 2–3" round cookie cutter or drinking glass. Place rounds on a baking sheet and bake for 12 minutes.

Serves 8
Serving Size 1

Calories: 262.42
Protein: 7.00 grams
Carbohydrates: 38.53 grams
Fiber: 3.38 grams
Fat: 9.66 grams

1½ cups all-purpose flour
1½ cups whole-wheat flour
4½ teaspoons baking powder
1½ teaspoons salt
1 tablespoon sugar
6 tablespoons cold butter
1¼ cups buttermilk

Cornmeal Dumplings

These square dumplings may be cooked in broth or added directly in a soup or stew instead of the water in this recipe. They are much more delicious than standard white-flour dumplings, and they're high in fiber.

1. Mix the flour, cornmeal, baking powder, and salt together in a food processor.

2. Add the butter and pulse until the mixture is sandy in texture.

3. Add the milk and process just until the dough comes together.

4. Roll out the dough on a floured surface ½" thick and cut into squares.

5. Bring a large pot of salted water to boil and drop the dumplings in. Cover and boil over medium high heat for 20–25 minutes. Drain and serve hot.

Serves 6

Calories: 192.61
Protein: 5.53 grams
Carbohydrates: 35.50 grams
Fiber: 1.98 grams
Fat: 2.89 grams

1¼ cups all-purpose flour
¾ cup cornmeal
1¼ teaspoons baking powder
¾ teaspoon salt
1 tablespoon cold butter
1 cup milk

Johnnycakes

*This is a thin, crunchy cornmeal flatbread or pancake that some
say got its name from journey cake, referring to a food that could be carried
by travelers. Being unleavened, it's much like a high-fiber cracker.*

Serves 4

Calories: 368.90
Protein: 8.12 grams
Carbohydrates: 41.64 grams
Fiber: 3.40 grams
Fat: 18.91 grams

1 cup stone-ground cornmeal
½ teaspoon salt
1½ cups milk
4 tablespoons butter, melted
nonstick spray

1. Combine cornmeal and salt in a bowl.

2. Microwave the milk for 12 seconds, just to take the chill off if it is cold from the refrigerator.

3. Add the milk and melted butter to the cornmeal and salt. Stir and let rest about 5 minutes.

4. Meanwhile, heat a nonstick griddle or a well-seasoned cast-iron skillet.

5. Spray the griddle or skillet and ladle 1 ounce of batter per cake onto it. Fry them 2 minutes per side. Serve hot.

Hoecakes

While the johnnycake is a Rhode Island favorite, the hoecake is a staple of Southern cooking. They were allegedly named "hoe" because they were originally fried on the flat blade of a hoe over an open fire. Some versions of hoecakes incorporate green onions or okra into the batter.

Whole-Wheat Dumplings

Like the cornmeal version, these dumplings may be cooked in broth or added directly to a soup or stew instead of cooked in water. Dumplings add fiber to a soup or stew and sop up the flavors of the liquid.

Serves 6

Calories: 178.31
Protein: 6.27 grams
Carbohydrates: 32.64 grams
Fiber: 3.00 grams
Fat: 2.93 grams

1 cup all-purpose flour
1 cup whole-wheat flour
1¼ teaspoons baking powder
¾ teaspoon salt
1 tablespoon cold butter
1 cup milk

1. Mix the flours, baking powder, and salt together in a food processor.

2. Add the butter and pulse until the mixture is sandy in texture.

3. Add the milk and process until dough just comes together.

4. Roll out the dough on a floured surface ½" thick and cut into squares.

5. Bring a large pot of salted water to boil and drop the dumplings in. Cover and boil over medium-high heat for 20–25 minutes. Drain and serve hot.

Dumplings

Dumplings are a substitute for bread that a busy cook can make in minutes. They are related to pasta and matzo balls, adding body to a thin soup. Make tiny ones for children—they will absolutely love them. Refer to little dumplings as "surprises" in your soup to get them to eat the vegetables around the dumplings.

Beet Green Dumplings

*These drop dumplings are dropped directly from a spoon
into simmering liquid instead of being rolled out and cut into squares.
The greens add fiber and a terrific taste to the dumplings.*

Serves 8

Calories: 68.87
Protein: 1.69 grams
Carbohydrates: 1.84 grams
Fiber: 0.23 grams
Fat: 6.28 grams

¼ cup butter
4 teaspoons all-purpose flour
2 teaspoons cream
1½ cups chopped cooked
    beet greens
3 eggs, beaten
½ teaspoon salt
½ teaspoon sugar
¼ teaspoon nutmeg
⅛ teaspoon white pepper

1. Melt the butter in a saucepan and stir in the flour.

2. Add the cream and beet greens and stir constantly until heated through. Remove the pan from heat and let cool for 5 minutes.

3. Quickly stir in the eggs, then add the salt, sugar, nutmeg, and white pepper.

4. Bring a large pot of salted water or soup to a boil and drop the dumplings in, using a large serving spoon and another spoon to scrape the dough off. Cover and simmer over medium heat for 5 minutes. Drain and serve hot.

Horseradish Sauce for Dumplings

When you serve dumplings as a side dish, garnish them with parsley, chives, and butter—or make a savory horseradish sauce. Start by making a basic béchamel sauce with 2 tablespoons butter, ¼ cup flour, and 1½ cups milk. Enrich it with a mixture of ½ cup sour cream and 2 tablespoons grated horseradish. Season to taste with salt and pepper and serve warm with the beet green dumplings as a side dish.

Whole-Wheat Pasta

This fresh pasta needs only a brief 3–5 minutes cooking time in boiling water. If you don't have a pasta machine, you can hand-roll the dough to achieve a rustic version of this high-fiber pasta.

1. Combine flours and salt. Make a well in the center.

2. Combine egg and water. Pour into the well in the flour mixture. Gradually bring the flour into the egg with a fork to form a dough. Knead dough for 10 minutes. Wrap in plastic.

3. Let rest 45 minutes before rolling with a pasta machine.

To Buy a Pasta Machine or Not to Buy One?

If you are interested in adding a variety of fibrous grains and flours to your diet, it's worthwhile to get yourself a pasta machine. They are very simple to use. The old-fashioned hand-cranked machines are fun to use. It's a great way to get the whole family involved. Kids are more likely to eat pastas that have spinach and whole grains in them if they are involved in making them.

Serves 2
Serving Size 4 ounces

Calories: 252.70
Protein: 10.46 grams
Carbohydrates: 45.92 grams
Fiber: 4.50 grams
Fat: 3.37 grams

½ cup whole-wheat flour
½ cup flour
½ teaspoon salt
1 egg, beaten
2 teaspoons water

Everyday Bran Muffin Batter

*This batter will keep for 6 weeks in the refrigerator, so you can
scoop and bake bran muffins fresh every morning. Be sure to enhance
the already high-fiber muffins with dried fruit and/or nuts.*

Serves 36

Calories: 100.55
Protein: 2.50 grams
Carbohydrates: 16.05 grams
Fiber: 2.30 grams
Fat: 3.74 grams

1 cup boiling water
3 cups bran
2½ cups all-purpose flour
2½ teaspoons baking soda
1 teaspoon salt
½ cup vegetable oil
1 cup sugar
2 eggs, beaten
2 cups buttermilk

1. Pour the boiling water over 1 cup bran and let it sit for 10 minutes.

2. Mix the flour, baking soda, and salt in a mixing bowl and set aside.

3. Mix the oil into the bran and water mixture, then add the remaining bran, sugar, eggs, and buttermilk. Add the flour mixture to the bran mixture and mix to combine. Store the batter in a covered container in the refrigerator for up to 6 weeks.

4. Bake muffins from this batter in a 400°F oven for 20 minutes.

Buckwheat Pasta

*A pasta machine is best for rolling this dough. Buckwheat is an excellent
source of fiber. It is high in iron and has a nutty taste.*

Serves 2
Serving Size 4 ounces

Calories: 255.58
Protein: 10.09 grams
Carbohydrates: 46.10 grams
Fiber: 3.12 grams
Fat: 3.58 grams

⅓ cup buckwheat flour
⅔ cup flour
½ teaspoon salt
1 egg, beaten
2 teaspoons water

1. Combine flours and salt. Make a well in the center.

2. Combine egg and water. Pour into the well in the flour mixture. Gradually bring the flour into the egg with a fork to form a dough. Knead dough for 10 minutes. Wrap in plastic.

3. Let rest 45 minutes before rolling with a pasta machine.

Yam Gnocchi

Gnocchi can be boiled without the step of rolling them down the tines
of a fork. You can just put a thumb indentation in each one instead.
You can freeze uncooked gnocchi for another meal.
Using the yams adds to the vitamin and fiber.

Serves 4
Serving Size ½ cup

Calories: 249.23
Protein: 8.53 grams
Carbohydrates: 45.79 grams
Fiber: 4.03 grams
Fat: 3.48 grams

1 baked yam
¾ cup flour
½ teaspoon salt
1 egg, beaten
¼ cup melted and browned
*   butter*
1 teaspoon chopped sage
¼ cup grated Parmesan
*   cheese*

1. Scoop the cooked yam flesh out of the skin and mash it with a fork or put it through a potato ricer or food mill. Toss the yam in a bowl with the flour and salt. Use a light touch.

2. Make a well in the center of the yam mixture and put the egg into it. Gradually incorporate the yam mixture into the egg to make a dough that comes together. Roll dough into 1"-thick logs and cut 1" pieces off the logs.

3. For the traditional indentations, roll each piece down the tines of a floured fork and flick it off with your thumb.

4. Bring a pot of salted water to a boil and add the gnocchi. Stir and cook until gnocchi floats to the top, about 5 minutes.

5. Drain the gnocchi and put it in a serving dish. Toss the gnocchi with the melted browned butter and sage to coat. Sprinkle the Parmesan cheese over it and serve immediately.

Gnocchi

Classic gnocchi is made with potatoes, but there are many variations that add flavor and high fiber to this wonderful dish. In Italy it's eaten as a pasta course as part of a big dinner. Yams can be used for lots of vitamin A as can pumpkins. Gnocchi can be savory, as in the Spinach Gnocchi (page 280), dressed with tomato sauce or herb butter. A pumpkin or yam gnocchi can be sweet, sprinkled with nuts and sugar or maple syrup.

Spinach Gnocchi

Serves 4
Serving Size ½ cup

Calories: 328.74
Protein: 10.88 grams
Carbohydrates: 48.42 grams
Fiber: 4.55 grams
Fat: 10.66 grams

1 large baked potato, about
   1 pound
¾ cup flour
½ teaspoon salt
1 egg, beaten
½ cup chopped cooked
   spinach
2 tablespoons olive oil
¼ cup grated Parmesan
   cheese

These Italian dumplings can be served with tomato sauce, Alfredo sauce, or simply as this recipe does, with a little olive oil and cheese. The potato and spinach will give your family iron and fiber.

1. Scoop the cooked potato flesh out of the skin and mash it with a fork or put it through a potato ricer or food mill. Use your hands to toss the potatoes in a bowl with the flour and salt. Use a light touch.

2. Make a well in the center of the potato mixture and put the egg and spinach into it. Gradually incorporate the potato mixture into the egg mixture to make a dough. Roll dough into 1"-thick logs and cut 1" pieces off the logs.

3. For the traditional indentations, roll each piece down the tines of a floured fork and flick it off with your thumb.

4. Bring a pot of salted water to a boil, add the gnocchi, stir, and then cook until gnocchi floats to the top, about 5 minutes.

5. Drain the gnocchi and put it in a serving dish. Toss the gnocchi with olive oil to coat. Sprinkle the Parmesan cheese over it and serve immediately.

Whole-Wheat Pizza Dough

Making your own pizza dough is fun and rewarding, and this recipe helps bring more fiber into your diet than standard pizza dough.

1. Combine yeast with the warm water, sugar, and ½ cup all-purpose flour. Let sit 10 minutes.

2. Add olive oil, cool water, salt, and 1 cup all-purpose flour. Combine with a wooden spoon.

3. Add the whole-wheat flour and mix to form dough.

4. Knead dough on a floured board for 5 minutes, adding flour as needed to prevent sticking.

5. Cover dough and set aside in an oiled bowl. Let dough rise in a warm place for 60 minutes. Punch down dough and divide in half. Roll the halves into balls and let rise, covered, for 60 minutes. Roll or stretch dough into pizza rounds.

6. Preheat the oven to 400°F. Bake the pizza on a pizza stone or cookie sheet for 12–15 minutes.

Whole-Wheat Pizza Dough

Once you've made it, you'll wonder why anyone would want to use all-purpose flour for pizza dough. The nutty flavor of the whole wheat, the added B-vitamins, and the crisp texture give you much more nutrition for the same amount of effort. Plus, you can top a whole-wheat pizza base with anything you like, from a white topping of cheeses to a red one with fresh tomatoes.

Serves 8

Calories: 171.08
Protein: 4.81 grams
Carbohydrates: 29.37 grams
Fiber: 2.65 grams
Fat: 4.09 grams

1 package yeast
½ cup warm water
½ teaspoon sugar
1½ cups all-purpose flour
1 ounce olive oil
½ cup cool water
1½ teaspoons salt
1 cup whole-wheat flour

Whole-Wheat Pie Dough

*If you can't find pastry flour, substitute all-purpose flour.
Rolled-out dough circles can be frozen or refrigerated in advance until
ready to use. Use these delicious high-fiber crusts for everything
from savory quiches to sweet fruit pies.*

Serves 8

Calories: 427.32
Protein: 4.29 grams
Carbohydrates: 27.63 grams
Fiber: 4.33 grams
Fat: 35.09 grams

1¼ cups pastry flour
1 cup whole-wheat flour
4½ teaspoons sugar
¾ teaspoon salt
1½ cups unsalted butter
½ cup ice water

1. Combine flours, sugar, and salt in a bowl.

2. Cut butter into ½"-thick slices.

3. Mix butter and dry ingredients with a pastry cutter until butter is in pea-size lumps.

4. Add ice water to flour-butter mixture and stir with a wooden spoon to combine. Form the dough.

5. Divide dough in half and form into 2 balls. Wrap in plastic and refrigerate for 60 minutes before rolling out into 10" circles.

Freezing Dough and Crusts

You can freeze dough; just wrap it well with plastic cling wrap or roll it out in circles and stack with waxed paper in between each circle. Once it's frozen hard, place the dough in a large baggie. You can freeze pie dough in a metal or glass pie plate—just be sure to prepare the pie plate with nonstick spray.

Sweet Cornmeal Tart Dough

This sweet pastry dough is used in the Polenta Pear Tart recipe (page 188). It's also excellent with apples, peaches, and berries. Mix berries into stone fruit tarts to add extra fiber, soluble and insoluble.

1. Cream the butter and sugar together with an electric mixer.

2. Add the egg yolks, one at a time, mixing to incorporate.

3. Mix the flour, cornmeal, and salt in another bowl.

4. Add the cornmeal mixture to the butter mixture and mix until smooth.

5. Divide dough in half and form into 2 balls. Wrap in plastic and refrigerate for 60 minutes before rolling out into 10" circles.

Serves 8

Calories: 195.78
Protein: 3.72 grams
Carbohydrates: 29.03 grams
Fiber: 0.85 grams
Fat: 7.25 grams

¼ cup unsalted butter, soft
½ cup sugar
2 egg yolks
1 cup all-purpose flour
⅓ cup cornmeal
½ teaspoon salt

Croutons

Any bread may be made into croutons to add crunch to salads and soups. If you toss some sesame seeds in with the butter, you will add even more flavor and toasty fiber.

Serves 8
Serving Size ½ cup

Calories: 233.58
Protein: 5.33 grams
Carbohydrates: 24.83 grams
Fiber: 3.66 grams
Fat: 13.71 grams

1 loaf whole-wheat bread
5 minced cloves garlic
½ cup melted unsalted butter
1 tablespoon kosher salt
1 teaspoon pepper

1. Preheat oven to 350°F. Remove crust from bread and cut loaf into cubes.

2. Put bread cubes and garlic in a large bowl.

3. Pour butter over bread cubes and toss to distribute the butter and garlic evenly.

4. Sprinkle salt and pepper on bread cubes and toss to distribute seasoning.

5. Bake seasoned bread cubes on a flat baking pan until toasted, 15–25 minutes. Cool and store in an airtight container.

Croutons

Making your own croutons is easy and delicious. Never throw away stale bread; you can always use it for making croutons. You can also use onion powder instead of garlic. Try making croutons with various dry herbs, such as rosemary, oregano, thyme, or tarragon. If you are planning to use the croutons in chicken or turkey stuffing, add celery salt, thyme, and dried sage.

Chapter 20
Condiments

Parsnip Marmalade

*This is an interesting marmalade with a hint of orange,
but no rind. Parsnips are sweet and fibrous and add a different dimension.
Try this with cooked carrots or parsnips.*

Serves 32
Serving Size ¼ cup

Calories: 100.36
Protein: 0.25 grams
Carbohydrates: 25.60 grams
Fiber: 0.87 grams
Fat: 0.06 grams

*4 cups peeled and grated
parsnips*
*¾ cup fresh squeezed
orange juice*
*2 tablespoons grated
orange zest*
*2 tablespoons grated
ginger root*
3½ cups sugar

1. Cook the parsnips in boiling water until tender, about 15 minutes.

2. Drain the cooked parsnips and put them in a saucepan with the orange juice, orange zest, ginger root, and sugar.

3. Stir and cook over medium heat until the sugar dissolves. Raise the heat and bring the mixture to a boil.

4. Cook for 45 minutes, stirring often to prevent the mixture from sticking to the bottom of the pan and burning.

5. Pour the finished marmalade into sterilized canning jars and screw on the lids. Let cool at room temperature.

Canning Technique

Preserves and other things that have a high sugar content don't need to be processed in a water bath. Even so, be sure to sterilize the jars and lids first. Pour the preserves into hot jars, wipe the rim if there is any spillage with a clean damp tea towel, and screw the lids on tightly. Let cool to room temperature. You will hear popping sounds as the jars cool, which ensures a vacuumed seal. Test by pressing down on the center of the lid. If it doesn't pop back up, you may store them for at least a year. If any pop back up, refrigerate them and use immediately.

Raspberry Jam

Frozen or fresh raspberries are good for this recipe; often frozen ones are riper than fresh if you get them from a store. If you strain the seeds out of the jam, you will lose the insoluble fiber. Only strain the seeds if you are cooking for someone with diverticulosis.

1. Cut the lemon in half and squeeze the juice out. Discard the seeds and retain the juice.

2. Put the lemon halves in a large saucepan with the raspberries and sugar. Bring to a boil over low heat, stirring to prevent scorching.

3. Simmer for 25 minutes, stirring often. Remove from heat, remove lemon halves, and stir in lemon juice.

4. Ladle or pour the jam into hot sterilized jars, filling to ¼" from the top. Wipe jar rims. Cover at once with metal lids and screw-on bands. Let cool at room temperature.

Serves 16
Serving Size ¼ cup

Calories: 161.13
Protein: 0.28 grams
Carbohydrates: 41.33 grams
Fiber: 2.15 grams
Fat: 0.17 grams

1 lemon
4 cups raspberries
3 cups sugar

Blackberry Jam

Serves 16
Serving Size ¼ cup

Calories: 164.78
Protein: 0.26 grams
Carbohydrates: 42.37 grams
Fiber: 1.96 grams
Fat: 0.14 grams

1 lemon
4 cups blackberries
3 cups sugar

Frozen or fresh berries are good for this recipe. Frozen ones are easier to come by than fresh most of the time. You can make variations on this by adding orange zest to the berries along with the lemon.

1. Cut the lemon in half and squeeze the juice out. Discard the seeds and retain the juice.

2. Put the lemon halves in a large saucepan with the blackberries and sugar. Bring to a boil over low heat, stirring to prevent scorching.

3. Simmer for 25 minutes, stirring often. Remove from heat, remove lemon halves, and stir in lemon juice.

4. Ladle or pour the jam into hot sterilized jars, filling to ¼" from the top. Wipe jar rims. Cover at once with metal lids and screw-on bands. Let cool at room temperature.

Jams and Preserves

Preserves and jams are exactly the same thing. When you make jam, you preserve the fruit by adding sugar, which thickens it. In the case of most jellies, you need to add pectin so that they will gel. Serve jam with a bowl of freshly roasted nuts to add crunch and fiber and cut the sweetness.

Strawberry Preserves

*Choose the ripest of fresh berries for this recipe. Frozen ones
are okay if ripe fresh ones are unavailable. You can get excellent strawberries
year-round now, just make sure they are ripe all the way through.
This treat does add some fiber to the diet.*

1. Cut the lemon in half and squeeze the juice into a bowl. Discard the seeds and reserve the juice.

2. Put the lemon halves in a large saucepan with the strawberries, vanilla bean, and sugar. Bring to a boil over low heat, stirring to prevent scorching.

3. Simmer for 25 minutes, stirring often. Remove from heat, remove vanilla bean and lemon halves, and stir in lemon juice.

4. Ladle or pour the preserves into hot sterilized jars, filling to ¼" from the top. Wipe jar rims. Cover at once with metal lids and screw-on bands. Let cool at room temperature.

Serves 16
Serving Size ¼ cup

Calories: 157.46
Protein: 0.23 grams
Carbohydrates: 40.44 grams
Fiber: 0.94 grams
Fat: 0.14 grams

1 lemon
*4 cups strawberries, cut in
    quarters*
½ vanilla bean
3 cups sugar

Apple Butter

Granny Smith is the apple of choice for this recipe because of its tartness and texture. However, you can use other varieties, such as Macintosh or a mixture. The concentrated apple pulp adds rich fiber and flavor to your morning muffin or toast.

Serves 16
Serving Size ¼ cup

Calories: 117.15
Protein: 0.24 grams
Carbohydrates: 28.05 grams
Fiber: 2.38 grams
Fat: 0.36 grams

8 cups unpeeled apples, cored
    and sliced
1⅓ cups apple cider
1 cup brown sugar
⅛ teaspoon salt
2 teaspoons cinnamon
¼ teaspoon ground cloves
½ teaspoon allspice
¼ cup brandy

1. Combine the apples and apple cider in a large pot. Cover and cook over medium heat for 20 minutes, stirring frequently.

2. Purée the apples and liquid in a food mill and return to the pot.

3. Add the brown sugar, salt, cinnamon, cloves, and allspice to the apple purée and cook uncovered over low heat for 3 hours. Stir often, especially toward the end of the cooking time to prevent sticking and burning.

4. Stir in brandy and remove from heat.

5. Ladle or pour the apple butter into hot sterilized jars, filling to ¼" from the top. Wipe jar rims. Cover at once with metal lids and screw-on bands. Let cool at room temperature. Refrigerate for one week before serving.

Granny Smith

One of the world's most famous apple varieties, Granny Smiths are bright green and shiny. They are very juicy and have a slightly tangy flavor. Granny Smiths were first cultivated in Australia in 1865 by Marie Ana Smith. They slowly made their way around the world, reaching the United States more than one hundred years after they were first cultivated.

Blueberry Butter

*Like the Apple Butter recipe, Granny Smith is the apple of choice
for this recipe because of its tartness and texture. Try mixing this with softened
butter to use on whole-grain pancakes or waffles.*

Serves 16
Serving Size ¼ cup

Calories: 225.56
Protein: 1.20 grams
Carbohydrates: 57.65 grams
Fiber: 2.33 grams
Fat: 0.48 grams

4 cups peeled apples,
  chopped
4 cups blueberries
1 cup brown sugar
2 cups sugar
1 teaspoon cinnamon
½ teaspoon nutmeg
¼ teaspoon allspice

1. Combine the apples, blueberries, sugars, and spices in a large pot and cook over medium heat until the sugar dissolves, stirring frequently.

2. Bring the mixture to a boil, then reduce the heat to low, and simmer for 45 minutes, stirring occasionally.

3. Pour into hot sterilized jars, filling to ¼" from the top. Wipe jar rims. Cover at once with metal lids and screw-on bands. Let cool at room temperature.

Fruit Butters

These delicious concentrates can also be made with prunes. They work well spread on pastry dough prior to baking. You can also add fruit butters to tarts for dark color and flavor. The concentrated fruit adds a sweet, strong touch of fiber to your breakfast. You can also add fruit butters to sweet sauces.

Mango Chutney

Sweet and spicy, somewhere between preserves, pickles, and hot sauce, mango chutney complements Indian food perfectly. It's also a nice high-fiber dip for cold shrimp cocktail.

Serves 6
Serving Size ¼ cup

Calories: 150.36
Protein: 0.68 grams
Carbohydrates: 38.66 grams
Fiber: 1.63 grams
Fat: 0.21 grams

¾ cup sugar
¾ cup white wine vinegar
2 mangoes
1 garlic clove, peeled
¼ small green pepper
½ small onion
2 tablespoons grated fresh
   ginger
½ teaspoon white pepper
¼ teaspoon ground
   cinnamon
⅛ teaspoon ground cumin
pinch of ground cloves

1. Combine the sugar and vinegar in a nonreactive saucepan and heat over low until sugar dissolves.

2. Peel and dice the mangoes, mince the garlic, and chop the green pepper and onion.

3. Add them to the pan along with the ginger, white pepper, cinnamon, cumin, and cloves.

4. Turn the heat up and simmer for 30 minutes, stirring occasionally.

5. Remove from heat and refrigerate in a covered container.

Chutneys

The flavor options for chutney are endless. The English brought the concept of a sweet and sour, spicy and hot, savory and highly textured fruit mixture back to Europe from India during the Raj. Nuts and onions can be added to chutney. Mangoes are a favorite East Indian ingredient. Mixing fresh and dried fruits give the chutney great texture, extra sweetness, and fiber.

Tomato Chutney

*Use canned tomatoes in this recipe since they are canned
at their sweetest ripeness and will be further cooked anyway. You will
get more fiber and texture from fresh tomatoes, however, and a few
green ones will give the chutney more fibrous zip.*

Serves 6
Serving Size ¼ cup

Calories: 142.00
Protein: 1.31 grams
Carbohydrates: 35.74 grams
Fiber: 1.37 grams
Fat: 0.30 grams

¾ cup sugar
¾ cup red wine vinegar
*3 cups diced, peeled
 tomatoes*
*1 garlic clove, peeled and
 minced*
¼ cup dried currants
½ cup minced shallots
*2 tablespoons grated fresh
 ginger*
½ teaspoon white pepper
pinch of ground cloves

1. Combine the sugar and vinegar in a nonreactive saucepan and heat over low heat until sugar dissolves.

2. Add the tomatoes, garlic, currants, and shallots to the pan along with the ginger, white pepper, and cloves.

3. Turn the heat up and simmer for 30 minutes, stirring occasionally.

4. Remove from heat and refrigerate in a covered container.

Relish the Difference

*Salsa is usually a fresh, uncooked chunky condiment; chutney is cooked
and has a chunky spreadable consistency. Relish is briefly cooked and
is both less sweet and crunchier than chutney. All of these condiments,
even the raw ones, actually "cook" in the sugar and acid of the vinegar,
lemon, or lime juice added to the recipes. Cooked or raw, they add fresh
flavors and fiber to any dish.*

Cranberry Chutney

This condiment makes a perfect match with smoked turkey, so use it when you make sandwiches. Add it to brown rice for a major fiber fix. You can serve it on the side when you are carving a pork roast.

Serves 12
Serving Size ¼ cup

Calories: 100.69
Protein: 0.31 grams
Carbohydrates: 26.06 grams
Fiber: 2.18 grams
Fat: 0.11 grams

¾ cup sugar
¾ cup cider vinegar
3 cups fresh cranberries
½ cup dried cranberries
½ cup chopped dried pears
½ cup diced sweet onion
1 teaspoon grated ginger root
½ teaspoon white pepper
¼ teaspoon ground cloves

1. Combine the sugar and vinegar in a nonreactive saucepan and heat over low until sugar dissolves.

2. Add the cranberries, dried cranberries, dried pears, and sweet onion to the pan along with the ginger, white pepper, and cloves.

3. Turn the heat up and simmer for 30 minutes, stirring occasionally.

4. Remove from heat and refrigerate in a covered container.

Pico de Gallo

You can add mango to this classic Mexican condiment, which literally translates from Spanish to English as "rooster's beak," referring to its vivid red and orange colors. It is used extensively in Argentina on steaks and roasts. Serve it with beef and pork to add fiber to a meat dish.

Serves 12
Serving Size ¼ cup

Calories: 11.99
Protein: 0.32 grams
Carbohydrates: 2.87 grams
Fiber: 0.49 grams
Fat: 0.09 grams

1 cup diced fresh red
    tomatoes, seeded
1 cup diced red onion
½ cup diced fresh yellow
    tomatoes, seeded
½ cup diced mango
1 teaspoon cayenne pepper
    sauce
1 tablespoon lime juice
1 tablespoon fresh cilantro,
    chopped
kosher salt to taste

1. Combine all of the ingredients in a bowl.

2. Serve as a dip for tortilla chips or as a garnish with tacos, nachos, or burritos.

Tomato Salsa

If you prefer a smoother salsa (this one is chunky), simply purée this recipe in a food processor briefly. The fiber in this salsa complements the fiber in corn tortillas or crisp corn chips.

1. Dice the tomatoes and sweet onion and combine in a large bowl. Cut the jalapeño pepper in half, remove the seeds, and then dice the flesh. Add to the bowl.

2. Mince the garlic clove, chop the cilantro, and add them to the bowl.

3. Add the vinegar, olive oil, and a pinch of salt. Stir well, taste, and add more salt if needed.

Serves 12
Serving Size ¼ cup

Calories: 10.03
Protein: 0.27 grams
Carbohydrates: 1.46 grams
Fiber: 0.30 grams
Fat: 0.48 grams

4 ripe tomatoes, seeded
¼ small sweet onion
1 jalapeño pepper
1 clove garlic, peeled
¼ bunch cilantro
1 tablespoon red wine vinegar
1 teaspoon olive oil
salt to taste

Bread and Butter Pickles

Cucumbers and onions are a good source of fiber; here they are seasoned and lightly cooked. Your own pickles will be far crisper than the ones that come in jars. Add pickle slices to ham or turkey sandwiches for fiber in the filling.

1. Layer cucumbers and onions with salt in a colander set in the sink and drain for 2 to 3 hours.

2. Combine vinegar, water, sugar, and spices in a large pot and bring to a boil.

3. Add drained cucumbers and onions and cook for 5 minutes.

4. Pack in sterilized pint jars and seal the lids in a water bath.

Serves 40
Serving Size ¼ cup

Calories: 32.02
Protein: 0.50 grams
Carbohydrates: 7.78 grams
Fiber: 0.67 grams
Fat: 0.12 grams

12 medium cucumbers, sliced ¼" thick
5 small onions, sliced ¼" thick
¼ cup pickling salt
1 cup cider vinegar
½ cup water
1 cup sugar
¼ teaspoon turmeric
1 teaspoon mustard seed
1 teaspoon celery seed

Corn Relish

This relish is an excellent accompaniment to fried or grilled chicken. It also adds fiber when mixed into boiled lima beans for a unique succotash. Stuff it into cherry tomatoes just before you roast them and give your family a big, healthful lift.

Serves 24
Serving Size ¼ cup

Calories: 100.33
Protein: 1.20 grams
Carbohydrates: 25.07 grams
Fiber: 1.38 grams
Fat: 0.30 grams

4 cups corn kernels
2 cups minced green bell peppers
2 cups minced red bell peppers
2 cups chopped sweet onion
2 cups diced peeled tomatoes
2 cups sugar
2 cups cider vinegar
2 tablespoons salt
1 teaspoon turmeric
2 teaspoons dry mustard
1 teaspoon celery seeds

1. Put the corn, peppers, onion, and tomatoes in a large pot and stir to combine.

2. Add the sugar, vinegar, salt, turmeric, dry mustard, and celery seeds and stir well.

3. Bring the mixture to a boil, stirring occasionally. Lower the heat and simmer for 30 minutes, still stirring occasionally.

4. Pack in sterilized pint jars, wipe the rims, and seal the lids in a water bath.

Relish for Fiber

Relishes are excellent sources of fiber when served with meats. They can be quite sour, like the dill pickle relish that goes on hot dogs. Relish for hamburgers tends to be sweet, with red peppers and tomatoes. Cranberry Relish (page 297) started as a New England staple and then spread around the country. You can add fiber to any dish with the properly tangy relish.

Cranberry Relish

*This is a Thanksgiving standard. It's an uncooked relish that is
great served chilled or at room temperature alongside sliced meats
such as turkey and pork. It is loaded with fiber and vitamin C.*

1. Cut the orange into 8 pieces. Put 4 pieces in a food processor with
   1 cup cranberries.

2. Process the cranberries and oranges until chopped but not puréed. Put
   the chopped mixture in a bowl and add the sugar.

3. Process the remaining orange pieces and cranberries until chopped and
   add them to the bowl. Stir the sugar into the cranberries and oranges.

4. Cover and refrigerate 3 days before serving.

Serves 10
Serving Size ¼ cup

Calories: 95.18
Protein: 0.19 grams
Carbohydrates: 24.87 grams
Fiber: 1.62 grams
Fat: 0.04 grams

*1 large seedless orange,
   unpeeled*
2 cups cranberries
1 cup sugar

Cranberry Raspberry Sauce

*This relish is a great answer for the child who seems not to
like meat or fish. It adds fiber and gives anyone, young or old, plenty
of delicious flavor. You may pour this into a gelatin mold when it is
hot and let it set in the refrigerator until cold.*

1. In a saucepan combine the sugar, water, and juice. Bring to a boil and
   simmer for 5 minutes.

2. Add the cranberries to the simmering liquid and stir over medium heat
   for 5 minutes, until the berries pop.

3. Stir the raspberry jam into the cranberries and remove them from the
   heat.

4. Let the sauce cool to room temperature; then chill it in the refrigerator.

Serves 16
Serving Size ¼ cup

Calories: 82.68
Protein: 0.06 grams
Carbohydrates: 21.39 grams
Fiber: 0.58 grams
Fat: 0.03 grams

1 cup sugar
½ cup water
*¼ cup cranberry-raspberry
   juice*
2 cups fresh cranberries
½ cup raspberry jam

Date Relish

This relish is good served with sliced smoked meats, shaved Parmesan cheese, and toast for bruschetta appetizers. It's excellent with Turkish and Greek dishes, adding flavor, texture, and lots of fiber.

Serves 6
Serving Size ¼ cup

Calories: 213.88
Protein: 1.87 grams
Carbohydrates: 41.30 grams
Fiber: 4.76 grams
Fat: 4.88 grams

4 cups diced onions
2 tablespoons canola oil
2 cloves garlic, minced
1 tablespoon grated ginger root
1 teaspoon salt
½ cup dry white wine
½ cup white wine vinegar
pinch of cayenne pepper
1½ cups chopped pitted dates

1. Put the onions and oil in a large pot and sauté over medium-low heat until the onions soften.

2. Add the garlic, ginger root, and salt and continue to sauté for another minute.

3. Add the wine, vinegar, and cayenne pepper. Raise the heat to medium-high and cook, stirring occasionally, for 10 minutes. Remove from heat.

4. Stir the dates into the onion mixture and let cool to room temperature.

5. Put the relish in a storage container and refrigerate.

Suggested Menus and Holiday Feasts

Every day, add one serving of either fruits or vegetables to every meal. Use fresh fruits, nuts, and raw vegetables for snacks.

SUNDAY

Sumptuous Brunch

Peach Yogurt Smoothies

Everyday Bran Muffin Batter for weekday breakfasts

Dinner

Bean Burrito Torte

Blackberry Clafouti

MONDAY

Quick Breakfast

Everyday Bran Muffin Batter

Scrambled Eggs with Ratatouille

Lunch on the Go

Sliced turkey, baby spinach, and sliced tomatoes on Whole-Wheat Hamburger Buns with Bread and Butter Pickles on the side

Family Dinner

Black Bean Soup

Curried Shrimp Salad in a Papaya

Raspberry Sorbet

TUESDAY

Quick Breakfast

Half-Grapefruit with Blueberry Sorbet

Toasted Whole Wheat Bread with Apple Butter

Lunch

Peanut Butter Banana Wrap

Dinner

Roast Chicken with Cranberry Relish

Wild Rice

Carrot Salad

Blueberry Clafouti

WEDNESDAY

Breakfast

Blueberry Lemon Smoothies

Toasted Strawberry Banana Oatmeal Bread with Raspberry Jam

Lunch

Crunchy Tuna Salad Melt on Rye

Dinner

Lentil Soup

Cornbread

Fresh Fig and Raspberry Compote

THURSDAY

Breakfast

Pomegranate Orange Juice

Blackberry Buckwheat Flapjacks

Lunch

Open-Face Ham Salad Sandwich

Dinner

Celery Soup

Grilled Cod with Pineapple Salsa

Wild Rice Salad

Walnut Biscotti

FRIDAY

Breakfast

Bran Muffins

Egg White Omelet Filled with Tomato Salsa

Lunch

Chunky Tuna Salad Melt on Rye

Bread and Butter Pickles

Dinner

Minestrone Vegetable Soup with Croutons

Sunflower Veggie Burgers on Whole-Wheat Hamburger Buns

Pineapple Upside-Down Cake

SATURDAY

Breakfast

Blueberry Cornmeal Pancakes

Lunch

Southwest Tortilla Soup

Open-Face Ham Salad Sandwich

Dinner

White Bean Soup

Spinach Gnocchi

Exotic Fruit Salad

Blueberry Sorbet

YOUR MENU

Breakfast

_____

_____

_____

Lunch

_____

_____

_____

Dinner

_____

_____

_____

Holiday Feasts

Here are some exciting alternatives to high-fat, high-calorie feasts. Treat your family to healthful alternatives to the typical holiday fare.

Easter Dinner
Shaved Fennel, Kumquat, and Frisée Salad
Pork Tenderloin with Blackberry Gastrique
Yam Gnocchi
Raspberry Rhubarb Crisp

Memorial Day Cookout
Game Hens on the Grill with Pico de Gallo
Green Lentil Salad
Blackberry Cobbler

Fourth of July Cookout
Sunflower Veggie Burgers on Whole-
    Grain Hamburger Rolls
Carrot Salad
Carrot Cake

Labor Day Brunch on the Porch
Gazpacho Mary
Double Corn Waffles with Mango Chutney
Raspberry Almond Turnovers

Rosh Hashanah
Beet and Cabbage Borscht
Sea Bass Wrapped in Savory Cabbage
Orange and Onion Salad
Fresh Fig and Raspberry Compote

Christmas Eve Dinner
Cabbage Rolls
Double Corn Waffles
Cabbage and Chicken Salad with Peanut Dressing
Fruitcake Bread Pudding with Hard Sauce

Chanukah Dinner
Carrot Salad
Walnut and Mushroom Loaf
Colcannon (use soymilk for kosher)
Cantaloupe Sorbet

New Year's Eve Dinner
Oysters on the Half Shell with Tomato Chutney
Waldorf Salad
Pork Loin with Brandied Prunes
Lasagna Florentine
Fruitcake Bread Pudding with Hard Sauce

Index

THE EVERYTHING SERIES!

BUSINESS & PERSONAL FINANCE

Everything® Accounting Book
Everything® Budgeting Book, 2nd Ed.
Everything® Business Planning Book
Everything® Coaching and Mentoring Book, 2nd Ed.
Everything® Fundraising Book
Everything® Get Out of Debt Book
Everything® Grant Writing Book, 2nd Ed.
Everything® Guide to Buying Foreclosures
Everything® Guide to Mortgages
Everything® Guide to Personal Finance for Single Mothers
Everything® Home-Based Business Book, 2nd Ed.
Everything® Homebuying Book, 2nd Ed.
Everything® Homeselling Book, 2nd Ed.
Everything® Human Resource Management Book
Everything® Improve Your Credit Book
Everything® Investing Book, 2nd Ed.
Everything® Landlording Book
Everything® Leadership Book, 2nd Ed.
Everything® Managing People Book, 2nd Ed.
Everything® Negotiating Book
Everything® Online Auctions Book
Everything® Online Business Book
Everything® Personal Finance Book
Everything® Personal Finance in Your 20s & 30s Book, 2nd Ed.
Everything® Project Management Book, 2nd Ed.
Everything® Real Estate Investing Book
Everything® Retirement Planning Book
Everything® Robert's Rules Book, $7.95
Everything® Selling Book
Everything® Start Your Own Business Book, 2nd Ed.
Everything® Wills & Estate Planning Book

COOKING

Everything® Barbecue Cookbook
Everything® Bartender's Book, 2nd Ed., $9.95
Everything® Calorie Counting Cookbook
Everything® Cheese Book
Everything® Chinese Cookbook
Everything® Classic Recipes Book
Everything® Cocktail Parties & Drinks Book
Everything® College Cookbook
Everything® Cooking for Baby and Toddler Book
Everything® Cooking for Two Cookbook
Everything® Diabetes Cookbook
Everything® Easy Gourmet Cookbook
Everything® Fondue Cookbook
Everything® Fondue Party Book
Everything® Gluten-Free Cookbook
Everything® Glycemic Index Cookbook
Everything® Grilling Cookbook
Everything® Healthy Meals in Minutes Cookbook
Everything® Holiday Cookbook
Everything® Indian Cookbook
Everything® Italian Cookbook

Everything® **Lactose-Free Cookbook**
Everything® Low-Carb Cookbook
Everything® Low-Cholesterol Cookbook
Everything® Low-Fat High-Flavor Cookbook
Everything® Low-Salt Cookbook
Everything® Meals for a Month Cookbook
Everything® Meals on a Budget Cookbook
Everything® Mediterranean Cookbook
Everything® Mexican Cookbook
Everything® No Trans Fat Cookbook
Everything® One-Pot Cookbook
Everything® Pizza Cookbook
Everything® Quick and Easy 30-Minute, 5-Ingredient Cookbook
Everything® Quick Meals Cookbook
Everything® Slow Cooker Cookbook
Everything® Slow Cooking for a Crowd Cookbook
Everything® Soup Cookbook
Everything® Stir-Fry Cookbook
Everything® Sugar-Free Cookbook
Everything® Tapas and Small Plates Cookbook
Everything® Tex-Mex Cookbook
Everything® Thai Cookbook
Everything® Vegetarian Cookbook
Everything® Whole-Grain, High-Fiber Cookbook
Everything® Wild Game Cookbook
Everything® Wine Book, 2nd Ed.

GAMES

Everything® 15-Minute Sudoku Book, $9.95
Everything® 30-Minute Sudoku Book, $9.95
Everything® Bible Crosswords Book, $9.95
Everything® Blackjack Strategy Book
Everything® Brain Strain Book, $9.95
Everything® Bridge Book
Everything® Card Games Book
Everything® Card Tricks Book, $9.95
Everything® Casino Gambling Book, 2nd Ed.
Everything® Chess Basics Book
Everything® Craps Strategy Book
Everything® Crossword and Puzzle Book
Everything® Crossword Challenge Book
Everything® Crosswords for the Beach Book, $9.95
Everything® Cryptic Crosswords Book, $9.95
Everything® Cryptograms Book, $9.95
Everything® Easy Crosswords Book
Everything® Easy Kakuro Book, $9.95
Everything® Easy Large-Print Crosswords Book
Everything® Games Book, 2nd Ed.
Everything® Giant Sudoku Book, $9.95
Everything® Giant Word Search Book
Everything® Kakuro Challenge Book, $9.95
Everything® Large-Print Crossword Challenge Book
Everything® Large-Print Crosswords Book
Everything® Lateral Thinking Puzzles Book, $9.95
Everything® Literary Crosswords Book, $9.95
Everything® Mazes Book
Everything® Memory Booster Puzzles Book, $9.95
Everything® Movie Crosswords Book, $9.95

Everything® Music Crosswords Book, $9.95
Everything® Online Poker Book
Everything® Pencil Puzzles Book, $9.95
Everything® Poker Strategy Book
Everything® Pool & Billiards Book
Everything® Puzzles for Commuters Book, $9.95
Everything® Puzzles for Dog Lovers Book, $9.95
Everything® Sports Crosswords Book, $9.95
Everything® Test Your IQ Book, $9.95
Everything® Texas Hold 'Em Book, $9.95
Everything® Travel Crosswords Book, $9.95
Everything® TV Crosswords Book, $9.95
Everything® Word Games Challenge Book
Everything® Word Scramble Book
Everything® Word Search Book

HEALTH

Everything® Alzheimer's Book
Everything® Diabetes Book
Everything® First Aid Book, $9.95
Everything® Health Guide to Adult Bipolar Disorder
Everything® Health Guide to Arthritis
Everything® Health Guide to Controlling Anxiety
Everything® Health Guide to Depression
Everything® Health Guide to Fibromyalgia
Everything® Health Guide to Menopause, 2nd Ed.
Everything® Health Guide to Migraines
Everything® Health Guide to OCD
Everything® Health Guide to PMS
Everything® Health Guide to Postpartum Care
Everything® Health Guide to Thyroid Disease
Everything® Hypnosis Book
Everything® Low Cholesterol Book
Everything® Menopause Book
Everything® Nutrition Book
Everything® Reflexology Book
Everything® Stress Management Book

HISTORY

Everything® American Government Book
Everything® American History Book, 2nd Ed.
Everything® Civil War Book
Everything® Freemasons Book
Everything® Irish History & Heritage Book
Everything® Middle East Book
Everything® World War II Book, 2nd Ed.

HOBBIES

Everything® Candlemaking Book
Everything® Cartooning Book
Everything® Coin Collecting Book
Everything® Digital Photography Book, 2nd Ed.
Everything® Drawing Book
Everything® Family Tree Book, 2nd Ed.
Everything® Knitting Book
Everything® Knots Book
Everything® Photography Book
Everything® Quilting Book

Everything® Sewing Book
Everything® Soapmaking Book, 2nd Ed.
Everything® Woodworking Book

HOME IMPROVEMENT

Everything® Feng Shui Book
Everything® Feng Shui Decluttering Book, $9.95
Everything® Fix-It Book
Everything® Green Living Book
Everything® Home Decorating Book
Everything® Home Storage Solutions Book
Everything® Homebuilding Book
Everything® Organize Your Home Book, 2nd Ed.

KIDS' BOOKS

All titles are $7.95

Everything® Fairy Tales Book, $14.95
Everything® Kids' Animal Puzzle & Activity Book
Everything® Kids' Astronomy Book
Everything® Kids' Baseball Book, 5th Ed.
Everything® Kids' Bible Trivia Book
Everything® Kids' Bugs Book
Everything® Kids' Cars and Trucks Puzzle and Activity Book
Everything® Kids' Christmas Puzzle & Activity Book
Everything® Kids' Connect the Dots Puzzle and Activity Book
Everything® Kids' Cookbook
Everything® Kids' Crazy Puzzles Book
Everything® Kids' Dinosaurs Book
Everything® Kids' Environment Book
Everything® Kids' Fairies Puzzle and Activity Book
Everything® Kids' First Spanish Puzzle and Activity Book
Everything® Kids' Football Book
Everything® Kids' Gross Cookbook
Everything® Kids' Gross Hidden Pictures Book
Everything® Kids' Gross Jokes Book
Everything® Kids' Gross Mazes Book
Everything® Kids' Gross Puzzle & Activity Book
Everything® Kids' Halloween Puzzle & Activity Book
Everything® Kids' Hidden Pictures Book
Everything® Kids' Horses Book
Everything® Kids' Joke Book
Everything® Kids' Knock Knock Book
Everything® Kids' Learning French Book
Everything® Kids' Learning Spanish Book
Everything® Kids' Magical Science Experiments Book
Everything® Kids' Math Puzzles Book
Everything® Kids' Mazes Book
Everything® Kids' Money Book
Everything® Kids' Nature Book
Everything® Kids' Pirates Puzzle and Activity Book
Everything® Kids' Presidents Book
Everything® Kids' Princess Puzzle and Activity Book
Everything® Kids' Puzzle Book
Everything® Kids' Racecars Puzzle and Activity Book
Everything® Kids' Riddles & Brain Teasers Book
Everything® Kids' Science Experiments Book
Everything® Kids' Sharks Book
Everything® Kids' Soccer Book
Everything® Kids' Spies Puzzle and Activity Book
Everything® Kids' States Book
Everything® Kids' Travel Activity Book
Everything® Kids' Word Search Puzzle and Activity Book

LANGUAGE

Everything® Conversational Japanese Book with CD, $19.95
Everything® French Grammar Book
Everything® French Phrase Book, $9.95
Everything® French Verb Book, $9.95
Everything® German Practice Book with CD, $19.95
Everything® Inglés Book
Everything® Intermediate Spanish Book with CD, $19.95
Everything® Italian Practice Book with CD, $19.95
Everything® Learning Brazilian Portuguese Book with CD, $19.95
Everything® Learning French Book with CD, 2nd Ed., $19.95
Everything® Learning German Book
Everything® Learning Italian Book
Everything® Learning Latin Book
Everything® Learning Russian Book with CD, $19.95
Everything® Learning Spanish Book
Everything® Learning Spanish Book with CD, 2nd Ed., $19.95
Everything® Russian Practice Book with CD, $19.95
Everything® Sign Language Book
Everything® Spanish Grammar Book
Everything® Spanish Phrase Book, $9.95
Everything® Spanish Practice Book with CD, $19.95
Everything® Spanish Verb Book, $9.95
Everything® Speaking Mandarin Chinese Book with CD, $19.95

MUSIC

Everything® Bass Guitar Book with CD, $19.95
Everything® Drums Book with CD, $19.95
Everything® Guitar Book with CD, 2nd Ed., $19.95
Everything® Guitar Chords Book with CD, $19.95
Everything® Harmonica Book with CD, $15.95
Everything® Home Recording Book
Everything® Music Theory Book with CD, $19.95
Everything® Reading Music Book with CD, $19.95
Everything® Rock & Blues Guitar Book with CD, $19.95
Everything® Rock & Blues Piano Book with CD, $19.95
Everything® Songwriting Book

NEW AGE

Everything® Astrology Book, 2nd Ed.
Everything® Birthday Personology Book
Everything® Dreams Book, 2nd Ed.
Everything® Love Signs Book, $9.95
Everything® Love Spells Book, $9.95
Everything® Paganism Book
Everything® Palmistry Book
Everything® Psychic Book
Everything® Reiki Book
Everything® Sex Signs Book, $9.95
Everything® Spells & Charms Book, 2nd Ed.
Everything® Tarot Book, 2nd Ed.
Everything® Toltec Wisdom Book
Everything® Wicca & Witchcraft Book, 2nd Ed.

PARENTING

Everything® Baby Names Book, 2nd Ed.
Everything® Baby Shower Book, 2nd Ed.
Everything® Baby Sign Language Book with DVD
Everything® Baby's First Year Book
Everything® Birthing Book

Everything® Breastfeeding Book
Everything® Father-to-Be Book
Everything® Father's First Year Book
Everything® Get Ready for Baby Book, 2nd Ed.
Everything® Get Your Baby to Sleep Book, $9.95
Everything® Getting Pregnant Book
Everything® Guide to Pregnancy Over 35
Everything® Guide to Raising a One-Year-Old
Everything® Guide to Raising a Two-Year-Old
Everything® Guide to Raising Adolescent Boys
Everything® Guide to Raising Adolescent Girls
Everything® Mother's First Year Book
Everything® Parent's Guide to Childhood Illnesses
Everything® Parent's Guide to Children and Divorce
Everything® Parent's Guide to Children with ADD/ADHD
Everything® Parent's Guide to Children with Asperger's Syndrome
Everything® Parent's Guide to Children with Asthma
Everything® Parent's Guide to Children with Autism
Everything® Parent's Guide to Children with Bipolar Disorder
Everything® Parent's Guide to Children with Depression
Everything® Parent's Guide to Children with Dyslexia
Everything® Parent's Guide to Children with Juvenile Diabetes
Everything® Parent's Guide to Positive Discipline
Everything® Parent's Guide to Raising a Successful Child
Everything® Parent's Guide to Raising Boys
Everything® Parent's Guide to Raising Girls
Everything® Parent's Guide to Raising Siblings
Everything® Parent's Guide to Sensory Integration Disorder
Everything® Parent's Guide to Tantrums
Everything® Parent's Guide to the Strong-Willed Child
Everything® Parenting a Teenager Book
Everything® Potty Training Book, $9.95
Everything® Pregnancy Book, 3rd Ed.
Everything® Pregnancy Fitness Book
Everything® Pregnancy Nutrition Book
Everything® Pregnancy Organizer, 2nd Ed., $16.95
Everything® Toddler Activities Book
Everything® Toddler Book
Everything® Tween Book
Everything® Twins, Triplets, and More Book

PETS

Everything® Aquarium Book
Everything® Boxer Book
Everything® Cat Book, 2nd Ed.
Everything® Chihuahua Book
Everything® Cooking for Dogs Book
Everything® Dachshund Book
Everything® Dog Book, 2nd Ed.
Everything® Dog Grooming Book
Everything® Dog Health Book
Everything® Dog Obedience Book
Everything® Dog Owner's Organizer, $16.95
Everything® Dog Training and Tricks Book
Everything® German Shepherd Book
Everything® Golden Retriever Book
Everything® Horse Book
Everything® Horse Care Book
Everything® Horseback Riding Book
Everything® Labrador Retriever Book
Everything® Poodle Book
Everything® Pug Book

Everything® Puppy Book
Everything® Rottweiler Book
Everything® Small Dogs Book
Everything® Tropical Fish Book
Everything® Yorkshire Terrier Book

REFERENCE

Everything® American Presidents Book
Everything® Blogging Book
Everything® Build Your Vocabulary Book, $9.95
Everything® Car Care Book
Everything® Classical Mythology Book
Everything® Da Vinci Book
Everything® Divorce Book
Everything® Einstein Book
Everything® Enneagram Book
Everything® Etiquette Book, 2nd Ed.
Everything® Guide to C. S. Lewis & Narnia
Everything® Guide to Edgar Allan Poe
Everything® Guide to Understanding Philosophy
Everything® Inventions and Patents Book
Everything® Jacqueline Kennedy Onassis Book
Everything® John F. Kennedy Book
Everything® Mafia Book
Everything® Martin Luther King Jr. Book
Everything® Philosophy Book
Everything® Pirates Book
Everything® Private Investigation Book
Everything® Psychology Book
Everything® Public Speaking Book, $9.95
Everything® Shakespeare Book, 2nd Ed.

RELIGION

Everything® Angels Book
Everything® Bible Book
Everything® Bible Study Book with CD, $19.95
Everything® Buddhism Book
Everything® Catholicism Book
Everything® Christianity Book
Everything® Gnostic Gospels Book
Everything® History of the Bible Book
Everything® Jesus Book
Everything® Jewish History & Heritage Book
Everything® Judaism Book
Everything® Kabbalah Book
Everything® Koran Book
Everything® Mary Book
Everything® Mary Magdalene Book
Everything® Prayer Book
Everything® Saints Book, 2nd Ed.
Everything® Torah Book
Everything® Understanding Islam Book
Everything® Women of the Bible Book
Everything® World's Religions Book

SCHOOL & CAREERS

Everything® Career Tests Book
Everything® College Major Test Book
Everything® College Survival Book, 2nd Ed.
Everything® Cover Letter Book, 2nd Ed.
Everything® Filmmaking Book
Everything® Get-a-Job Book, 2nd Ed.
Everything® Guide to Being a Paralegal
Everything® Guide to Being a Personal Trainer
Everything® Guide to Being a Real Estate Agent
Everything® Guide to Being a Sales Rep
Everything® Guide to Being an Event Planner
Everything® Guide to Careers in Health Care
Everything® Guide to Careers in Law Enforcement
Everything® Guide to Government Jobs
Everything® Guide to Starting and Running a Catering Business
Everything® Guide to Starting and Running a Restaurant
Everything® Job Interview Book, 2nd Ed.
Everything® New Nurse Book
Everything® New Teacher Book
Everything® Paying for College Book
Everything® Practice Interview Book
Everything® Resume Book, 3rd Ed.
Everything® Study Book

SELF-HELP

Everything® Body Language Book
Everything® Dating Book, 2nd Ed.
Everything® Great Sex Book
Everything® Self-Esteem Book
Everything® Tantric Sex Book

SPORTS & FITNESS

Everything® Easy Fitness Book
Everything® Fishing Book
Everything® Krav Maga for Fitness Book
Everything® Running Book, 2nd Ed.

TRAVEL

Everything® Family Guide to Coastal Florida
Everything® Family Guide to Cruise Vacations
Everything® Family Guide to Hawaii
Everything® Family Guide to Las Vegas, 2nd Ed.
Everything® Family Guide to Mexico
Everything® Family Guide to New England, 2nd Ed.
Everything® Family Guide to New York City, 3rd Ed.
Everything® Family Guide to RV Travel & Campgrounds
Everything® Family Guide to the Caribbean
Everything® Family Guide to the Disneyland® Resort, California Adventure®, Universal Studios®, and the Anaheim Area, 2nd Ed.
Everything® Family Guide to the Walt Disney World Resort®, Universal Studios®, and Greater Orlando, 5th Ed.
Everything® Family Guide to Timeshares
Everything® Family Guide to Washington D.C., 2nd Ed.

WEDDINGS

Everything® Bachelorette Party Book, $9.95
Everything® Bridesmaid Book, $9.95
Everything® Destination Wedding Book
Everything® Father of the Bride Book, $9.95
Everything® Groom Book, $9.95
Everything® Mother of the Bride Book, $9.95
Everything® Outdoor Wedding Book
Everything® Wedding Book, 3rd Ed.
Everything® Wedding Checklist, $9.95
Everything® Wedding Etiquette Book, $9.95
Everything® Wedding Organizer, 2nd Ed., $16.95
Everything® Wedding Shower Book, $9.95
Everything® Wedding Vows Book, $9.95
Everything® Wedding Workout Book
Everything® Weddings on a Budget Book, 2nd Ed., $9.95

WRITING

Everything® Creative Writing Book
Everything® Get Published Book, 2nd Ed.
Everything® Grammar and Style Book, 2nd Ed.
Everything® Guide to Magazine Writing
Everything® Guide to Writing a Book Proposal
Everything® Guide to Writing a Novel
Everything® Guide to Writing Children's Books
Everything® Guide to Writing Copy
Everything® Guide to Writing Graphic Novels
Everything® Guide to Writing Research Papers
Everything® Improve Your Writing Book, 2nd Ed.
Everything® Writing Poetry Book